Mastering Arduino

A project-based approach to electronics,
circuits, and programming

Jon Hoffman

BIRMINGHAM - MUMBAI

Mastering Arduino

Acquisition Editor: Ben Renow-Clarke, Suresh Jain
Project Editor: Radhika Atitkar
Content Development Editor: Alex Sorentinho
Technical Editor: Gaurav Gavas
Proofreader: Safis Editing
Indexer: Tejal Daruwale Soni
Graphics: Tom Scaria
Production Coordinator: Sandip Tadge

First published: September 2018

Production reference: 1270918

Published by Packt Publishing Ltd.
Livery Place
35 Livery Street
Birmingham
B3 2PB, UK.

ISBN 978-1-78883-058-4

www.packt.com

I would like to thank my wife, Kim; without her support none of my books would have been possible. I would also like to thank my two daughters who have both been my inspiration and driving force since the days they were born.

-Jon Hoffman

Packt Upsell

`mapt.io`

Mapt is an online digital library that gives you full access to over 5,000 books and videos, as well as industry leading tools to help you plan your personal development and advance your career. For more information, please visit our website.

Why subscribe?

- Spend less time learning and more time coding with practical eBooks and Videos from over 4,000 industry professionals

- Improve your learning with Skill Plans built especially for you

- Get a free eBook or video every month

- Mapt is fully searchable

- Copy and paste, print, and bookmark content

packt.com

Did you know that Packt offers eBook versions of every book published, with PDF and ePub files available? You can upgrade to the eBook version at www.packt.com and as a print book customer, you are entitled to a discount on the eBook copy. Get in touch with us at customercare@packtpub.com for more details.

At www.packt.com, you can also read a collection of free technical articles, sign up for a range of free newsletters, and receive exclusive discounts and offers on Packt books and eBooks.

Contributors

About the author

Jon Hoffman has over 25 years of experience in the field of Information Technology. Over those years, Jon worked in the areas of System Administration, Network Administration, Network Security, Application Development, and Architecture. Currently, Jon works as an Enterprise Software Manager for Syntech Systems.

Jon has developed extensively for the iOS platform since 2008. This includes several apps that he has published in App Store, apps that he wrote for third parties and numerous enterprise applications. What really drives Jon is the challenges in the Information Technology field, and there is nothing more exciting to him than overcoming a challenge.

Some of Jon's other interests are baseball and basketball. Jon also really enjoys TaeKwonDo, where he and his oldest daughter earned their Black Belts together early in 2014. Kim (his wife) earned her Black Belt at the end of 2014.

About the reviewers

Dr. Pratik Desai is a computer scientist and an engineering leader. His fields of expertise include the Internet of Things, Artificial Intelligence, and Connected Cars. He is a pioneer researcher in IoT and the published author of *Python Programming for Arduino*. In his spare time, Pratik likes tinkering with sensors and working on Python projects.

Ejike is a developer with a serious love of sharing his skills and knowledge with his fellow developers and beginners in the industry. He has spent his few years as a lead instructor in computer programming and has enjoyed the most part of his life doing live trainings with over hundreds of students. Ejike derives joy in building the next generation of software and hardware developers who do amazing things in the industry today. He led the team of developers who participated in Forbes' *Under 30 Change the World Challenge*, judged by a panel of professionals at the *Wharton school of the university of Pennsylvania* in 2015.

His love for computer programming in his early stage in life got Ejike into Java, C, C#, C++, Python, MikroC, Arduino, and lots of other programming languages and embedded system designs. He began to think that he is crazy until I started developing advance projects for clients and getting amazing job offers from reputable companies across America, Asia, and Africa.

The worst part of Ejike's life as a software developer is seeing himself coding always in his dreams.

The best part of his life as a developer is NOT building advanced and complicated projects with different programming languages combine together, but, building the next generation of developers and seeing them excel in the industry like him and other senior developers around him. He is always happy each time his students get across to him to tell him how they successfully got employed by one reputable firm or the other, and how they pick up fast in their respective companies to become senior developers with mouth-watering salaries!

Ejike's courses are one of the most comprehensive ones in the market today!

Packt is searching for authors like you

If you're interested in becoming an author for Packt, please visit `authors.packtpub.com` and apply today. We have worked with thousands of developers and tech professionals, just like you, to help them share their insight with the global tech community. You can make a general application, apply for a specific hot topic that we are recruiting an author for, or submit your own idea.

Table of Contents

Preface

Mastering Arduino is an all-in-one guide to getting the most out of your Arduino. This practical, no-nonsense guide teaches you all of the electronics and programming skills that you need, to create advanced Arduino projects. This book is packed full of real-world projects for you to practice on, bringing all of the knowledge in the book together and giving you the skills to build your own robot from the examples in this book. The final two chapters discuss wireless technologies and how they can be used in your projects.

The book begins with the basics of electronics, making sure that you understand components, circuits, and prototyping before moving on. It then performs the same function for code, getting you into the Arduino IDE and showing you how to connect the Arduino to a computer and run simple projects on your Arduino.

Once the basics are out of the way, the next 10 chapters of the book focus on small projects centered around particular components, such as LCD displays, stepper motors, or voice synthesizers. Each of these chapters will get you familiar with the technology involved, how to build with it, how to program it, and how it can be used in your own projects.

Who this book is for

Mastering Arduino is for anybody who wants to experiment with an Arduino board and build simple projects. No prior knowledge is required, as the fundamentals of electronics and coding are covered in this book.

What this book covers

Chapter 1, *The Arduino*, introduces the reader to the Arduino by giving a brief history of the Arduino and going over the different versions. We also look at the headers and what the different pins are used for.

Chapter 2, *Basic Electronics*, introduces the reader to the basics of electricity and electronics. We also introduce the reader to basic electronic components and discuss what they can be used for.

Chapter 3, *Circuit Diagrams*, introduces the reader to circuits and circuit design. It also introduces the reader to circuit properties such as voltage, current, and resistance and how they affect the circuit. We also introduce the reader to the Fritzing tool that can be used for circuit design.

Chapter 4, *Basic Prototyping*, introduces the reader to prototyping and shows them how they can create basic prototypes of their projects. We also discuss the tools needed to create prototypes with the Arduino.

Chapter 5, *Arduino IDE*, introduces the reader to the Arduino IDE and the Arduino Web Editor. We will show the reader how they can use the both the IDE and the Web Editor to program the Arduino.

Chapter 6, *Programming Arduino - The Basics*, gives the reader an introduction to the language used to program the Arduino and the layout of the files.

Chapter 7, *Programming Arduino - Beyond the Basics*, shows the reader how they can interact with the pin headers of the Arduino. We also go over more advance topics such as structures, unions, and classes.

Chapter 8, *Motion Sensor*, is the first "project" chapter. We show how to use the HC-SR01 motion sensor with the Arduino.

Chapter 9, *Environment Sensors*, helps the reader build a basic weather station using a temperature and humidity sensor and a rain sensor.

Chapter 10, *Obstacle Avoidance and Collision Detection*, teaches the reader how to use crash sensors, infrared obstacle avoidance sensors, and ultrasonic range finders to sense objects nearby.

Chapter 11, *Fun with Lights*, teaches the reader how to use the Arduino to control RGB Leds and NeoPixels.

Chapter 12, *Fun with Sound*, shows how the reader can use piezo buzzers and an 8-ohm speaker with the Arduino tone library to create sounds and music. It also teaches the reader learn how to play RTTTL (Ring Tone Text Transfer Language) ring tones with the Arduino.

Chapter 13, *Using LCD Display*, teaches the reader how to connect and use the Nokia 5110 LCD display with the Arduino.

Chapter 14, *Speech Recognition and Voice Synthesizing*, teaches the reader how to use the MOVI speech recognition and voice synthesizing shield to create a voice activated temperature device that will tell them the temperature.

Chapter 15, *DC Motors and Motor Controllers*, teaches the reader how to use DC motors with the L298 motor controller and L293D h-bridge motor driver.

Chapter 16, *Servo Motors*, teaches the reader how to use servo motors with an external power supply to create a robotic claw.

Chapter 17, *Using a Relay*, shows the reader how a relay can be used to allow the Arduino to control an AC powered device.

Chapter 18, *Remotely Controlling the Arduino*, shows the reader how to use both a RF (radio frequency) and an IR (infrared) remote controls to control the Arduino.

Chapter 19, *Creating a Robot*, shows the reader how to take the knowledge they gained in previous chapter and use it to design a robot. We do not actually design a robot, we show how the parts can be used so that the reader can design their own creation.

Chapter 20, *Bluetooth LE*, teaches the reader about Bluetooth LE and how to use the HM-10 Bluetooth LE radio module with the Arduino.

Chapter 21, *Bluetooth Classic*, teaches the reader about Bluetooth Classic and how to use the HC-05 Bluetooth radio module with the Arduino.

To get the most out of this book

- This book assumes no previous knowledge of electronics, programming, or the Arduino. Everything that is needed is covered in this book.

Download the example code files

You can download the example code files for this book from your account at www.packt.com. If you purchased this book elsewhere, you can visit www.packt.com/support and register to have the files emailed directly to you.

You can download the code files by following these steps:

1. Log in or register at www.packt.com.
2. Select the **SUPPORT** tab.
3. Click on **Code Downloads & Errata**.
4. Enter the name of the book in the **Search** box and follow the onscreen instructions.

Once the file is downloaded, please make sure that you unzip or extract the folder using the latest version of:

- WinRAR/7-Zip for Windows
- Zipeg/iZip/UnRarX for Mac
- 7-Zip/PeaZip for Linux

The code bundle for the book is also hosted on GitHub at `https://github.com/PacktPublishing/Mastering-Arduino`. In case there's an update to the code, it will be updated on the existing GitHub repository.

We also have other code bundles from our rich catalog of books and videos available at `https://github.com/PacktPublishing/`. Check them out!

Download the color images

We also provide a PDF file that has color images of the screenshots/diagrams used in this book. You can download it here: `https://www.packtpub.com/sites/default/files/downloads/9781788830584_ColorImages.pdf`.

Conventions used

There are a number of text conventions used throughout this book.

`CodeInText`: Indicates code words in text, database table names, folder names, filenames, file extensions, pathnames, dummy URLs, user input, and Twitter handles. Here is an example: "Mount the downloaded `WebStorm-10*.dmg` disk image file as another disk in your system."

A block of code is set as follows:

```
#define BUTTON_ONE 12
#define LED_ONE 11

void setup() {
  pinMode(BUTTON_ONE, INPUT);
  pinMode(LED_ONE, OUTPUT);
}
```

When we wish to draw your attention to a particular part of a code block, the relevant lines or items are set in bold:

```
display.clearDisplay();
display.drawPixel(10, 10, BLACK);
display.display();
```

Any command-line input or output is written as follows:

```
at+nameBuddy
at+name?
```

Bold: Indicates a new term, an important word, or words that you see onscreen. For example, words in menus or dialog boxes appear in the text like this. Here is an example: "Select **System info** from the **Administration** panel."

 Warnings or important notes appear like this.

 Tips and tricks appear like this.

Get in touch

Feedback from our readers is always welcome.

General feedback: Email customercare@packtpub.com and mention the book title in the subject of your message. If you have questions about any aspect of this book, please email us at customercare@packtpub.com.

Errata: Although we have taken every care to ensure the accuracy of our content, mistakes do happen. If you have found a mistake in this book, we would be grateful if you would report this to us. Please visit www.packt.com/submit-errata, selecting your book, clicking on the Errata Submission Form link, and entering the details.

Piracy: If you come across any illegal copies of our works in any form on the Internet, we would be grateful if you would provide us with the location address or website name. Please contact us at copyright@packt.com with a link to the material.

If you are interested in becoming an author: If there is a topic that you have expertise in and you are interested in either writing or contributing to a book, please visit `authors.packtpub.com`.

Reviews

Please leave a review. Once you have read and used this book, why not leave a review on the site that you purchased it from? Potential readers can then see and use your unbiased opinion to make purchase decisions, we at Packt can understand what you think about our products, and our authors can see your feedback on their book. Thank you!

For more information about Packt, please visit `packt.com`.

The Arduino
1

Have you ever looked at a gadget and wondered how it worked? Do you want to create your own cool and exciting electronics project but do not know how to get started? Your decision to start reading this book is an excellent first step.

In this book, we will teach you everything you need to get started with the Arduino. Everything from basic electronics and prototyping to setting up the Arduino development environment and programming is covered. This book also has numerous sample projects to show you how to use this knowledge with real-world examples. Before we get to all that fun stuff, let's a look at the Arduino itself and get familiar with it.

In this chapter, you will learn:

- What the Arduino boards are
- How to power the Arduino boards
- What Arduino shields are
- What the pins on the Arduino boards do
- Learn about generic and compatible Arduino boards

Arduino is a company, development boards, community and a way of thinking. As you will soon find out, Arduino is also the name of a bar in northern Italy. While we could begin this book by writing several chapters on everything that the Arduino name stands for, that is not what this book is about. This book is about teaching you how to use the Arduino development board to build fun and exciting projects. Anywhere in this book, unless noted otherwise, when we refer to the Arduino we will be referring to the Arduino development boards. However, we do believe to really understand the Arduino board, you should at least have a basic understanding of its history; therefore, we will start off by giving you a brief history of the board and its predecessors.

History of the Arduino

In 2003 Hernando Barragan started working on a project called **Wiring** for his master's thesis at the **Interaction Design Institute Ivrea** (**IDII**) in Italy. At that time students used a microcontroller board that cost USD $100 and needed additional hardware and software to use. Massimo Banzi and Casey Reas, who is known for work on the Processing language, were supervisors for his thesis. The name was *Wiring: Prototyping Physical Interaction Design*.

You can view the thesis here: `http://people.interactionivrea.org/h.barragan/thesis/thesis_low_res.pdf`.

The purpose of the thesis was to create a low-cost and easy-to-use tool so non-engineers could create digital projects. To do this, Hernando wanted to abstract away the complicated details of the electronics to let the user focus on their project. This meant that it had to be work by simply plugging the device into a host computer and have an easy-to-use interface to program it.

The first prototype used the **Parallax Javelin Stamp** microcontroller, which used a subset of the Java programming language. This solution required the Parallax proprietary tools to compile, link and upload the projects to the microcontroller; therefore, it did not meet the requirements of the project because the wiring was going to be an open source project.

The second prototype used the Atmel ARM-based **91R40008 microcontroller**. Hernando obtained better results with this new microcontroller; however, he determined that the microcontroller was far too complex, and it was almost impossible to solder it by hand to a circuit board.

The third prototype used the **Atmel ATmega128** microcontroller with the **MAVRIC** microcontroller board. Hernando had great success using this microcontroller. He used a tool written by Brian Dan called **Avrdude** to easily upload new programs to the board.

Avrdude is still used today and can be found here: `http://www.nongnu.org/avrdude/`.

FTDI's hardware was chosen for the USB to serial communication because it had easy-to-obtain drivers for Linux, Windows and macOS platforms. This allowed the Wiring project to be compatible with all three major platforms.

In 2004, the IDII ordered and paid for 25 Wiring circuit boards. These boards were manufactured by SERP. They included the ATmega128 microcontroller, FTDI USB to serial hardware, onboard LED connected to a pin and serial RX/TX LEDs. Usability tests were performed using these boards and the results were great.

After graduating with distinction in 2004, Hernando moved back to his native Colombia to teach at the Universidad de Los Andes where he continues to work on Wiring. In May 2005, Hernando ordered 200 circuit boards and begin assembling the first Wiring boards outside of IDII. He sold these boards for approximately USD $60. By the end of 2005 Wiring was being used in various parts of the world.

Also, in 2005, the first Arduino board was created. The Arduino board used the less expensive ATmega128 microcontroller to reduce cost. The Arduino team forked the Wiring code and added support for this board.

The initial Arduino core team consisted of Massimo Banzi, David Cuartielles, Tom Igoe, Gianluca Martino and David Mellis. Hernando was not invited to participate in this project. There are several accounts from different individuals involved about why he was not invited.

I do not have any first-hand knowledge about which of these stories are true and which are false; therefore, for this book, I will leave it at the known truth of *Hernando was not invited to participate in the Arduino project.*

The Arduino team strongly believed in open source hardware and software. They believed that by opening the platform up, many more people would have access to and be involved with it. Another reason for opening the platform up was that IDII had used up its funding and was going to be shut down. By open sourcing the platform they knew it would survive and would not be exploited by others.

The team initially decided on a price of USD $30 for the board. They figured it would make it easily accessible to students as well individuals. They also decided to make the board blue, which was different from most other boards at the time, which were green. Another design decision that helped add to the popularity of the board was giving it lots of input and output pins. Most boards at the time limited the number of I/O to reduce costs.

Initially, the team ordered 300 printed circuit boards to conduct a usability test. They handed these boards out to students at IDII with three simple instructions: look up the assembly instructions online, build your board and use it to create something. They had great success with this test because the students were able to assemble the boards and create numerous projects with it.

Shortly after this test, people began to hear about this board and wanted one for themselves. The project started to take off; however, it was still missing a name. While discussing the name, the team was having drinks at a local a bar frequented by Massimo Banzi. The bar's name was *Bar Di Re Arduino* and the new board became known as the Arduino.

What is the Arduino?

At the heart of the Arduino is the microcontroller. A microcontroller is a standalone, single-chip integrated circuit that contains a CPU, read-only memory, random access memory and various I/O busses. Most Arduino boards use the Atmel 8-bit AVR microcontroller.

The Arduino UNO R3, which is the primary board used in this book, uses the ATmega328 chip. This chip is an 8-bit RISC-based microcontroller that features 32 KB of flash memory with read-write capabilities, 1 Kbyte EEPROM, 2 Kbytes SRAM, 23-general purpose I/O lines and 32 general-purpose registers. Do not be too concerned if you do not understand all those specifications because we will be interacting with the microcontroller using the interface that the Arduino board provides us. It is good to know these specifications as you begin to develop more complex applications because they do put limits on what we can do.

All the hardware and software that make up the Arduino platform are distributed as open source and licensed under the GNU **Lesser General Public License** (**LGPL**) or the GNU **General Public License** (**GPL**). This allows for the manufacture and distribution of Arduino boards by anyone and has led to numerous *generic*, lower cost, Arduino compatible boards.

 You can find more information about the license and the Arduino boards on the Arduino website here: `https://www.arduino.cc`.

Touring the Arduino UNO R3

The Arduino is an open source hardware and software platform that is incredibly powerful yet easy to use. You can look at and download the code from any of the Arduino repositories on GitHub here: `https://github.com/arduino`. This platform has captured the imagination of electronic enthusiasts and the maker community everywhere. It enables people to inexpensively experiment with electronic prototypes and see their projects come to life. These projects can range from simply making an LED blink or recording the temperature to controlling 3D printers or making robots.

While there are numerous models of the Arduino, in this book we will primarily be using the very popular Arduino UNO R3 board. The following photograph shows the Arduino Uno's board layout with the main connectors identified:

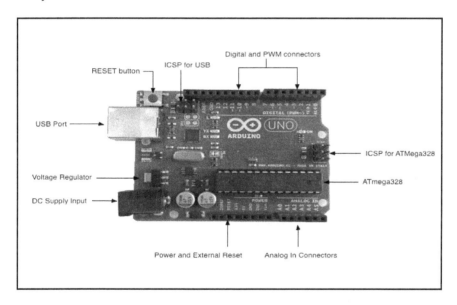

 For the purposes of this book, anytime we refer to the Arduino Uno board or the Uno board we are referring to the Arduino Uno R3 depicted in the preceding photograph.

As we can see, the Arduino Uno of today still uses the blue color that the original Arduino designers chose to help their boards stand out. The following is a list of major components of the Arduino Uno:

- **DC supply Input**: The DC supply input can be used with an AC-to-DC power adapter or a battery. The power source can be connected using a 2.1 mm center-positive plug. The Arduino Uno operates at 5 volts but can have a maximum input of 20 volts; however, it is recommended to not use more than 12V.
- **Voltage Regulator:** The Arduino uses a linear regulator to control the voltage going into the board.
- **USB Port:** The USB port can be used to power and program the board.
- **RESET button:** This button, when pressed, will reset the board.
- **ICSP for USB:** The in-circuit serial programming pins are used to flash the firmware on the USB interface chip.
- **ICSP for ATmega328:** The in-circuit serial programming pins are used to flash the firmware on the ATmega microcontroller.
- **Digital and PWM connectors**: These pins, labeled 0 to 13, can be used as either a digital input or output pins. The pins labeled with the tilde (~) can also be used for **Pulse-Width Modulation** (**PWM**) output.
- **Analog In Connectors:** The pins, labeled A0 to A5, can be used for analog input. These pins can be used to read the output from analog sensors.
- **Power and External Reset:** These pins in this header, provide ground and power for external devices and sensors from the Arduino. The Arduino can also be powered through these pins. There is also a reset pin that can be used to reset the Arduino.
- **ATmega328:** The microcontroller for the Arduino Uno board.

The Digital/PWM/Analog in/Power/Reset connectors are collectively known as the pin headers. The pins in these headers allow the Arduino to communicate with external sensors and other devices. Let's look at the different ways that we can power the Arduino board.

Powering the Arduino

The Arduino can be powered in one of three ways: through the VIN/GND pins, the DC Supply Input port or the USB port.

Using the VIN/GND pins to power the Arduino

The VIN and GND pins in the power and external reset header can be used to power the Arduino with an external battery. Powering the Arduino in this way is mainly used when we wish to connect a battery, in series, with a switch to turn the power to the Arduino on and off. The following photograph illustrates this:

It is not recommended that we power the Arduino in this manner unless we are looking for the most expensive and short-lived way to power the Arduino. We could use six AA batteries in series, which will provide the same voltage as the 9V battery in the preceding photograph but would give us approximately four times the capacity. It is still not recommended that we power the Arduino in this manner as it would be fairly expensive.

Unless there is a specific need to use a battery to power the Arduino, I would avoid using them.

Using the DC supply input to power the Arduino

The DC supply input connector can be used with an AC-to-DC power adapter or a battery to power the Arduino. The connector has a female 2.1 mm center-positive plug. While the Arduino operates at 5 volts a maximum input of 20 volts can be used; however, as was stated earlier, it is recommended to not use more than 12V.

We can use an AC-to-DC adjustable power adapter like the one shown in the following photograph to power the Arduino using the DC supply input connector:

With this adapter, you can adjust the output power to the desired voltage. You can find power supplies similar to this online or at most stores that sell electronic items.

Using the USB connector to power the Arduino

Using the USB connector to power the Arduino is the way that I usually power it. It is by far the easiest and safest way to power the Arduino and the least expensive. You can power the Arduino directly from the USB port on your computer or from a USB rechargeable power bank like the one shown in the following photograph:

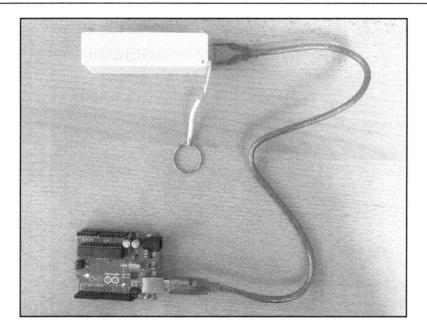

This is a very affordable and simple way to power the Arduino. It can also be used for robotic or similar projects that need the mobility to move around; however, we do need to be careful when we connect shields or other accessories to the Arduino that the USB connector can draw enough power. As an example, later in this book, we will look at the MOVI speech synthesizing and voice recognition shield that draws too much power for the Arduino to be powered by the USB connector while the shield is connected.

Now that we have mentioned Arduino shields, let's look at what they are and see the types of functionality they can provide.

Arduino shields

An Arduino shield is a modular circuit board that plugs directly into the pin headers of the Arduino board. These shields will add extra functionality to the Arduino board. If we are looking to connect to the internet, do speech recognition, control DC motors or add other functionality to the Arduino, there is probably a shield that can help us. While we are not required to use shields, they do make adding extra functionality to our Arduino boards very easy.

The following photograph shows examples of a few shields. We will be using shields in some of our sample projects later in this book:

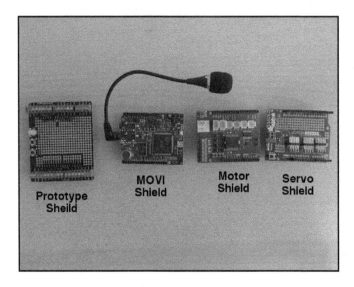

A shield fits on top of the Arduino by plugging directly into the pin headers. We can also stack one shield on top of another if they do not use the same resources. Here is how an Arduino looks with two shields attached:

An Arduino shield makes it incredibly easy to add functionality to an Arduino Uno. Most shields usually have great documentation as well, which makes programming them also very easy. The drawback to shields is they usually cost more than purchasing the components and connecting them to the Arduino with a breadboard.

Some shields, such as the MOVI speech synthesizing and voice recognition shield and the Sparkfun Xbee radio module shield, add functionality that cannot simply be added as a single component. For functionality like this, a shield or an external circuit board would be required.

Let's take a closer look at the pin headers for the Arduino Uno R3.

Arduino pin

There is a total of 31 pins in the Arduino Uno pin headers. Most of these pins can be configured to perform different functions. The following diagram shows what the various pins can be used for:

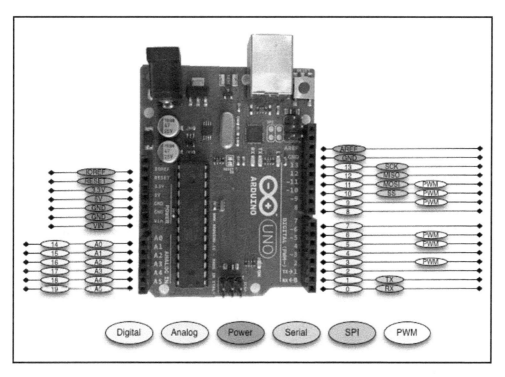

Let's look at what the different pins do.

Digital pins

The digital pins on the Arduino are the ones that are used the most when connecting external sensors. These pins can be configured for either input or output. These pins default to an input state; therefore, when we are using a pin for input we do not need to explicitly declare them as input pins; however, it is good practice to do so because it will make it easier for someone reading our code to understand what the pin is being used for.

The digital pins will have one of two values: HIGH (1), which is 5V, or LOW (0), which is 0V. Once we start to program the Arduino, we will see how to read from or write to these pins.

Analog input pins

The Arduino Uno contains a built-in **Analog-To-Digital** (**ADC**) converter with six channels, which gives us six analog input pins. The ADC converts an analog signal into a digital value. While the digital pins have two values, either high or low, the analog input pins have values from 0 to 1023 relative to the reference value of the Arduino. The Arduino Uno has a reference value of 5V.

The analog input pins are used to read analog sensors such as rangefinders and temperature sensors. The six analog pins can also be configured as digital pins if we run out of digital pins in our project.

PWM pins

Where the analog input pins are designed to read analog sensors (input), the PWM pins are designed for output. PWM is a technique for obtaining analog results with digital output.

Since a digital output can be either on or off, to obtain the analog output the digital output is switch between HIGH and LOW rapidly. The percentage of the time that the signal is high is called the **duty cycle**. The following diagram illustrates this concept:

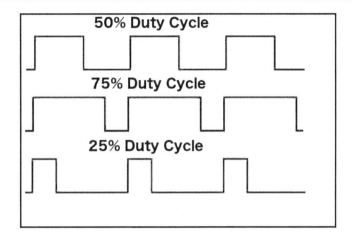

We have the ability to set the frequency of how fast the signal can switch between HIGH and LOW. This frequency is measured in Hertz and sets how many times the signal can switch per second. For example, if we set the frequency to 500 Hz, that would mean that the signal could switch 500 times a second.

We will be using the PWM pins for several examples in this book and will examine them more when we learn how to program the Arduino.

Power pins

The Arduino has several power pins. They are as follows:

- **VIN**: This pin is used when we power the Arduino board using an external power supply. This is the pin used in the *Using the VIN/GND pins to power the Arduino* section of this chapter.
- **GND**: These are the ground pins.
- **5V**: This is 5V out and is used to power most sensors.
- **3.3V**: This is 3.3V out and can be used to power sensors that are compatible with 3.3V. A list of some compatible 3.3V sensors can be found here: `https://www.dfrobot.com/wiki/index.php/3.3V_Compatible_Device_List`.
- **Reset**: This pin can be used to reset the Arduino board by an external source.
- **ioref**: This is the reference voltage for the board. For the Arduino, this will be 5V.

Serial pins

These pins can be used for serial communication. The RX (digital pin 0) is used to receive while TX (digital pin 1) is used to transmit. These pins are connected directly to the USB-to-TTL serial chip. One note, you should not connect these pins directly to an RS-232 serial port because you will damage your board.

SPI pins

The **Serial Peripheral Interface** (**SPI**) pins are used for a synchronous serial data protocol that is used by microcontrollers for communicating with peripheral devices. This protocol always has one master with one or more slave devices. The pins are:

- **MISO**: The **Master in Slave out** pin is used to send data from the slave to the master device.
- **MOSI**: The **Master out Slave in** the pin is used to send data from the master to the slave device.
- **SCK**: The **serial clock** synchronizes the data transmission and is generated by the master.
- **SS**: The **slave select** pin tells the slave to go active or to go to sleep. This is used to select which slave device should receive the transmission from the master.

Now that we have quickly looked at the pins on the Arduino Uno R3 let's look at some of the different Arduino boards.

Different Arduino boards

There are a number of different official Arduino boards and modules that can be used for various purposes. To see all the different boards, you can go to that Arduino product page (https://www.arduino.cc/en/Main/Products) where they list all the official Arduino boards.

While the Arduino Uno R3 is the most popular Arduino board within the maker community, the following lists some of the other popular boards:

Arduino Micro

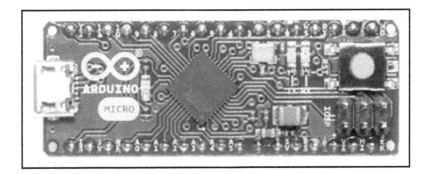

The Arduino Micro is the smallest board in the Arduino family. It is based on the ATmega32U4 microcontroller. This board features 20 digital I/O pins of which 7 can be used for PWM output and 12 can be used as analog input. The Micro and the Nano (which we will see a little later) can be used for a project where the Arduino Uno may be too big.

Arduino Mega 2560

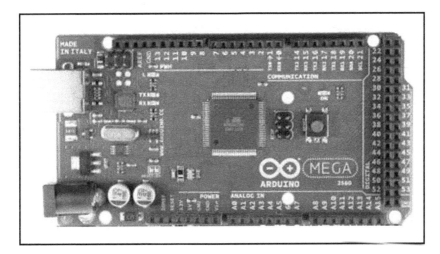

The Arduino Mega 2560 is designed for the most complex projects. It features 53 digital I/O pins, 16 analog input pins and 15 PWM output pins. It also has 4 serial UARTs for serial connections. If you want to create a complex project like a robot, the Mega is the board you will want to start with.

Lilypad

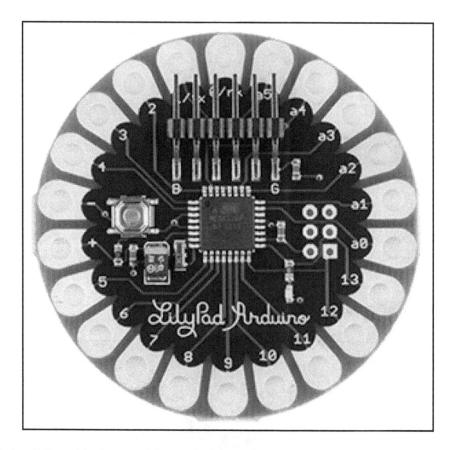

The Arduino Lilypad is designed for wearable projects. It can be sewn into fabrics and use power supplies and sensors that are also sewn into fabrics. The Lilypad is based on the ATmega168V or ATmega328V (low power versions). This board features 16 digital I/O, 6 analog inputs and 6 PWM outputs.

Arduino Nano

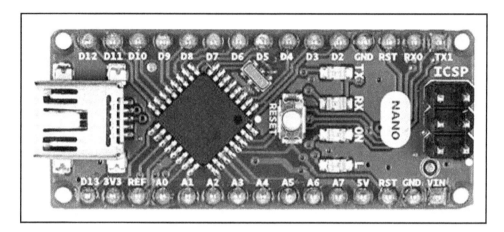

There are a lot of similarities between the Nano and the Micro. The Micro was released in 2012 while the Nano was released in 2008. The Nano features 14 digital I/O pins, 8 analog input pins and 6 PWM output pins. With those specifications, you may think that you should use the Micro board over the Nano however if you look at most online retailers like Amazon or eBay you can find the Nano for about half the price of the Micro.

You will also find that the Nano is easier to obtain than the Micro because there are so many generic Nano boards. We will also be using the Nano for some of the projects in this book.

Generic boards

At the beginning of this book, we noted that the Arduino is an open source hardware and software platform. All the original hardware design files are released under the Creative Commons Attribution Share-Alike license. This license allows both personal and commercial derivatives of all the Arduino boards if they credit Arduino and release their design under the same license. This has led to many lower price *generic* boards.

If you search for an Arduino board on most online retailer sites, the majority of the boards will not actually be genuine Arduino boards. If you look at the Arduino Uno board in the following photograph, you will notice an infinity sign with a plus (+) and minus (-) in it. That is the official Arduino logo and any board that has this logo is a genuine Arduino board.

In this book, we will be using mostly generic Arduino boards as they are cheaper and usually easier to obtain. The following photograph shows what some generic Arduino boards look like. The first photograph shows two generic Arduino Uno boards:

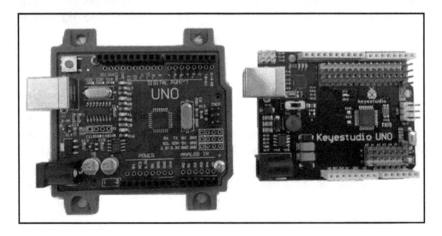

The next photograph shows a generic Arduino Mega 2560 board:

You will notice that these generic boards do not contain the Arduino logo; however, they still contain the name of the official board. While the previous generic boards look very similar to the official Arduino boards, that is not required. Some manufacturers chose to take the Arduino reference design and add additional functionality to their boards. The board in the following photograph is an example of this:

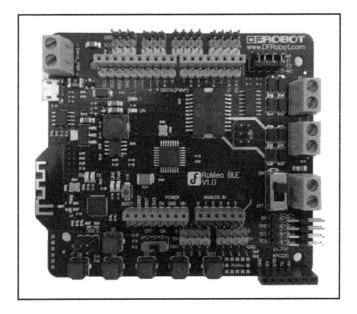

The DFRobot RoMeo BLE board is an Arduino-compatible robot control board with Bluetooth LE 4.0. This board takes the design of the Arduino Uno and adds a number of extra features, such as built-in Bluetooth and an integrated two-way DC motor driver.

No matter what your project is, you can probably find either a genuine Arduino board or a generic/compatible one that will fit your needs.

Summary

In this chapter, we gave a brief history of the Arduino, which included its development from a master's thesis paper to a full commercial project. This included a tour of some different Arduino boards. We also showed the different ways that the Arduino boards can be powered and gave a brief explanation of the various pin types.

In the next chapter, we will give you a brief introduction to electronics and commonly used components.

Basic Electronics

2

For as long as I can remember, I have been fascinated by electronics. When I was seven or eight years old, I can remember taking apart a hand-held transistor radio and struggling for several days to put it back together without letting my parents know I took it apart. Even though I would take little devices apart and put them back together, I really did not understand basic electronics until I took a basic electronics course in high school. That class gave me enough knowledge to begin to understand how the electronic devices that I have been taking apart actually worked. It also laid the foundation for all electronic projects that I have done since.

What you will learn in this chapter:

- What the four building blocks of an electronic circuit are
- What a multimeter is
- What some of the more popular basic electronic components are
- What the properties of electricity are
- How to use Ohm's law
- How to calculate power

While the Arduino board was originally designed to abstract away the complicated details of the electronics to let the user focus on their project, we still need a basic understanding of electronics and electricity to connect external components to the Arduino board and to make sure we do not damage the board with those components. This chapter, along with `Chapter 3`, *Circuit Diagrams* and `Chapter 4`, *Basic Prototyping*, are designed to give you a basic understanding of electronics, electricity, and circuits so you can build your own prototypes and work with the examples in the later chapters of this book.

All electronics and electricity covered in this book is related to **direct current** (**DC**), which is different from the **alternating current** (**AC**) that comes from wall outlets. DC current is the flow of electrical charge in one direction while AC current changes direction periodically. We only cover DC current in this book because it is inherently safer than AC current and the Arduino with its components are powered by DC power sources. We can power the Arduino by plugging a power adapter into a wall, as we saw in Chapter 1, *The Arduino*; however, the power adapter converts the AC power source to a DC power source.

Let's start exploring basic electronics by looking at the four main building blocks of any electronic project.

Electronic building block

When I want to build something, whether it is prototyping something with the Arduino, coding an application or building wooden steps to our back door, I usually try to break the project down into individual blocks. It really helps me focus on each individual part of the design rather than getting overwhelmed by the whole design. We can usually break an electronic project into four separate blocks. The following diagram illustrates how these blocks work together:

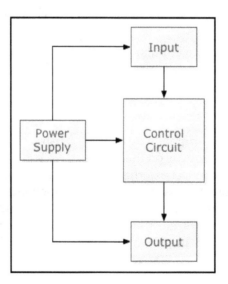

Let's look at each one of these blocks starting with the power supply.

Power supply

The power supply is the source of electricity for the project. For most of the experiments in this book, the power supply will be some low-voltage DC power supply like the power sources discussed in the *Powering the Arduino* section of `Chapter 1`, *The Arduino*. We will also show how to use a 12V battery to power DC motors using a motor controller board in the later chapters of this book.

Input

The input block will contain electronic components that give the control circuit information. These components give the control circuit the ability to sense the outside world. Some examples of input components would be:

- **Buttons or switches:** Buttons and switches can be used to turn the flow of electricity on or off. When they are in the off-state electricity will not flow through the circuit; however, when they are in the on-state electricity does flow through the circuit.
- **Temperature sensors:** Temperature sensors adjust the amount of resistance in a circuit based on the temperature causing the voltage to vary by the temperature. By reading the amount of voltage coming in, the control circuit can calculate the current temperature.
- **Range finders:** There are many types of range sensors; however, the basic idea is the voltage that is outputted by the sensor varies depending on how close an object is to it. Like the temperature sensor, the control circuit can then calculate the distance based on the voltage coming in.
- **Proximity sensor:** This is a sensor that is triggered when something gets within a certain distance of the sensor. A proximity sensor is usually either ON (full voltage) or OFF (no voltage).

Output

The output block will contain electronic components that do something. These components give the circuit the ability to interact with the outside world or to do something. Some examples of output components are:

- **Motors:** Motors allow the circuit to turn something like a fan or wheels. This type of component turns electrical power into power that does work.

- **LEDs:** An LED can be used as indicators to give visual feedback to the user. This type of component will turn electrical power into light.
- **Speaker:** A speaker can be used to give audio feedback to the user. This type of component will turn electrical power into sound.

Control circuit

The control circuit block is the electronic component that receives information from the input components, processes that information and controls the output components. For the purposes of this book, the control circuit will be the Arduino but keep in mind it is not required that we use the Arduino for the control circuit. We could create our own control circuit or use another type of microcontroller board like the **Raspberry Pi** or **BeagleBone Black**.

This block diagram gives us a high-level view of our Arduino projects. The first thing that we will need to understand is what ties these blocks and the components in the blocks together. For this, we will need to have a basic understanding of electronics and electricity. Let's begin by looking at some tools and common electronic components. We will start by looking at probably the most important tool we have, in our toolbox, to help us with electronic projects: the multimeter.

Multimeter

A multimeter, also known as a Volt-Ohm-Milliameter, is an electronic measuring instrument that is typically used to measure voltage, current, and resistance. There are analog multimeters that operate by moving a pointer to display the measurement, but today most multimeters are digital with an LCD that is used to display exactly what the measurement is.

A multimeter can cost as low as USD $10 and up to USD $400 for a really nice Fluke 87V. Unless you are planning on using the multimeter for professional purposes, I would recommend getting a low-cost multimeter like the ones shown in the following photograph:

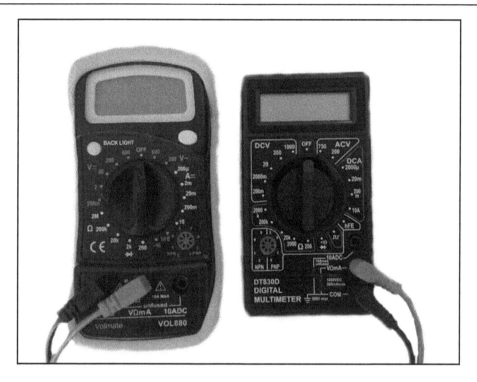

The digital multimeter has three main parts, which are the display, selection knob, and the probe ports.

The display will show what the measurement is. Some of the higher-end multimeters have a backlit display to make it easier to read in low light.

The selection knob is used to select what we wish to measure. Most multimeters will read resistance (ohms), voltage (volts), and current (amps). Some of the higher-end meters will have the ability to measure additional items and have additional features.

Probes are plugged into the probe ports, which are usually located on the front of the meter. The black probe should be plugged into the port labeled COM and the red probe will be plugged into one of the other ports depending on what is being measured. Really there is no difference between the red and black probes; however, it is good practice to always connect black probes and wires to common/ground and the red probes and wires to power since this is the standard.

Digital multimeters are very easy to use. We start off by selecting what we wish to measure using the selection knob. Then connect the black probe to one end of the circuit and the red probe to the other and the multimeter will display the measurement. The following photograph shows how we would measure the remaining voltage of a 9V battery:

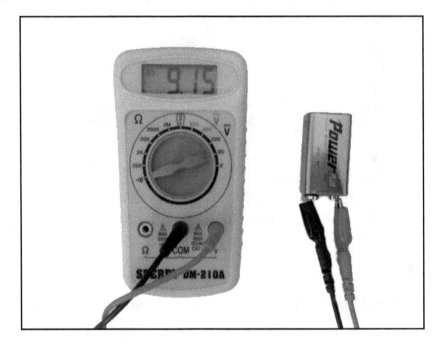

You will notice that the selector knob is set to 20V, therefore, the meter will measure up to 20V. The following photograph shows how we could measure the resistance of a resistor:

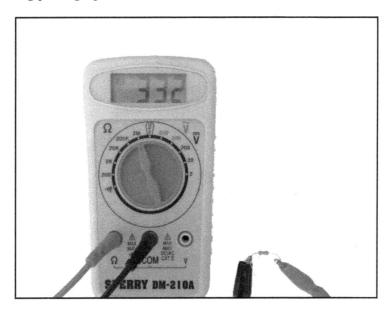

In this photograph, we are measuring a 330K Ohm resistor. If we happen to set the selection knob to low, we would overload the multimeter but almost all meters have protection, therefore, they will not be damaged by overloading them. When you overload a meter they typically show a 1 all the way to the left of the display as the following photograph shows:

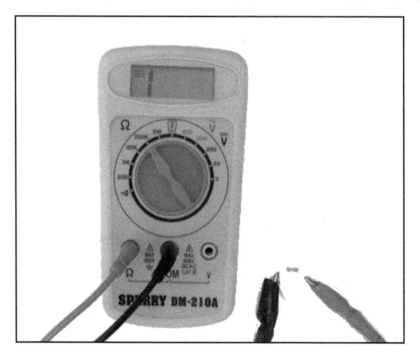

In the preceding photograph, we are trying to measure a 330K Ohm resistor with the selection knob set for a maximum of 200K Ohms. If you are not comfortable using a multimeter I would recommend searching for *multimeter video tutorials* and watching a couple videos on how to use them.

Electronic components

There are numerous types of electronic components that we will be using in our projects. These components can be obtained for a relatively low cost from many online retailers. It is important to be familiar with what some of the more popular components because they will be used in many of the circuits we create. Let's start off by looking at the component that we will be using is almost all circuits that we create, the resistor.

Resistor

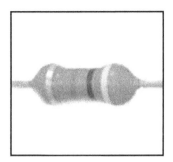

The resistor will be used in almost every circuit that we create. A resistor is an electronic component that has a specific amount of electrical resistance that never changes. The resistor limits the flow of electrons in the circuit. We will see how resistance works a little later in this chapter.

Potentiometer

The potentiometer, also known as a pot, is a variable resistor. A potentiometer allows for the creation of a circuit where the user can change the resistance. Potentiometer comes in various shapes, sizes, and values but they all have three connectors. The resistance between the two outer connectors is fixed and is the maximum resistance of the potentiometer. The resistance between the center connector and either outer connection various as the user turns the knob.

The potentiometer has lots of usages including audio control, motion control for servo motors and control brightness of a light.

Switches

There are several types of switches that can be used depending on the need. The preceding photograph shows, from left to right, a push button, micro and toggle switch.

The **push button** switches are switches that are activated by pressing a button. These switches are usually used to start or stop some action. Some examples usages for a push button switch would be to start a robot in motion, start a led blinking or capture the current measurement from a sensor.

The **microswitch** is a switch that is activated by a light force being applied to a lever or button on the switch. These switches are widely used in many household and industrial applications. Some examples of uses for a micro switch are end stops for a 3D printer, detecting if the door of a microwave is closed, and collision detection for robots.

The **toggle switch** is activated and deactivated by moving the lever to the on or off position. The toggle switch is mainly used to turn items on and off like a light switch.

Transistor

Transistors are tiny switches that can be triggered by an electric signal. Transistors are the building blocks for the digital world that we live in today. Integrated circuits are made up of many tiny transistors. The transistor gives up the digital on/off a signal that all digital devices rely on.

A transistor has three connectors, which are known as the collector, base, and emitter. For NPN transistors collector is the leftmost pin followed by the base and emitter. For PNP transistors the leftmost pin is the emitter followed by the base and collector. The collector should be connected to an input power source. The emitter should be connected to a common ground in the circuit. The base, when a certain amount of voltage is applied, triggers the flow of electricity through the transistor. The base is what acts as a switch to turn the flow of electricity on or off.

 For a DC circuit, like the ones we will be using in this book, all of the components need to be connected to a common ground. For example, if you have a battery that powers the Arduino and a battery that powers the DC motors, the ground (negative) terminals will need to be connected together so all of the components are connected to the same ground. This is known as having a common ground in the circuit.

LED

The **Light Emitting Diode** or **LED** for short, is a two-lead semiconducting device that emits light when a certain amount of current is passed through. When using a LED, we need to be very careful not to apply too much current because it is very easy to blow one. For most LED, the recommended voltage would be 5 volts.

Most LEDs have two different size connectors. The long connector is the anode and should be connected to a power source. The short connector is a cathode and should be connected to a common ground.

Capacitor

Capacitors come in many shapes, sizes and capacities. The preceding photograph displays two small capacitors that could be used in low-power circuits like we will be using in this book.

A capacitor stores and discharges electricity similar to a battery, except the capacitor charges and discharges rapidly often in seconds or fractions of seconds. The capacitor is used in almost all electronic devices for various reasons. The capacitor can be used to smooth the flow of electricity, filter the flow of electricity to only allow so much through or for a large quick burst of electricity like a camera flash.

We should be very careful when dealing with capacitors to make sure they are fully discharged before handling them to avoid getting an electrical shock.

Integrated circuit

An **integrated circuit**, or **IC** for short, is a semiconductor wafer that contains thousands or millions of tiny resistors, transistors, and capacitors that are used to perform certain functions. There are millions of different types of IC and one example is the Atmel ATmega128 microcontroller used in the Arduino. Virtually all electronics have some integrated circuits in them.

Now that we have seen the more popular electronic components that will make up the projects in this book, let's see what electricity is.

What is electricity?

Everything in the universe is made up of atoms. Atoms are made up of three primary components, which are the proton, neutron, and electron. The protons and neutrons make up the nucleus of the atom while the electrons orbit the nucleus like the moon orbits the Earth. The proton has a positive charge and the electron has a negative charge.

Electricity is created when particles become charged. Some particles become positively charged while others becomes negatively charged. Particles with opposite charges attract each other while particles with the same charge repel each other.

Since the electrons are in constant motion, occasionally an electron will escape from its atom and joins another atom. The atom that the electron escaped from now will have a net positive charge while the atom that gained the electron while having a net negative charge. Electricity is this flow of electrons.

The electrical conductivity of a metal is measured by how easily an electron can escape from its atom. Copper, Silver, and Gold are some of the best conductive materials because they have only a single valence, or outer shell, an electron that moves with little resistance.

If we connected a copper wire from one end of a battery to the other, as shown in the following diagram, the flow of electrons would go from the negatively charged end to the positively charged end.

Do not actually do this, the wire could get very hot and the battery will drain very quickly.

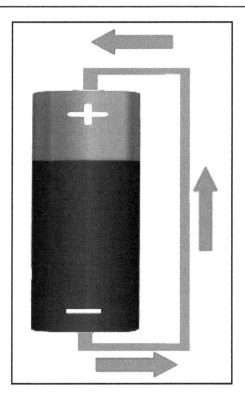

The reason that electricity flows in this manner is oppositely charged particles attract therefor the positively charged end attracts the electrons causing them to flow from the negatively charged end. One of the easiest ways to envision the flow of electrons is to look at how water flows through a pipe. Now let's look at some properties of electricity starting with how we would measure the flow of electrons.

Current

Current, in an electronic circuit, is the flow of the charged particles (electrons). The current is measured by the number of charged particles passing the point of the circuit, that is being measured, per second.

Current is measured in amperes and can be measured with most standard multimeters. One ampere is equal to 6.241×10^{18} electrons passing the point being measured per second.

If we think of electricity as water flowing through a pipe, the following diagram will help visualize what current is:

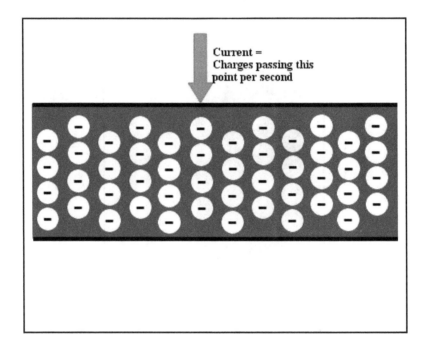

Voltage

Voltage is the amount of potential energy between two points, where one point has more charged particles than the other. The difference in this charge is called the voltage. We can think of the voltage as the pressure within the circuit to push the charged particles through the circuit. Voltage is measured in volts.

To continue with the water in a pipe analogy, we can think of voltage as the water pressure within the pipe pushing the water through. The following diagram illustrates this:

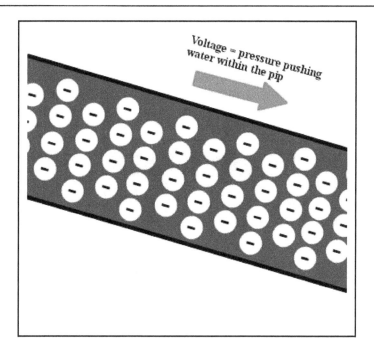

Resistance

Resistance is how much the flow of current is reduced or impeded. All circuits have some resistance from the wire and components that make up the circuit; however, most circuits include resistors that add extra resistance to the circuit. These resistors enable us to limit the flow of charged particles within the circuit. Resistance is measured in Ohms.

Using the water in a pipe analogy again, resistance is the smallest part of the pipe that is impeding the water flow.

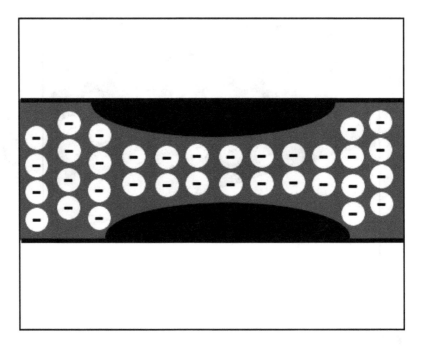

Now let's see how these three properties work together by examining Ohm's law.

Ohm's law

Ohm's law stated that the current flowing through a circuit is directly proportional to the voltage applied to the circuit. This means that if the voltage of the circuit increases, then the current will also increase if the resistance stays the same.

Ohm's law also states that current flowing through a circuit is inversely proportional to the resistance of the circuit. This means that if the resistance of a circuit increases, then the current flow will decrease if the voltage stays the same.

The standard formula for Ohm's law states that the current is equal to the voltage divided by the resistance:

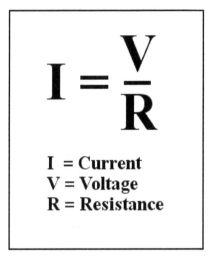

$$I = \frac{V}{R}$$

I = Current
V = Voltage
R = Resistance

While the preceding formula is how Ohm's law is usually introduced, it really consists of three formulas:

$I = V/R$

$R = V/I$

$V = I*R$

In this book, we will use the $R = V/I$ the most to calculate the resistance needed to limit the current flow of the circuits. We limit the current flowing in a circuit by adding resistors to it.

There is one other formula that we should know when working with electronic components. This formula is used to calculate power.

What is power?

Power is the amount of electrical energy transformed into another type of energy (heat, light or work) per second. Power is an important concept because it is what allows our electric circuit to do something. For example, if we created a circuit with a battery and a resistor, the resistor will convert the electrical energy to heat (or thermal) energy. All resistors also have a maximum power rating that they can handle therefore to ensure that we do not damage the resistors in a circuit we will need to know how to calculate power. Power is calculated by multiplying the voltage by the current and is measured in Watts.

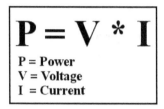

$$P = V * I$$

P = Power
V = Voltage
I = Current

Most of the low-cost resistors that we can get from online retailers are rated at 1/4 (or 0.25) Watts so we will assume that the resistors we are using for the projects in this book are rated at that 1/4 Watt. Now let's say in our project we are running a voltage of 10V across a 100 Ohm resistor, do you think the resistor will be able to handle it? To figure this out, the first thing we need to do is to calculate the current using Ohm's law. We will use the formula $I = V/R$ to calculate the current ($I = 10V/100$ Ohms) and come up with a current of 0.1 Amps. We can now use the formula $P = V*I$ to calculate the power ($P=0.1A * 10V$) which would equal 1 Watt, which is four times what the resistor is rated for, therefore the resistor will get very hot and may even get damaged.

Resistor color codes

The value of a resistor is marked on its body using color bands. The majority of the resistors contain four bands but there are also some resistors that have five and six bands. The following picture shows what a resistor with four bands looks like:

With a four-band resistor the first two bands, from left to right, indicate the resistor's value. The third band is the multiplier and the fourth band is the tolerance. Resistors that have five bands use the first three bands to indicate the resistor's value, then the fourth band is the multiplier and the fifth band is the tolerance. The following table shows the color values:

Color	Value	Multiplier	Tolerance
Black	0	1	
Brown	1	10	
Red	2	100	
Orange	3	1K	
Yellow	4	10K	
Green	5	100K	
Blue	6	1M	
Violet	7	10M	
Grey	8	100M	
White	9	1G	
Gold		0.1	5%
Silver		0.01	10%

The resistor pictured the beginning of this section has four bands coloured Yellow-Violet-Orange-Silver, which means the resistor is a 47K Ohm with 10% tolerance. We know this because the first two bands (Yellow and Violet) have values of 4 and 7. We then use the third band (Orange) as the multiplier which is 1K. This gives us a resistance value of 47 multiplied by 1K or 47K. The fourth band (Silver) indicates a tolerance of 10%.

Summary

In this chapter, we gave a very brief introduction to electricity and some of the more popular electronic components that we will be using later in this book. This chapter will give you enough knowledge to get you started building very basic prototypes. It is recommended that once you start more advanced projects you do further reading on electricity and electronic components.

In the next chapter, we will look at circuits and how to read circuit diagrams.

3
Circuit Diagrams

As a boy, the more I took apart the hand-held transistor radios and games the easier it became to identify the various parts that were on the circuit boards. It was a lot harder, however, to figure out how all the parts worked together. While it was possible to take electronic devices apart and put them back together without a basic understanding of the circuit, it was impossible to figure out how the devices actually worked. Once I understood how circuits worked, not only was I able to begin to understand how the electronic devices worked but I was also able to build simple circuits on my own.

In this chapter, you will learn:

- What a circuit is
- What open, closed, and short circuits are
- What Fritzing diagrams are
- What schematic diagrams are
- What the differences between series and parallel circuits are

Before we can begin developing our own electronic projects we need to have a basic understanding of what circuits are and how to design them. In this chapter, we will look at the knowledge we need to begin designing and creating basic circuits.

What is a circuit?

A circuit is a circular path in which electrical current flows. In Chapter 2, *Basic Electronics* we described electrical current as the flow of electrons. The circuit is the path in which these electrons flow, powering the components that make up the circuit. The point where the electrons enter the circuit, and the current starts, is called the **source**. The point where the electrons exit the circuit is called the **return**. Everything between the source and the return, the components and wires that make up the remainder of the circuit, is called the **load**.

In a closed circuit, the current has a complete path from the source to the return allowing the current to flow through the circuit. The following diagram shows a closed circuit where a switch is closed allowing the current to flow through the circuit. In this circuit, we are powering a light bulb. This makes the light bulb the load:

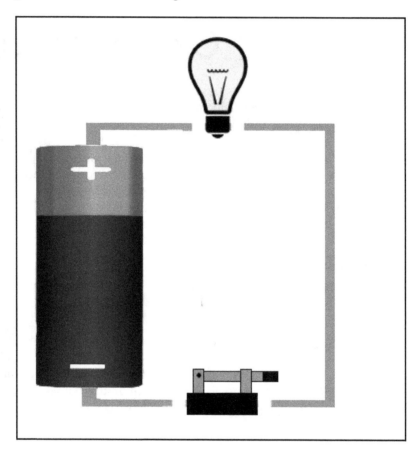

An open circuit is one that has a break in the circuit that prevents the current flow. The following diagram shows an open circuit where the switch is open, thereby preventing the current flow:

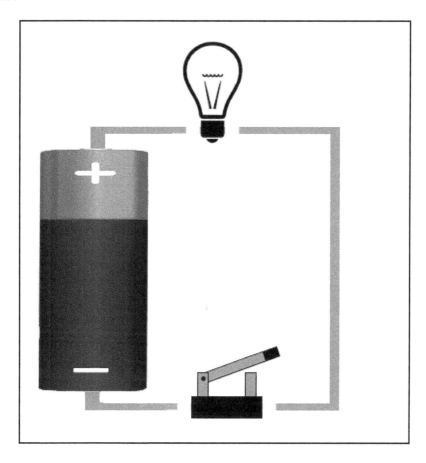

The last two examples show how a typical light switch works in your house. When you turn the switch on, the circuit is closed, which turns the light on; however, when you turn the switch off, the circuit is open, which turns the light off.

Most multimeters have a continuity mode that can be used to test if you have an open circuit or not. If your multimeter has a continuity mode, you should see a symbol that looks somewhat like this:

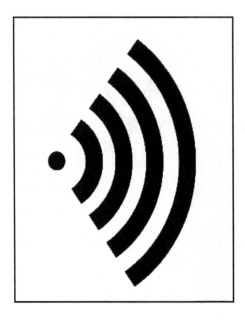

If you set your multimeter to continuity mode and touch the two leads together the meter will emit a tone. This tone lets you know that you have a closed circuit. To test if your circuit is closed or open, put the multimeter into continuity mode and place the two leads from the multimeter at different points in your circuit, and if there is a connection between the two points the meter will emit the tone.

The most dangerous circuit is a short circuit. A short circuit is one that allows the current to flow through the circuit with little to no resistance. This is usually a circuit with no load.

 You should never create a circuit like this because you run the risk of starting a fire.

The following diagram shows what a short circuit looks like:

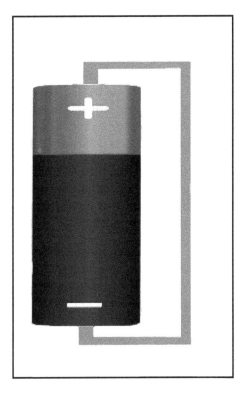

While the preceding diagrams look nice, it would be almost impossible to show complex circuits with diagrams like these. It is also hard for someone else to understand these diagrams without an explanation, because there are no standard symbols defined. The standard way to represent a circuit is with a schematic diagram.

A schematic diagram, when referring to electronic circuits, is a diagram that contains representations of the elements in the circuit. Each type of electrical component has a standard symbol that is used when representing it on a schematic diagram. These diagrams will show how each component is connected giving anyone that reads the diagram an understanding of how the circuit works.

All the circuit diagrams in this book will be created using the very popular, and free, **Fritzing** application, which can be downloaded here: `http://fritzing.org/home/`. At the time this book was written, the latest version of Fritzing is 0.9.3b and is the version used to create all of the diagrams in this book and the diagrams that come with the downloadable code. Let's look at what Fritzing is before we look at the types of diagrams it can produce.

Fritzing

Fritzing is an open-source initiative to develop software to design electronic hardware. This software is designed in the same spirit as the Arduino where it abstracts away the complexity of diagramming the circuit, so the user can focus on the design itself. There will be a **Fritzing sketch** in the downloadable code, for all projects in this book. A Fritzing sketch is a project within the Fritzing application that represents the circuit being created. These projects can contain both circuit diagrams and code if the project includes a microcontroller like the Arduino. We will not be using the coding section of Fritzing in this book and instead will use the standard Arduino IDE, but it is good to know it is there.

The Fritzing sketches included in the downloadable code will allow you to examine the design of each project closer and enables you to adjust the design if you want to. We will also be including either a Fritzing diagram or a schematic diagram in the book itself for each project to show how to create the circuit. Both types of diagrams will be generated from the Fritzing sketch.

Fritzing is a very powerful tool and it is recommended that you spend some time learning how to create your own diagrams with it. This chapter is focused on how to read both the Fritzing and schematic diagrams that are included in this book. If you wish to learn how to use the Fritzing software, their website has a very good tutorial that you can find here: `http://fritzing.org/learning/`. Let's start with the Fritzing diagrams.

Fritzing diagrams

A Fritzing diagram is a picture representation of what the circuit should look like, similar to the open, closed and short circuit diagrams previously shown in this chapter; however, the Fritzing diagram has standard symbols to represent each part and a compact design making it easier to design more complex circuits. The following Fritzing diagram shows an Arduino connected to a LED and resistor on a breadboard:

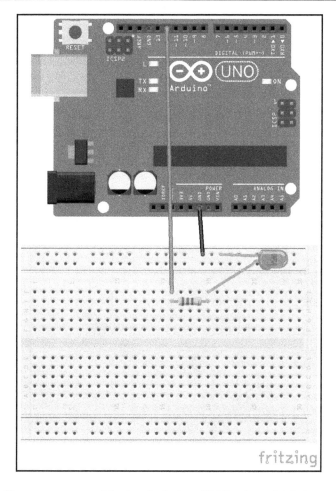

The circuit in this diagram starts with the Arduino GND pin, which is connected to the top rail of the breadboard. The cathode connector of the LED is also connected to the top rail, which connects it to the common ground from the Arduino. The anode connector of the LED is connected to a 220 Ohm resistor, which is connected to the digital 12 pin of the Arduino. This is a pretty easy diagram to understand because the diagrams look like the components themselves. Fritzing diagrams are used a lot when showing diagrams on electronic websites and blogs because it is easier for a beginner to understand how to connect the circuit.

Now let's look at the schematic diagram.

Schematic diagrams

While the Fritzing diagrams used images to represent the circuit, schematic diagrams use symbols. This allows for a more compact diagram, which makes it easier to represent complex circuits. The following diagram shows the symbols for some of the more common electronic components in a schematic diagram:

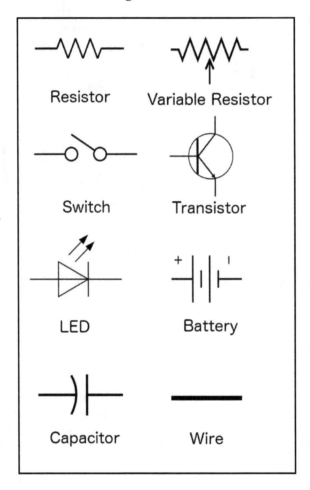

We would use these symbols to represent the components in a circuit. To see what a schematic diagram would look like, let's create a simple circuit that contained a battery, resistor and LED. The Fritzing diagram for this circuit would look like this:

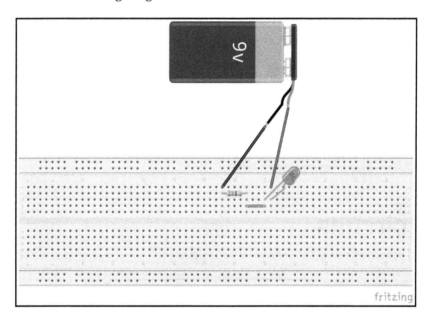

In this diagram, it is easy to see what components are needed and how they are connected; however, in more complex circuits it can be harder to see how everything is connected. The image from the Fritzing diagram also doesn't show the value of the components. A schematic diagram offers a much clearer view of the circuit and if the author of the diagram chooses to, show the values of each component. The following diagram shows the same circuit in a schematic diagram:

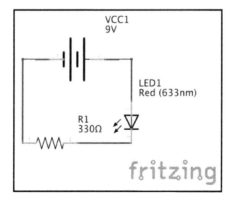

This diagram shows us how the components are connected and all the values of the components. We will be using both Fritzing diagrams and schematic diagrams throughout this book, so we can get familiar with both kinds. Both types of diagrams will be generated from the Fritzing sketches that comes with the downloadable code for this book.

Parallel and series circuits

There are two types of circuits that we can create. These are parallel and series circuits. A series circuit is a circuit where current only has one path to flow from the source to the return. A parallel circuit is a circuit that has multiple paths for the current flow. It is important to understand both types of circuits because the properties are different between them. Let's see look at the series circuit first.

Series circuits

The following schematic diagram shows a series circuit:

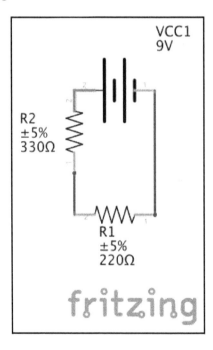

The preceding diagram shows a series circuit where the current only has one path from the source to the return. In this circuit, the load consists of two resistors. One resistor has a value of 330 ohms and the other has a value 220 ohms. Now let's look at several properties of a series circuit.

Resistance

The total resistance of a series circuit is the sum of the resistance of each component of the load. In the example circuit, the load consists of two resistors with values of 220 ohms and 330 ohms. If we add these two values together we get a total resistance of 550 ohms.

Voltage

The total voltage of a series circuit is the sum of the voltage of each power source connected in series. In the example circuit, there is only one power source, which is a 9V battery, therefore, the total voltage is 9 volts. If we used 4 AA batteries (1.5 volts each) in series, rather than the 9-volt battery, we would have a total voltage of 6 volts because 1.5V + 1.5V + 1.5V + 1.5V would equal 6 volts.

Current

In a series circuit, the same current flows through each part of the circuit. This means that we can measure the current at any point within the circuit and it will be the same as any other point in the circuit.

In the example circuit, we know the total voltage (9 volts) and we know the total resistance (550 ohms) therefore we can calculate the current of the circuit using Ohm's law, where $I=V/R$. This formula would give us a current of 9 volts/550 ohms or 0.0164 amps (16.4 milliamps).

Now let's look at the properties of a parallel circuit.

Parallel circuits

The following schematic diagram shows a parallel circuit:

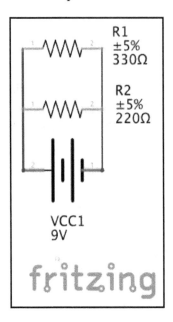

The preceding diagram shows a parallel circuit where the current has multiple paths to the return. The current can either flow through the branch with the 220-ohm resistor, the branch with the 330-ohm resistor or both branches.

In this sample circuit, as with the series circuit, the load consists of two resistors with values of 330 ohms and 220 ohms, however, this time the resistors are connected in parallel rather than series. The properties of a parallel circuit are very different than the properties of a series circuit. Let's look at these properties.

Resistance

The total resistance of a parallel circuit will always be less than the total resistance of any branch within the circuit and adding additional branches will always decrease the total resistance of the circuit.

To calculate the total resistance of a parallel circuit, take the sum of the reciprocal of the resistance for each component in the circuit and that equals the reciprocal of the total resistance. Sounds confusing? It really isn't. Here is the formula:

$$\frac{1}{R_t} = \frac{1}{R_1} + \frac{1}{R_2} + \frac{1}{R_3}$$

This formula will go out to however many resistance values are needed. In the example circuit, there are two resistors with values to 220 ohms and 330 ohms. Therefore, to calculate the resistance of the circuit we would take the reciprocal of 1/220 + 1/330, which would equal 132 ohms.

Rather than trying to calculate the resistance of a parallel circuit by hand, there are plenty of online calculators that you can use.

Voltage

Each branch of a parallel circuit will have the same voltage. If we measured the voltage across either branch of the sample circuit it would show a voltage of 9 volts.

Current

In a parallel circuit, current will be different in each branch. The total current of the circuit (the current coming out of the power source) will be equal to the sum of the current in each branch. This means that current coming out of the power source will equal the sum of the current running through the 220-ohm resistor branch and the 330-ohm resistor branch.

Let's look at this with Ohm's law to see how this works. To calculate current with Ohm's law we use the formula $I=V/R$, which means the current equals the voltage divided by the resistance. Earlier, in the resistance section, we calculated that the resistance in the circuit was 132 ohms and we know that the voltage is 9 volts, therefore, the total current will equal 9 volts/132 ohms or 0.0682 amps (68.2 milliamps).

We can also use Ohm's law to calculate the current in each branch knowing that the voltage for each branch will be the same 9 volts. The current in the branch that contains the 220-ohm resistor would be 9 volts/220 ohms or 0.0409 amps (40.9 milliamps). The current in the branch with the 330-ohm resistor would be 9 volts/330 ohms or 0.0273 amps (27.3 milliamps).

We can now add the current from the branch that contains the 220-ohm resistor to the current from the branch that contains the 330-ohm resistor to get the total current of 40.9 milliamps + 27.3 milliamps, which equals the same 68.2 milliamps coming out of the power source.

Now that we understand the difference between parallel and series circuits, there is one more concept we need to understand before we can get started building things. This concept is a voltage drop.

Voltage drop

Voltage drop is defined as the amount of voltage lost through each component in the circuit due to impedance. Impedance is the amount of opposition that the circuit and component present to the current flow. We will see why voltage drop is important in the next section where we light up a LED.

Light up LED

Now that we have discussed the basics of electrical circuits, let's build our first circuit. In this circuit, we will simply light up a LED. We will start off with a look at the schematic diagram, which will tell us how to build the circuit:

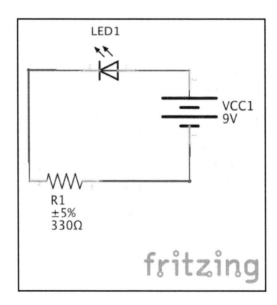

In this diagram, we can see that the circuit consists of one 9-volt power source (9-volt battery) one LED and one resistor. One of the first questions people new to circuits ask is how we calculate the value of the resistor. To calculate this value, we need to know what the forward voltage for the LED is and the maximum current it can take without blowing. The forward voltage is the voltage amount required before the LED will conduct electricity and the voltage drop that will occur. If you purchase the LED from a good electronic store, they should have a datasheet that will tell you the forward voltage and the maximum current the LED can take.

I would recommend writing these items down, so you will have it later when you forget where you purchased the LEDs from.

We use the forward voltage and maximum current in the following formula to figure out what size resistor we need:

$$R = \frac{V_S - V_{LED}}{I_{LED}}$$

In this formula, the voltage marked with the **S** is the voltage source, which is 9V in this example. The voltage and current marked with **LED** is the forward voltage and maximum current, respectively, for the LED. The LED I am using for this example is 3.4 volts and 20 milliamps. This gives a value of (9 - 3.4 volts)/20 milliamps, which are 280 ohms. Since I do not have a resistor with a value of 280 ohms, I rounded it up to the next highest value with is 330 ohms as shown in the schematic.

The following photograph shows how I connected everything:

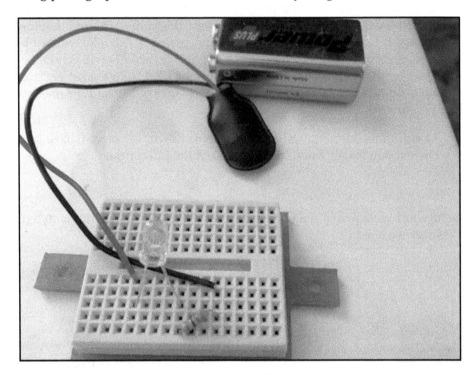

If you have everything connected correctly the LED will light up when the battery is connected.

Summary

In this chapter, we introduced what circuits are and described the differences between closed, open and short circuits. We also showed how to read both a Fritzing and a schematic diagram. We finished the chapter by seeing the differences between parallel and series and creating our first circuit to light up a LED.

In the next chapter, we will look at how we can prototype circuits and what tools and skills we need.

4
Basic Prototyping

Prototyping is where all of our ideas come to life. When I started working with microcontrollers I really wanted to design and build my whole project and watch it magically work. I realized that all I was doing was overwhelming myself and quickly learned how to break the larger projects into much smaller projects. I could then create prototypes for each of these smaller projects to verify they worked before incorporating them into the larger project.

In this chapter, we will learn:

- Where to set up a work area
- All about breadboards
- What Dupont (jumper) cables are
- How to prototype a project

Prototypes are used to prove the specifications for a working concept or process rather than theoretical ones. Prototypes, as we are referring to it in this book, is a model to test a concept or process. Prototyping is the process of creating and testing the prototypes.

When working with the Arduino and other microcontrollers, it is important to understand how to prototype especially when working with larger projects. These larger projects can usually be broken up into multiple smaller projects. We can then prototype each of these smaller projects to make sure they work as expected before incorporating them into the larger project. Before we look at how to prototype, we need to set up a good work area to do prototyping in.

Setting up a work area

When you first start building projects with the Arduino, it is important to find a good work area to not only build these projects but also store the parts and the prototypes that you create. When I first started using microcontrollers like the Arduino I used the living room table as my work area while I was watching baseball on the TV and quickly realized that the living room was not the ideal place to work in because all of the tools and components needed to build these projects quickly took over the room. In this section, we will look at what makes a good work area.

The first item we need to consider when deciding on a work area is static electricity. While static electricity isn't as big as a problem as a lot of people make it out to be, it is something that we need to consider when setting up an area to do prototyping in. I personally have not lost a single electronic component to static electricity in the past fifteen to twenty years; however, I also don't wear fluffy sweaters, pet my dog and rub my feet on shag carpet while I am working with electronic components. As a general rule, we should try to avoid areas that are prone to static like areas with thick carpet.

Some tips to avoid static electricity when working with the Arduino or other electronic components:

- Touch something metal to discharge any static electricity that has built up prior to touching an electronic component.
- Avoid, if possible, having carpet in your work area or wearing rubber soled shoes.
- Be careful of the material of your clothing. Wool sweaters or socks can cause static buildup, so opt for cotton instead.
- Avoid petting any furry pets while working.
- If your work area is dry, use a humidifier to add moister to the air.

Another concern when picking a work area is to have a table or bench large enough to hold your projects and preferably one that you can store the projects on for extended periods of time. When I was using the living room table as my work area, I quickly realized how inconvenient it was to have to clean up every night.

You will also want to make sure you have plenty of light in your work area. Even if your work area has sufficient lighting I would recommend investing in a clip-on table light that you can clip to the edge of the table when you need extra lighting. Trust me there will be times when you need extra lighting to make the small print on the electronic components stand out.

The final thing you will want to look for in your work area is plenty of storage. The more prototyping you do the more parts you will acquire, and you will need someplace close by to store them. When I first started working with microcontrollers, I stored most of my small parts in a couple small plastic toolboxes. This worked out very well in the beginning, but I eventually outgrew those toolboxes and bought some small parts cabinets for the smaller components and larger plastic storage bins for larger components.

Before you begin working with the Arduino, it is well worth the time to set up a proper work area. I did not do that in the beginning and it made building my prototypes significantly harder. Now let's look at two of the most important items, after the microcontroller, that you will be using when you are prototyping. The two items are the breadboard and Dupont cables.

Using a solderless breadboard

It is a good idea to avoid connecting LEDs, resistors and other electronic components directly to the Arduino because you can easily damage the headers on the Arduino and the circuit quickly turn into an unorganized mess. When prototyping, it is a lot easier to connect the components together using a solderless breadboard.

A solderless breadboard enables us to connect electronic components together without the need to solder. You can get a good solderless MB-102 breadboard for under ten US dollars. They are also reusable, which makes them perfect for creating prototypes and experimenting with circuit designs.

I would recommend not skimping too much on your breadboards because you will be using them so much. You can find some very cheap and small breadboards like the one in the following photograph; however, it is a lot harder to organize your circuit design with these smaller breadboards. I do use these for quick and small prototyping, but I would not recommend having these as your main breadboards.

For prototyping with the Arduino, it also isn't necessary to get breadboards with built-in power connectors like the one shown in the following photograph:

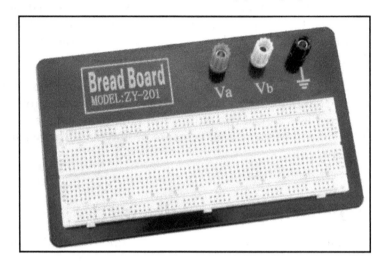

I would recommend getting an MB 102 breadboard like the one shown in the following photograph:

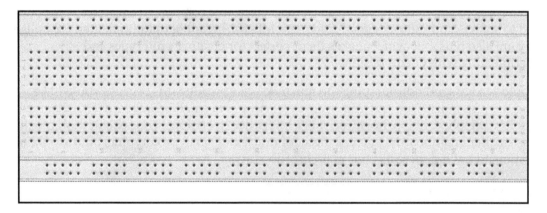

The MB-102 breadboard contains two positive and two negative power pails which makes it easy to connect the power and ground pins from the Arduino to the electronic components needed for the prototype. In the following photograph, we highlighted the four power rails where the rails highlighted with red are the positive rails and the rails highlighted in black are the negative rails. The positive rails are usually marked, on the breadboard, with a + sign and the negative rail is marked with a - sign:

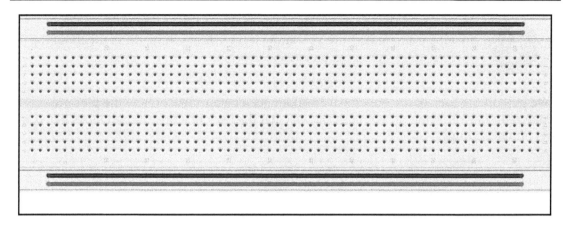

The power rails run horizontally across the breadboard where all of the connectors along the horizontal rail are usually connected together. This means, as an example, that if we connect one of the voltage pins on the Arduino to any of the pins along the positive rail, then all of the connectors along that rail will have to be connected to the voltage pin on the Arduino.

The pins in the middle of the board are connected together vertically; however, the connection does not cross the center of the breadboard. The following photograph shows how the pins in the middle of the board are connected:

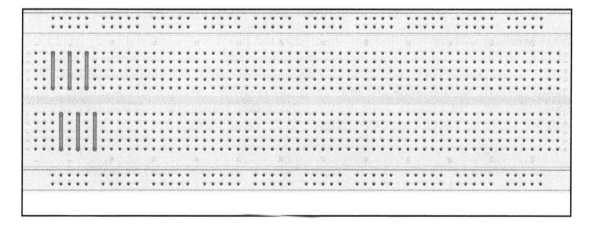

While the preceding photograph only shows how six of the vertical rows are connected, all of the vertical rows are connected in this manner. One thing to make note of is how we described the MB-102 breadboard is how the majority of them are configured; however, not all of them are configured in this manner.

Always read the specifications when you purchase components like a breadboard to make sure you know if there is anything different about the one you are purchasing. It can save you hours of troubleshooting.

If we pull off the back of the breadboard we can get a better view of how the pins are connected. The following photograph shows what the back of a breadboard looks like if we peel off the padding:

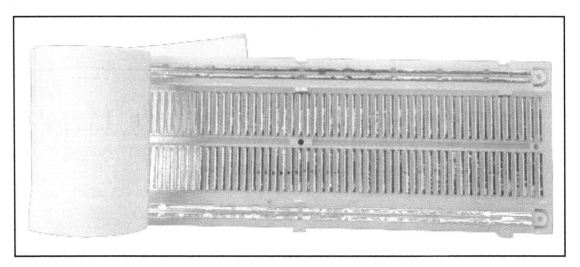

When working with the Arduino, we can usually run power and ground directly from the Arduino to the power rails on the breadboard; however, there are times where we may need external power. For those times, they do make external power adapters that can connect directly to the breadboard and enable us to use USB, AC adapters, and other power sources to power the projects. The following photograph shows one such adapter and also how we would connect these power adapters to the breadboard:

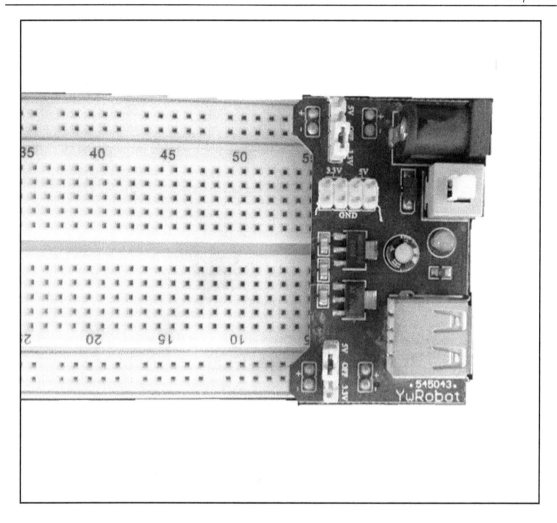

Now the question is how you connect components together using the breadboard and the answer is Dupont (jumper) cables.

Dupont (jumper) cables

Dupont cables, also known as jumper wire, are used to wire components together when using a solderless breadboard. These cables come in three types: male-male, male-female and female-female. When using these cables with a solderless breadboard, and the Arduino, we typically use cables that have male connectors on both ends; however, there are some components that already have male connectors on them, so it is worthwhile having some male-female cables as well. The following photograph shows what the male connectors look like at the end of the Dupont cables:

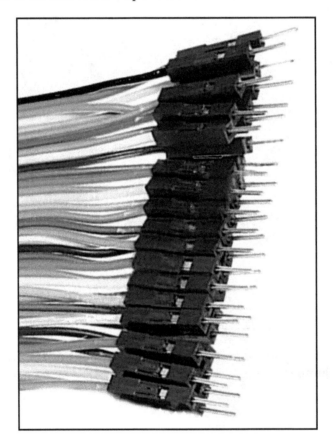

It is pretty cheap to purchase premade Dupont cables but if you want to customize the length you can make them yourself by purchasing a crimper and some ends. These cables are not that hard to make but I would recommend starting off by purchasing premade ones.

Prototyping

Prototypes are used to prove the specifications for a working concept or process rather than theoretical ones. A prototype, as we are referring to it in this book, is a model to test a concept or process. For simple concepts or process, we may create a prototype for the whole system but for my complex systems, we will want to break the system down into individual components and create a prototype for each component.

Prototypes with the Arduino usually consist of one Arduino microcontroller with one breadboard used to connect the components to the Arduino. For these prototypes, I use a holder that I designed and printed out with my 3D printer. The following photograph shows the holder with an Arduino Uno, Nano and a breadboard in it:

The holder is designed to hold an MB-102 breadboard, an Arduino Nano and either an Arduino Uno or Mega. If you have access to a 3D printer I included the STL file for this holder in the downloadable code for this book so you can print one for yourself. Holders like this are especially useful when we need to move the prototype because it keeps everything together and organized.

Before we can start building a prototype, we need to have an idea of what we want to build. This idea may be something as simple as blinking an LED or as complex and creating an autonomous robot. The idea is always the first step when beginning a project.

The second step is to break up the idea into the different building blocks that were discussed in Chapter 2, *Basic Electronics*. After we have broken up the project into the different blocks we would then diagram the circuits that need to be prototyped. After the diagrams are complete, we can then begin building the prototypes. Let's look at these steps a little closer, starting with the four building blocks of an electronic circuit.

Four building blocks of an electronic project

In Chapter 2, *Basic Electronics*, we discussed the four building blocks of an electronic project. The following diagram shows these four blocks:

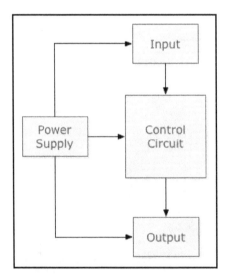

It is really easy to break a simple prototype, like a circuit to turn an LED on and off, into the individual blocks but for more complex projects it becomes harder because of the different components.

By separating the components into the different blocks, it becomes easier to see how to break a larger project into separate prototypes. For example, if we wanted to create an autonomous robot we could see that one of the inputs is a sonic rangefinder that will detect obstacles in front of the robot, while the output that will be affected by the input from the rangefinder would be the motors that move the robot. In this example, we would probably want to change the direction of the motors if the rangefinders detect an obstacle in front. We could then create a prototype to test how this particular system worked.

In this step, we are defining what the inputs and outputs are and what outputs are trigger based on these inputs. This is also where we define most of the logic for the project, so we can set up the prototypes.

When you first start building these projects, you will want to create a diagram for each project. Once you gain experience, for most smaller to medium projects, you will not need to write anything down at this step. This step will become just breaking the project down in your heads and figuring out what the inputs and outputs are. For larger projects, we may want to create flowcharts and even diagrams that show how we want everything to work together. Once we get into the projects in this book, we will see different ways to separate the components into their individual blocks and how to define the logic for the inputs and outputs.

After we have broken our project down into the individual prototypes with the separate inputs and output circuits, we would then want to create circuit diagrams for each of these prototypes.

Creating a diagram

Once we have defined the inputs and outputs of the circuit and the logic for the project, the next step is to diagram the circuits. We will want to make sure that we diagram all of the circuits that we create even the most basic ones. This will help us figure out resistors needed and to visualize how we want to organize and connect the component.

When creating the circuit diagrams, I would recommend using the Fritzing software that was described in `Chapter 3`, *Circuit Diagrams*. Now let's look at the final step, building the prototype.

Building the prototype

The final step is actually building a working prototype. This is where all of the hard work from the first three steps come together and you are able to see if the prototype works as expected.

All of us would prefer to skip the first few steps and go right to building the prototype; however, you will be more successful and damage fewer parts if you take your time and go through each of these steps when creating your prototypes.

Now let's see how we would go through these steps and build our first prototype. You will want to follow along and build this prototype yourself because we will be using it in the next couple of chapters as we learn to program the Arduino.

First prototype

The first prototype that we will build is pretty simple and designed to be used in the next couple chapters where we learn to program the Arduino. This prototype will have one button that will be used to turn a LED on or off, another LED that we can turn on or off and a TMP36 temperature sensor.

In this prototype, we will have two inputs (a push button and temperature sensor) and two outputs (the two LEDs). We will use the 5V output from the Arduino to power the components. Here is the Fritzing diagram of this prototype:

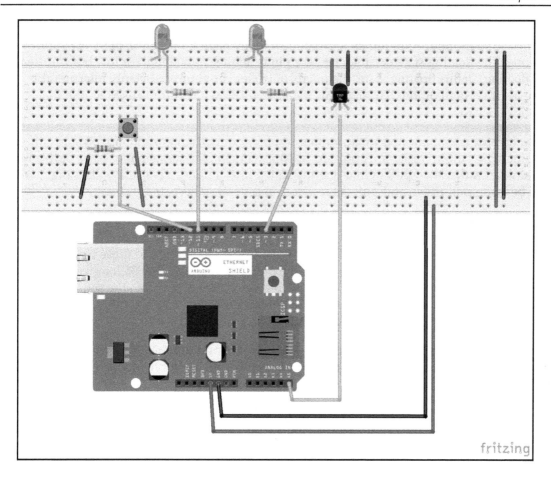

In this diagram, starting from left to right, we have the button, the two LEDs, and the TMP36 temperature sensor. Each of the LEDs has the same 330-ohm resistor that used in `Chapter 3`, *Circuit Diagram*. Since the power from the Arduino is only 5 volts, we could lower the value of the resistor to 100 ohms, but the 330-ohm resistors will work fine as well.

The resistor that we are using the button is called a pull-down resistor because one end is connected to ground. A digital logic circuit can really have three states: high, low, and floating. The floating state occurs when the pin is neither pulled high or low but is instead left floating. In this floating state, the microcontroller could unpredictably interpret this state as either high or low. To solve this issue, a pull-down resistor is used to pull the floating state low.

If the resistor was connected to the voltage supply, rather than ground, it would be considered a pull-up resistor. A pull-up resistor works in the same manner as a pull-down resistor but rather than pulling the floating stated low, a pull-up resistor pulls it high. We will be using pull-down and pull-up resistors in several projects in this book.

The push button is connected to pin 12 of the Arduino; therefore, we will be able to read the state of the button by checking the state of pin 12. The LEDs are connected to pins 11 and 3; therefore, we will be able to turn them on by sending a digital high to those pins or turn them off by sending a digital low. Finally, the output pin on the TMP36 temperature sensor (the middle pin) is connected to the analog 5 pin since the output from the sensor in analog. The voltage and ground pins on the TMP36 temperature sensor are connected to the voltage and ground rails on the breadboard.

The Fritzing diagram makes the prototype look so nice and organized; however, most prototypes do not look like that. The following is what the prototype looked like when I built it for this book:

It is nice to have your prototype neat and looking good, but it is not necessary as long as you can work with it. It is especially hard to have the prototype neat when you only have one or two lengths of Dupont (jumper) cables.

You will also notice the short wires that run across the power rails. On this breadboard, the power rails are not connected all the way across horizontally. This is an example of a breadboard that is configured a little differently. You can tell that the power rails do not run all the way across because the red and blue lines on the breadboard have a gap halfway across; therefore, we used small cables to connect the two sides. There are times that we need different power sources so having the power rails split like this can be very helpful but for this prototype, since we are using the same power source for all components, we connected the power rails together.

Summary

In this chapter, we looked at the basics of prototyping and what steps we should take when we create prototypes. The sample prototype that we did at the end of this chapter was pretty basic, but we still went through each of the steps to make sure we had everything correct. We will be walking through each of these steps in the projects chapters later in this book.

Now that we have created our first prototype, we need to learn how to program the Arduino. The next three chapters are written to teach you how to program the Arduino. We will start off by showing you how to download and install the Arduino IDE.

Arduino IDE
5

I have been programming computers, as a hobby or professionally, for over 37 years. In that time, I have used many different **Integrated Development Environments (IDE)** and text editors to write code. I wrote my first Hello World program on a teletype that did not use either an IDE or a text editor. When I bought my first computer, which was a Commodore VIC-20, I used the BASIC programming language in programming mode to write my programs. When you were in programming mode, you entered the code line by line and each line went into memory as you entered it, there wasn't a nice editor or IDE. I wasn't until I learned to program in the C programming language, on an IBM PCjr, that I used my first real IDE. Now I wonder how I managed to write anything with one.

In this chapter, you will learn:

- What an Arduino Sketch is
- What the Arduino IDE is
- What the Arduino Web Editor is
- How to write your first sketch

Before we look at the Arduino IDE and Web Editor, let's look at what an Arduino Sketch is to help us understand why we need these tools.

Arduino Sketch

When we program the Arduino, the code is put into a project. These projects are called **sketches** and a sketch is stored in a **Sketchbook**. A sketch is designed to be as simple and straightforward as possible by abstracting away a lot of the technical aspects of programming the Arduino by using the prebuilt functions.

The coding language used to program the Arduino is very similar to the C programming language. We will be looking at how to program the Arduino in Chapter 6, *Programming the Arduino – The Basics* and Chapter 7, *Programming the Arduino – Beyond the Basics*. This chapter is to get you familiar with what sketches are and to look at the tools we can use.

Before a sketch can be uploaded to an Arduino, the Arduino IDE or Web Editor must go through several steps to build the application. The first step to building a sketch is to perform some preprocessing, which turns the sketch into a C++ (see-plus-plus) program, which is passed to the compiler to turn this human-readable C++ code into machine-readable instructions (object files). These object files are then linked against the standard Arduino libraries that provide the basic functionality for the Arduino. The results of this linking are a single hex file that can be uploaded to the Arduino and ran. The nice thing is the Arduino tools perform all of this automatically when we tell them to upload the sketch to the Arduino board.

If we were to put a definition on what an Arduino Sketch is, we would say that it is the project that contains the human-readable code that can be built and uploaded to an Arduino. Now let's look at two tools that we can use to help us write and build these sketches, starting with the Arduino IDE.

Arduino IDE

The Arduino IDE is an integrated development environment that can be installed locally on Windows, macOS and Linux-based computers. The IDE can be downloaded from the Arduino software page at this URL: `https://www.arduino.cc/en/Main/Software`. At the time this book is written, the latest stable version of the IDE is 1.8.5.

The following images show what the IDE will look like when it is first run:

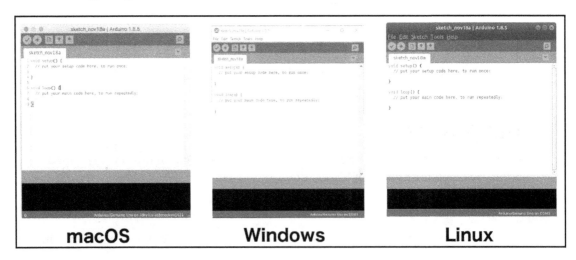

We will start using the IDE at the end of this chapter where we will build our first sketch. We will be using it, as well as the Web Editor extensively throughout the rest of this book. For now, let's briefly explore the IDE so we can familiarize ourselves with some of its basic functionality.

Exploring the IDE

There are four areas that make up the main development window of the IDE. The following screenshot shows these four areas:

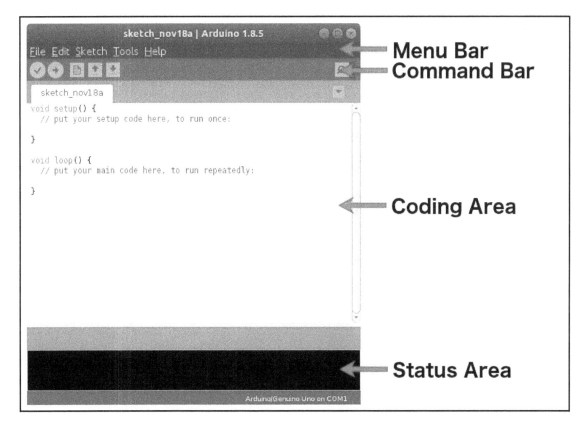

The **menu bar** for the IDE functions like menu bars in other applications, where you click on one of the options, and a submenu appears with more options. We will look at some of the commonly used menu options as we go through this book.

The **command bar** provides quick access to five of the most commonly used commands. These commands are, from left to right, verify, upload, new, open and save. The verify command will attempt to compile the sketch in order to verify that there is nothing wrong with the code. The upload command will attempt to build and upload the sketch to the attached Arduino. The new command will create a new sketch. The open command will open a sketch. Finally, the save command will save the sketch.

 Note: In order to upload a sketch, you must have an Arduino connected to the computer you are working on and configured in the IDE otherwise you will receive an error. We will look at how to do this in the *Configuring the Arduino within the IDE* section.

The **coding area** is where we write the code for the Arduino. You will notice that when we start a new sketch, two functions (setup and loop) are automatically created in the main tab. We will be working with these functions a lot in this book. We will be looking at what these two functions do at the end of this chapter when we create our first sketch.

The **status area** is used by the IDE to let us know what is happening when the IDE is doing something like compiling, uploading or verifying a sketch.

In order to upload a sketch to an Arduino, we need to connect the Arduino to the computer the IDE is running on with a USB cable and configure it in the IDE. Configuring the Arduino within the IDE requires us to tell it what type of Arduino we are using and what port it is on. Let's see how to do this.

Configuring the Arduino within the IDE

To connect an Arduino to the IDE the first thing the IDE needs to know is what type of Arduino is being used. To do this we click on the **Tools** option in the menu bar and select the **Board** option as shown in the following screenshot:

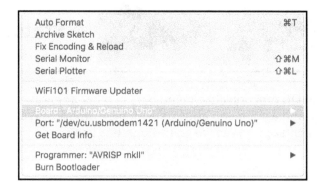

When the **Board** option is selected the IDE displays a list of compatible boards. This list will look similar to the following screenshot:

From this list, select the board that you are using for your project. Once the board is selected, the next thing that the IDE needs to know is what port the Arduino is connected too. To select the port, click on the **Tools** menu option from the menu bar and then select the **Port** option as shown in the following screenshot:

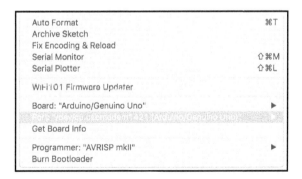

When the **Port** option is selected from this menu, the IDE displays a list of the ports it is aware of. This list should look something similar to this:

```
Serial ports
/dev/cu.Bluetooth-Incoming-Port
/dev/cu.JonsiPad-WirelessiAP
/dev/cu.JonHoffmansiPhone-Wirel
✓ /dev/cu.usbmodem1421 (Arduino/Genuino Uno)
```

You will probably have a different list of ports; however, it is usually obvious which port should be selected because it displays the name of the board attached to a port if it sees the board. Most of the time the IDE will automatically select it the correct port for you.

Once the board and port are selected, the IDE is ready to upload the compiled sketch to the board.

Now that we have seen how to use the Arduino IDE, let's look at how to set up and use the Arduino Web editor.

Arduino web editor

The Arduino Web Editor enables us to create and upload sketches within most web browsers. Officially the Web Editor is supported with the Chrome, Firefox, Safari and Edge browsers with the installation of a plugin.

 The Web Editor is part of and can be accessed from the Arduino Create project here: `https://create.arduino.cc`

Before you can install the plugin and use the Web Editor, you will need to create a free Arduino account. Once we are logged in to our account, the site will walk you through installing the plugin. Once the plugin is installed, you should see a page similar to this:

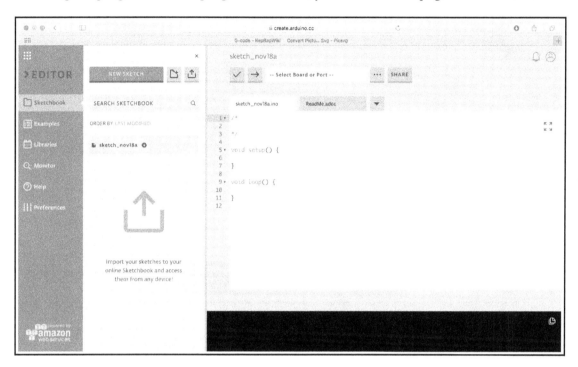

Let's explore the Web Editor to see how to use it.

Exploring

The four main areas of the Web Editor are shown in the following screenshot:

The **menu bar** of the web editor enables us to quickly access certain items like examples, libraries, and the serial monitor. We will look at these items later in this chapter.

The **command bar** provides quick access to commonly used commands and gives us the ability to select the board we are using. The icon with the checkmark will verify the sketch while the icon with the arrow compiles and uploads the sketch to the Arduino. The icon with the three dots opens up a menu that enables us to save, rename, download, and delete the current sketch.

The **coding area** is where we write the code for the Arduino. As with the Arduino IDE, you will notice that the setup() and loop() functions were automatically created when a new sketch is started.

The **status area** is used by the IDE to let us know what is happening when the IDE is doing something like compiling, uploading or verifying a sketch. Let's see how to configure Arduino within the Web Editor so we can upload sketches to it.

Configuring the Arduino within the IDE

In order to upload a sketch to an Arduino, we need to connect the Arduino to the computer the Web Editor is running on with a USB cable. After the Arduino is connected to the computer, we can select the Arduino and port within the Web Editor by clicking on the **Select Board or Port** section. If the Web Editor recognizes the Arduino board, you should see the Arduino board and port listed in the drop-down menu. The listing will look like this screenshot:

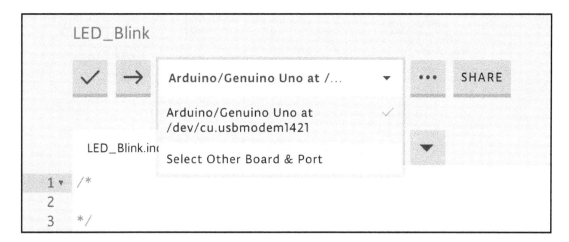

If you see the Arduino, select it and you will then be able to upload compiled sketches it. The best way to learn the Arduino IDE or Web Editor is to use it and we will be using both extensively throughout this book.

Let's look at some of the features of the Arduino IDE and the Web Editor starting with the examples that are included.

Examples

There are numerous examples that are included with the Arduino IDE and the Web Editor. These examples are simple sketches that demonstrate the Arduino commands and how to use them. These examples range from the very basic sketches that demonstrate how to read and write digital I/O to more advance sketches that show how to use sensors. While these examples are designed to demonstrate the Arduino commands they can also be used as examples of how to write good code for the Arduino.

To access the examples within the Arduino IDE, click on the **File** option in the menu bar and then go to the **Examples** option. You will see a list of categories for the examples that look similar to the following screenshot:

If you go to any of the categories, you will see a list of examples for that categories. If you select an example, such as the `DigitalReadSerial` example under the **Basics** category, the code for the example will load in a new window and the sketch will look similar to the following screenshot:

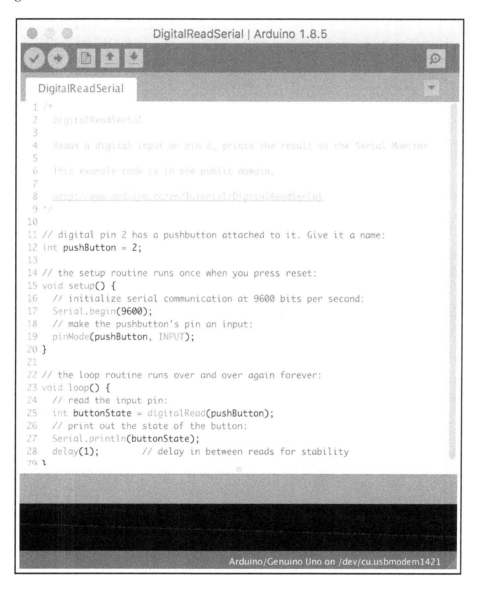

With the Web Editor, to load an example select the **Examples** option from the menu bar. As with the Arduino IDE we will see the same list of example categories. This list will look similar to the following screenshot:

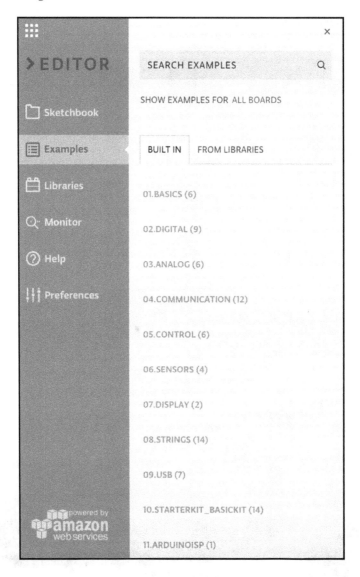

We can then select any of the categories to see the list of examples. What makes the examples in the Web Editor different from the examples in the Arduino IDE is that most of the examples in the Web Editor also include layout (Fritzing) and schematic diagrams showing how to create a circuit that can be used with the example. For example, if we select the same `DigitalReadSerial` example that we select in the Arduino IDE, not only will we see the code for the sketch, but we will also see the layout as shown in the following screenshot:

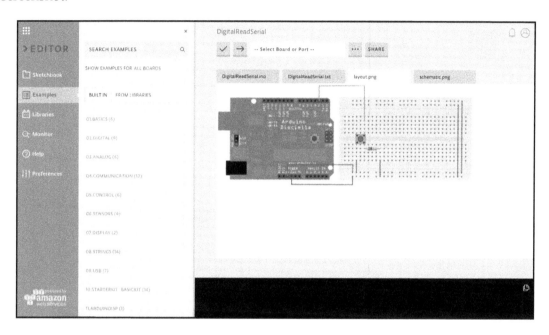

The diagrams that are included with the Web Editor are great for beginners because they show how to build the circuit without having to fully understand the code for the example.

There are numerous external libraries that can be used with the Arduino. Let's take a look at what libraries are.

Arduino libraries

Like most development platforms, the Arduino environment can be extended with libraries. These libraries provide extra functionality, that we can use in our sketches, such as providing access to specific hardware, manipulating data and adding extra features like a task scheduler (Arduino Cron Library). There are numerous libraries that are built in to the IDE and Web Editor, but we can also download other libraries or build our own.

To access the libraries in the Arduino IDE, we select the **Sketch** option from the menu bar and then select the **Include Library** option. This will show another menu that lets you load a library or manage libraries. This menu should look similar to the following screenshot:

If you select any of the built-in libraries, the header files will automatically be included in your sketch. We will learn more about header files in Chapter 6, *Programming the Arduino – The Basics* and Chapter 7, *Programming the Arduino – Beyond the Basics*.

Selecting the **Manage Libraries** option enables us to download and install other libraries that are not included with the standard installation of the Arduino IDE. When a library is downloaded and installed, it will then appear in the quick list of Arduino libraries and can be used just like the built-in libraries. A number of these libraries also install example code that can be accessed from the examples section of the IDE.

To access the libraries in the Web Editor, select the **Library** option from the menu bar and a list of available libraries with a search bar will appear to the right of the menu bar. The interface will look like the following screenshot:

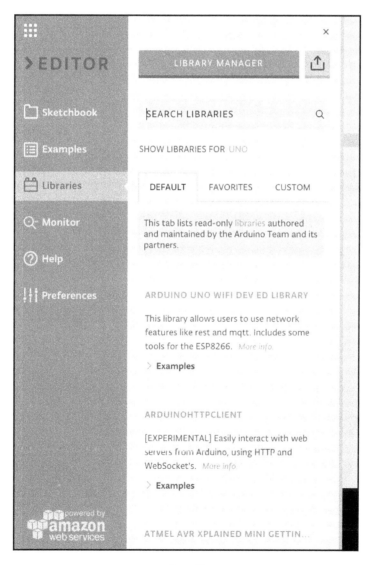

There are hundreds of libraries included within the Web Editor. This makes accessing the libraries easier than with the Arduino IDE because we do not need to install them. The Web Editor also makes it easier to share sketches that require libraries. When sharing a sketch that was created with the Arduino IDE, the person that receives the sketch needs to install the correct versions of the required libraries. This can occasionally become complicated and confusing. With the Web Editor, when we share a sketch, the Web Editor will ensure that the correct libraries are used when the sketch is compiled.

To add a library to a sketch, search for the library from within the search bar and when the library appears in the list, hover the mouse over it and an **INCLUDE** button will appear as shown in the following screenshot:

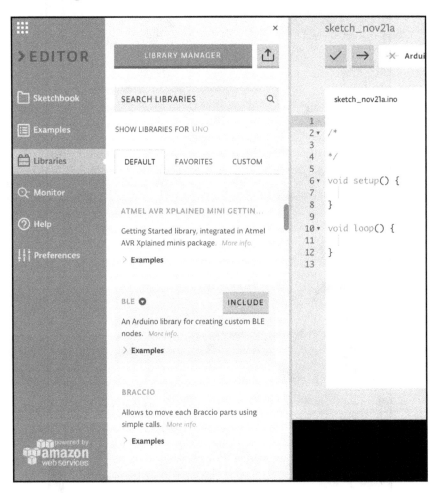

Click on the **INCLUDE** button and the required headers will appear in the code and the library will be included with the sketch.

Before we create our first sketch, let's look at what the serial monitor is.

Serial monitor

The serial monitor sends and/or receive text, usually through the USB cable. This enables us to receive debug messages or send text from the keyboard within the Web Editor or the Arduino IDE. We will see how to do both of these when we create our first sketches at the end of this chapter.

To use the serial monitor with the Arduino IDE or with the Web Editor, you must first connect an Arduino to the computer and establish communication between the Arduino and the IDE or Editor.

To begin using the serial monitor within the Arduino IDE, click on the serial monitor icon in the upper right-hand corner of the IDE. The following screenshot highlights the serial monitor icon:

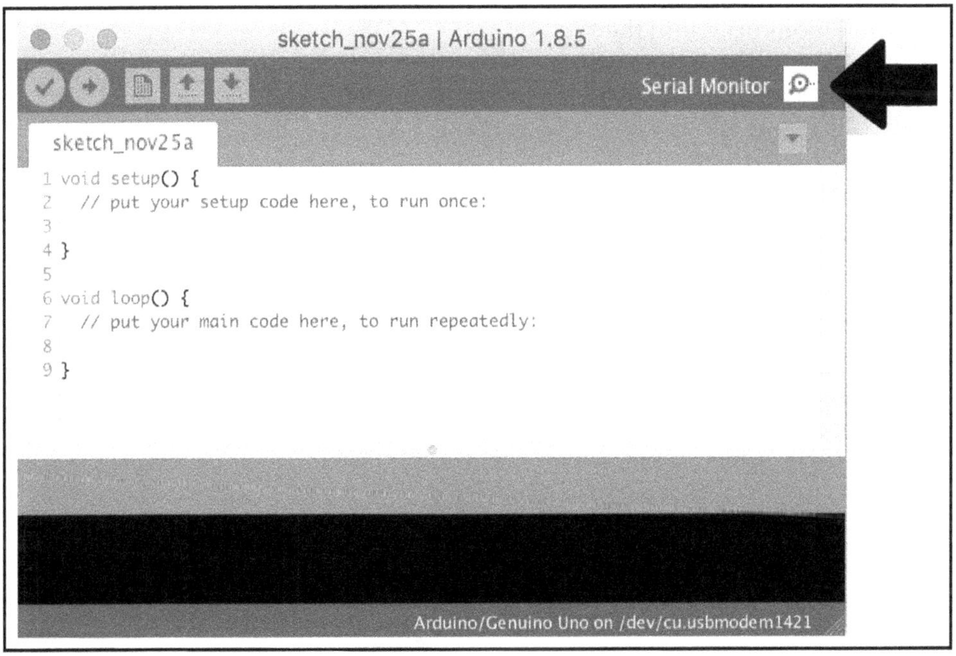

The serial monitor will open up in a separate window, as shown in the following screenshot:

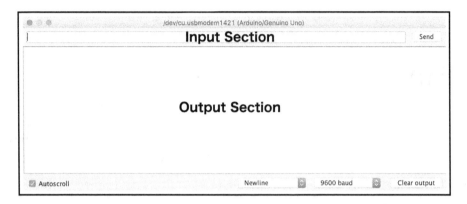

The input section enables us to send text to the Arduino. To do this, type the text into the input box and click the **Send** button or hit enter to send it. The text from the Arduino will appear in the output section.

To use the serial monitor with the Web Editor, click on the **Monitor** option in the menu bar and the serial monitor will appear to the right of the menu bar. The following screenshot shows the serial monitor within the Web Editor:

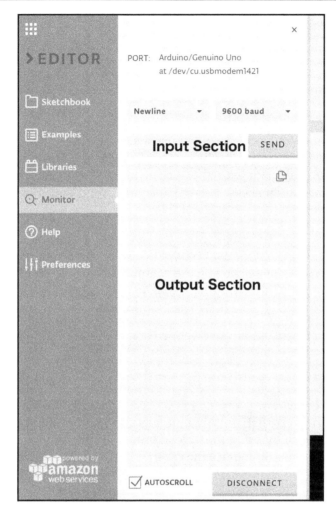

Just like the serial monitor in the Arduino IDE, to send text to the Arduino type in into the input box within the input section and then click on the **SEND** button or press enter to send it. The output from the Arduino will appear in the output section.

Now that we have a basic understanding of how the Arduino IDE and Web Editor works, let's create some sketches.

Hello World

For our first Sketch, we will create the traditional *Hello World* application with the Arduino. This application will output the words "Hello World" to the serial monitor; however, before we create this application we need to understand what the `setup()` and `loop()` functions do.

The `setup()` function is run once and only once when the application first starts. This function enables us to initiate any variables or hardware when the application first starts. After the `setup()` function completes, the `loop()` function is then called for the first time. When the `loop()` function finishes it will be called again and will continue to loop until the Arduino is powered down.

Let's demonstrate how these functions work. We will need to start off by creating a new sketch in either the Arduino IDE or the Web Editor. To create a new sketch with the Arduino IDE we can use the **New** icon on the command bar or select **File** | **New** from the menu bar. To create a new sketch with the web IDE, click on the Sketchbook option from the menu bar and then click on the **NEW SKETCH** button.

Once a new sketch is created, add the following code to the `setup()` function:

```
Serial.begin(9600);
Serial.println("Hello World");
```

We will then need to connect an Arduino to the computer and establish a connection between the Arduino and the IDE or Web Editor as described previously in this chapter. We can then run the sketch by using the upload button on the command bar for both the Arduino IDE and the Web Editor. Once the code is compiled and uploaded to the Arduino you should see the words `Hello World` outputted once to the serial monitor.

Now let's remove the `Serial.println("Hello World");` line from the `setup()` function and put it in the `loop()` function so our code looks like this:

```
void setup() {
  Serial.begin(9600);
}
void loop() {
    Serial.println("Hello World");
}
```

We can then upload the sketch and we should see the worlds `Hello World` is printed to the serial monitor over and over again. The text will continue to be printed until we unplug the Arduino from the computer.

In the last two examples, we used the `Serial.println()` function to output text to the serial monitor. This function will output the text and then add a newline at the end. We could also use the `Serial.print()` function, which will output the text but will not add a newline at the end.

The output to the serial monitor should look similar to this:

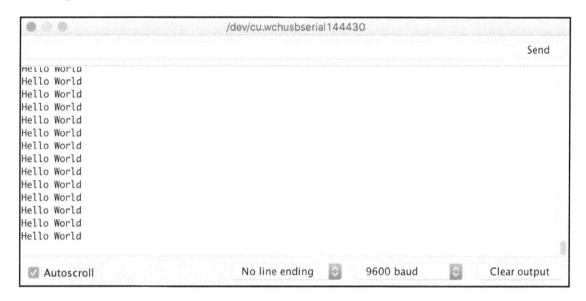

Now that we have seen how to output text from the Arduino to the serial console, let's see how the Arduino can receive a text from the Serial Monitor by creating an echo application.

Echo

An echo application will read the text in from the Serial Monitor and will then output it back.

The text will be entered into the input field, as shown in the following screenshot:

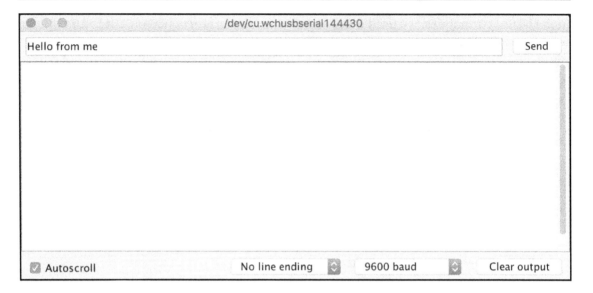

And the text will be echoed, as shown in the following screenshot:

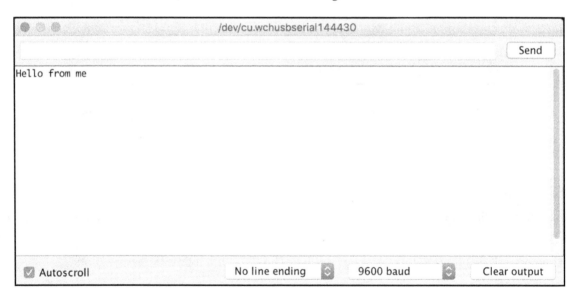

We will start off by creating a new sketch and add the following code to it:

```
byte bytesIn;

void setup() {
  Serial.begin(9600);
```

```
  }

void loop() {
  if (Serial.available()) {
    bytesIn = Serial.read();
    Serial.write(bytesIn);
  }
}
```

In this code, we start off by defining a variable named `bytesIn` of the byte type. Then within the `setup()` function the data rate for the serial data transmission is set to 9600 baud.

Within the `loop()` function we use the `Serial.available()` function to see if there is any data stored in the serial queue. The `Serial.available()` function returns the number of bytes available for reading in the serial receive buffer. If there are bytes available to read, the code then uses the `read()` function to read the bytes and then uses the `write()` function to write the bytes back to the Serial Monitor.

The difference between the `write()` function used in this code and the `println()` function used in the previous examples is the `println()` function will print the data as human-readable ASCII text while the `write()` function will write the data as bytes. In this example, if we used the `println()` function we will see the ASCII equivalent of the characters that were entered rather than the characters themselves.

Summary

In this chapter, we saw how to set up the Arduino IDE and the Web Editor. We also learned the basic functionality of both. At the end of this chapter, we saw how to use the Serial Monitor to send and receive data to and from the Arduino.

In the next chapter, we will begin to learn how to program the Arduino.

Programming the Arduino - The Basics

6

I have been programming as long as I can remember, everything from teletypes and mainframes to personal computers and embedded devices. I have programmed games, business applications, websites and mobile apps but I can honestly say that I enjoy programming microcontroller boards like the Arduino the most.

The reason for this is with microcontrollers my programs can interact with the outside world through various sensors and motors rather than programming for simple human interaction. With microcontrollers we are only limited by our imagination and ingenuity however before we can begin conquering the world, we must first learn the basics of the Arduino programming language.

In this chapter, you will learn:

- What variables and constants are and how to use them
- What math functions the Arduino programming language offer
- How to add comments to our code
- How to make decisions with the Arduino programming language
- How to create loops to repeat blocks of code

In Chapter 5, *Arduino IDE* we learned how to use the Arduino IDE and the Web Editor. We also examined the setup() and loop() functions and learned how to use them. In this chapter and Chapter 7, *Programming the Arduino–Beyond the Basics*, we will learn about the Arduino programming language and how to use the language to develop applications for the Arduino. Let's start off by looking at the curly brackets.

Curly brackets

The left curly brackets ({) defines where a block of code starts and the right curly bracket (}) defines where it ends. We saw these brackets when we looked at the `setup()` and `loop()` functions; however, curly brackets are not limited to defining the code within a function they are also used to define other blocks of code as well. We will see examples of this in the *Decision making* and *Looping* sections of this chapter.

Whenever there is a left curly bracket there must also be a right curly bracket. We say that the curly brackets are balanced when we have an equal number of left and right curly brackets. Unbalanced curly brackets can lead to crypt compiler errors. If you are receiving very crypt and hard to understand compiler errors, you may want to begin your troubleshooting by verifying that the curly brackets are balanced.

Now let's look at semicolons.

Semicolons

A semicolon is used at the end of every statement to separate one statement from the next. If a statement does not end with a semicolon it will result in a compile-time error. The error text for forgetting a semicolon is pretty obvious and will include the line number of the statement that is missing it.

Semicolons are also used in the `for` loop to separate the different elements. We will look at the `for` loop in the *Looping* section of this chapter. Now let's look at how we can add comments to our code.

Comments

There are two types of comments that can be used to within our Arduino code. These are block comments and line comments. Block comments are used when the text of the comment will span multiple lines and are usually used before function calls to let the reader know what a function does. The line comments are used when a short one-line comment is needed and are usually used within function blocks to let the reader know what a specific line of code is doing.

A block comment begins with /* and ends with */. The following code shows what a block comment would look like:

```
/* This is a block comment
   This comment can span multiple lines
   This type of comment is usually found outside function calls
*/
```

A line comment starts with // and goes until the end of the line. The line comment can start at the beginning of the line or it may be after a statement ends. The following examples show what a line comment would look like:

```
// This is a single line comment
Serial.println("Hello World"); // comment after statement
```

It is always a good idea to add comments to your code to let the reader know what certain blocks of code are doing. Now let's look at what variables are.

Variables

A variable is used to store information that can be referenced or manipulated within the code. A variable is given a unique name which can then be used to access the information. The name of the variable should be something that describes what the variable is so anyone that looks at the code will understand what the variable is used for. Camel case should be used when naming a variable.

Camel case is used when creating a name out of multiple words are phases where the first letter of the name is lowercase, but the beginning of each remaining word is uppercase. Some examples of camel case are ledOne, myVariable and redLedOnRightSide.

When a variable is declared it is usually a good idea to give it an initial value. This helps to avoid accidentally accessing the variable prior to initializing it. To declare a variable, we define the type of variable followed by the name of the variable and then if we are going to give it an initial value we add the equal sign followed by the initial value. The following code shows how we would do this:

```
int myInt = 0;
```

In the preceding line of code, we declared a variable named myInt of the integer (int) type with an initial value of 0. Let's look at some of the more popular built-in data types that we can use with the Arduino language.

Data types

There are numerous, built-in, data types in the Arduino programming language. In this section, we will look at the most commonly used ones. Let's begin by looking at the Boolean type.

Boolean

The Boolean data type can contain one of two possible values, `true` or `false`. The following example shows how to declare a variable to be of the Boolean type:

```
boolean myBool = true;
```

The preceding code declares a variable named `myBool` of the Boolean type and sets an initial value of `true`. Boolean types are used a lot within a standard Arduino program and all comparison operations, as we will see later in this chapter, return a Boolean value.

Byte

The byte data type is an 8-bit numerical value that ranges from 0 to 255. The following shows how we would declare a variable of the byte type:

```
byte myByte = 128;
```

The preceding code declares a variable named `myByte` of the `byte` type with an initial value of `128`.

Integer

The integer is the primary data type used to store numerical data when a decimal value is not needed. A variable of the integer type can contain numbers ranging from -32,768 to 32,768. An integer is defined using the `int` keyword.

We can declare an integer to be unsigned by using the `unsigned` keyword. An unsigned integer can range from 0 to 65,535 whereas the normal integer has a range of -32,768 to 32,768. The following code shows how we would define both a regular integer and an unsigned integer:

```
int mySignedInt = 25;
unsigned int myUnsignedInt = 15;
```

In the preceding code, we declared a variable named `mySignedInt` of the integer type with an initial value of `25`. We also declared a second variable named `myUnsignedInt` of the unsigned integer type with an initial value of `15`.

 On some Arduino boards like the Due or SAMD, the integer can store values larger than the 32,768 and smaller than the -32,768 value. Since most of the boards have an integer range of -32,768 to 32,768, I would recommend always assuming that is the range you can use.

Long

The long data type can store integers from -2,147,483,648 to 2,147,483,647. The following code shows how we would define a long variable:

```
long myLong = 123,456,789;
```

In the preceding code, we declared a variable named `myLong` of the `long` type and gave it a value of 123,456,789. It is good practice to avoid using the long data type unless it is necessary to store larger numbers because it uses more memory than the integer type.

Double and float

Double and float data types are floating point numbers which means they are numbers that can contain a decimal point. Both the double and float types can hold values ranging from -3.4028235E+38 to 3.4028235E+38.

On most platforms, the float data type has a precision of six or seven decimal digits while the double data type usually has fifteen digits; however, this is not true on the Arduino platform. On the Arduino platform, the double and float types are exactly the same, therefore they both have the precision to six or seven decimal digits.

There are two very good reasons not to use a double or float value unless you absolutely need a decimal number. The first reason is with precision inaccuracy, as an example 6.0 divided by 3.0 may not always equal 2. You may end up getting something like 1.9999999999. The second reason is floating point math is much slower than integer math.

The following code shows how to define both a double and float variable:

```
double myDouble = 1.25;
float myFloat = 1.5;
```

In the preceding code, we declare a variable named `myDouble` of the `double` type with a value of `1.25`. We also declare a variable named `myFloat` of the `float` type with a value of `1.5`.

Character

The char data type is usually described as the data type that stores a character, however, this is not technically correct. The char data type stores a character as a numeric value based on the ASCII chart. When a char variable is defined, it can be defined with either the number that represents the character or the character itself as shown in the following code:

```
char myChar = 'A';
char myChar = 65;
```

In the preceding code, both lines declare a variable named `myChar` of the `char` type with a capital A as the value. Having a type that can hold only a single character is useful, but it would be more useful if we could store entire words or sentences. Later in this chapter, we will see how we can store words or sentences by using an array of characters.

Arrays

An array is an ordered collection of variables which are of the same type. Each variable in the array is called an **element**, and these elements can be accessed by the location (index) in the array. When an array is defined we must declare the type of variables that will be stored in it. There are several ways that an array can be defined. The following examples show some of the basic ways to define an array:

```
int myInts[10];
int myInts[] = {1, 2, 3, 4};
int myInts[8] = {2, 4, 6, 8, 10};
```

Each of these examples defines an array of integers. The first example defines an uninitialized array of ten integers. Be careful when defining uninitialized arrays because the memory locations are never initialized, which could lead to very unexpected results.

The second example defines an array of four integers were all of the elements are initialized with values. This array is automatically sized to the number of elements that is in the initialization array.

The last example defines an array of eight integers where the first five elements are initialized with values, but the last three elements are not initialized. Once again, I would recommend not defining an array like this because the last three elements are not initialized. In a moment, we will see what happens when we attempt to access an element in an array whose value was not initialized but first we need to see how we would access elements in an array.

We access an element in an array by the index. We put the index of the element we wish to retrieve between two square brackets as shown in the following code:

```
int myInts[] = {1, 2, 3, 4};
int myInt = myInts[1];
```

In the preceding code, we begin by defining an array of four integers and initialize all four values. In the next line, we retrieve the element at index 1 and put the value in the myInt variable.

It would be incorrect to think the myInt variable contains the number 1 because arrays are zero indexed which means the first value would be at index 0 therefore the myInt variable contains the number 2. The following code shows how this works:

```
int myInts[] = {1, 2, 3, 4};
int myInt0 = myInts[0]; // contains 1
int myInt1 = myInts[1]; // contains 2
int myInt2 = myInts[2]; // contains 3
int myInt3 = myInts[3]; // contains 4
```

What this code shows is when we declared an array of four integers the valid indexes for this array start at 0 and end at 3. Now that we know how to access an array let's see what happens when we access elements that aren't initialized. Add the following code in the setup() function of a sketch and run it:

```
int myInts[5];
Serial.println(myInts[0]);
Serial.println(myInts[1]);
Serial.println(myInts[2]);
Serial.println(myInts[3]);
Serial.println(myInts[4]);
```

In the Serial Monitor, you will see five values printed out but they can be any valid integer value because the elements were never initialized. Assigning a new value to an element in the array is exactly like assigning a value to any variable. The following code shows this:

```
int myInts[2];
myInts[0] = 0;
myInts[1] = 1;
```

In the preceding code, we defined an array of two integers and then assigned the value of 0 to the first element and a value of 1 to the second element.

We can also create multi-dimensional arrays, which are basically arrays of arrays. The following code shows two ways that we would define a 3 × 4 array of integers:

```
int myInts[3][4];
int myInts[][] = { {0,1,2,3}, {4,5,6,7}, {8,9,10,11} };
```

Elements in a multidimensional array are accessed by the indexes just like a single dimensional array. The following code shows how to do this:

```
int myInt = myInts[1,2]; // The value would be 6
```

Now that we have seen how to use arrays, let's see how we can use character arrays to store words and sentences.

Character arrays

We saw earlier in this chapter that we can use the character (char) type to store a single character; however, what if we wanted to store whole words or sentences? We can use an array of characters to do this. Character arrays can be initiated exactly like other arrays as the following code shows:

```
char myStr[10];
char myStr[8] = {'A', 'r', 'd', 'u', 'i', 'n', 'o', '\0'};
```

Generally, character arrays are called **strings**. In the preceding code, we define an uninitialized string that can contain up to ten characters and also a character array that contains the word *Arduino*.

You may notice that at the end of the *Arduino* string there is a \0 character. This character represents a null. When defining a string we should always terminate the string with the null character, this is called **Null Termination**. By ending the string with a null character, functions like the serial.println() function know where in memory the string ends. Without the null characters, these functions would continue to read memory until a null character is encountered, which will cause a lot of garbage to appear in the console.

There are easier ways to declare a string as the following code shows:

```
char myStr[] = "Arduino";
char myStr[10] = "Arduino";
```

In the preceding code, the first line initializes a string containing the word Arduino and the array is automatically sized with the null terminator added at the end. In the second line, we initialize a string that contains the word Arduino and contains additional space. The null terminator is added at the end of the work Arduino.

The Arduino language does contain a separate string object; however, you will find that character arrays are used a lot in the sample code. We will look at the string object in `Chapter 7`, *Programming the Arduino – Beyond the Basics.*

Now that we have seen how to use variables and arrays, let's look at how to define a constant.

Constants

A constant is a value that never changes. In the Arduino programming language, we have two ways to declare constants. We can use the `const` keyword or the `#define` component.

The `#define` component enables us to give a name to a constant value prior to the application being compiled. The compiler will replace all references to these constants, with the assigned value, prior to the application being compiled. This means that the defined constants do not take up any program space in memory, which may be an advantage if you are trying to squeeze a large program into an Arduino Nano.

The `#define` component does have some drawbacks where the biggest drawback being if the name that is defined for the constant is also included in some other constant or variable name then the name would be replaced by the value defined in the `#define` component. For this reason, when I use the `#define` to define a constant I usually use all capital letters for the name.

The following code shows how to use the `#define` component. You will note in the following code that with the `#define` component there is no semicolon at the end of the line. When using a directive like `#define`, you do not need to use a semicolon:

```
#define LED_PIN 8
```

The second way to declare a constant is to use the `const` keyword. The `const` keyword is a variable qualifier that modifies the variable's behavior making it read-only. This will enable us to use the variable exactly as we would any other variable except that we are unable to change the variable's value. If we attempted to change the value, we would receive a compile-time error.

The following code shows how to use the `const` keyword:

```
const float pi = 3.14;
```

The `const` keyword is generally preferred of the `#define` component; however, with devices with limited memory the `#define` can be used. Now let's see how we can perform math functions in the Arduino programming language.

Arithmetic functions

The Arduino programming language includes operators that enable us to calculate the sum, difference, product and quotient of two operands. To use these operators, the two operands must be of the same type. This means, as an example, we have the ability to calculate the sum of two integer variables; however, we are unable to calculate the sum of a float variable and an integer variable without casting one of the variables forcing them to be of the same type. We will look at casting a little later in this chapter.

The following example shows how we calculate the sum, difference, product, and quotient of two variables:

```
z = x + y; // calculates the sum of x and y
z = x - y; // calculates the difference of x and y
z = x * y; // calculates the product of x and y
z = x / y; // calculates the quotient of x and y
```

When we perform a division operation there are times where we only need the remainder. For this, we can use the modulo operator. If we divided 5 by 2 the result would be 2.5, therefore with the modulo operator the result will be 5 since that is the remainder. The following code example shows how to use the modulo operator:

```
z = x % y // z will contain the remainder of x divided by y
```

The Arduino programming language also includes compound assignment operators that enable us to combine the arithmetic and variable assignment operations. This enables us to perform an arithmetic operation and assign the result to the original variable. The following code shows the compound operators in the Arduino programming language:

```
x++; // increments x by 1 and assigns the result to x
x--; // decrements x by 1 and assigns the result to x
x += y; //increments x by y and assigns the result to x
x -= y; //decrement x by y and assigns the result to x
x *= y; //multiplies x and y and assigns the result to x
x /= y; //divides x and y and assigns the result to x
```

There are also numerous math functions that enable us to perform various common math functions. The following code shows some of the more common functions:

```
abs(x) // returns the absolute value of x
max(x,y) // returns the larger of the two values
min(x,y) //returns the smaller of the two values
pow(x,y) // returns the value of x raised to the power of y
sq(x) // returns the value of x squared
sqrt(x) // returns the square root of the value
```

Now that we have seen the arithmetic operators and functions that the Arduino programming language provides, let's look at the comparison operators.

Comparison operators

The Arduino programming language includes comparison operators that enable us to compare the values of two operands. The comparison operators return a Boolean value indicating if the comparison was true or false. The following code shows how we would use these operators:

```
x == y // returns true if x is equal to y
x != y // returns true if x is not equal to y
x > y // returns true if x is greater than y
x < y // returns true if x is less than y
x >= y // returns true if x is greater or equal to y
x <= y // returns true if x is less than or equal to y
```

Now that we have seen the comparison operators that the Arduino programming language provides, let's look at the logical operators.

Logical operators

There are several logical operators included in the Arduino programming language. These operators are the AND, OR and NOT operators. The NOT operator enables us to reverse a comparison operation. The AND and OR operators enable us to combine multiple comparison operators into one step. The following code shows how to use the logical operators:

```
(x > 5 && x < 10) // true if x is greater than 5 and less than 10
(x > 5 || x < 1) // true if x is greater than 5 or less than 1
!(x == y) // returns true if x is not equal to y
```

Now let's see how we can cast a variable.

Casting

The cast operator will convert the variable type to a different type. This will enable us to perform operations, like arithmetic operations, on variables of different types. For example, if we want to add two variables where one is of the float type and the other is of the integer type, then we will need to cast one of them, so the two variables are of the same type.

One thing to note is when we cast a float value to an integer value the value is truncated and not rounded. This means that if the float variable contains the value 2.9 and we cast it to an integer, the value will be 2. With this in mind, we generally want to cast integer values to float values rather than float values to integer values even if it means the operation will take longer.

The following code shows how we could cast an integer variable as a float variable to perform arithmetic calculations:

```
int x = 5;
float y = 3.14;
float z = (float)x + y;
```

There are very few useful applications that we can write that do not have some sort of logic in them. This logic is usually performed by deciding what to do based on some input. This requires our applications to make decisions. Let's see how we can do this with the Arduino programming language.

Decision making

In the Arduino programming language, we make decisions with the `if` statement. The `if` statement will check if a condition is true and if so will execute the block of code within the curly brackets.

The following shows the syntax for the `if` statement:

```
if (condition) {
  // Code to execute
}
```

We can use an `else` statement after the `if` statement to execute a block of code if the condition is not true.

The following shows the syntax for the `if/else` statement:

```
if (condition) {
  // Code to execute if condition is true
} else {
  // Code to execute if condition is false
}
```

The condition, in the `if` statement, can be any Boolean value or an operation that returns a Boolean result. You will find that the majority of the `if` statements in your code will contain comparison operations. Let's look at some code that will illustrate this:

```
if (varA > varB) {
  Serial.println("varA is greater than varB");
} else {
  Serial.println("varB is greater or equal to varA");
}
```

In the preceding code, we used the greater than (>) comparison operator to see if `varA` is greater than `varB`. If the comparison operation returned `true` then the code sends the `varA is greater than varB` message to the console. If the comparison operation returned false then the `varB is greater or equal to varA` message is sent to the console.

We can also string the `if` statements together by using an `if` statement with an `else` statement. The following code illustrates this:

```
if (varA == varB) {
  Serial.println("varA is equal to varB");
} else if (varA > varB) {
  Serial.println("varA is greater than varB");
} else {
  Serial.println("varB is greater than varA");
}
```

In the preceding code, we used the equal (==) comparison operator to see if `varA` equaled `varB` and if so we send the `varA is equal to varB` message to the console. If they were not equal, we then used the greater than (>) comparison operator to see if `varA` is greater than `varB` and if so we send the `varA is greater than varB` message to the console. If neither one of the two comparison operations were successful we then send the `varA is equal to varB` message to the console.

When using the `else` and `if` statements together, the code will execute the first block of code that returns a `true` condition and will then ignore the remainder of the `else` statements.

Using the `if` and `else` statements is the most common way to perform logic within an application; however, the code can get very messy if we have more than two or three conditions to check. Just imagine if the last `if`/`else` example has ten different conditions that we needed to check. If there is a need to check more than two or three conditions, we can use the `switch`/`case` statements.

The `switch`/`case` statement takes a value, compares it to the several possible matches, and executes the appropriate block of code based on the first successful match. The `switch` statement is an alternative to using multiple `else-if` statements when there could be several possible matches. The `switch` statement is preferred over the `else-if` statements if there are three or more possible matches. The `switch` statement takes the following format:

```
switch (var) {
   case match1:
     // Code to execute if condition matches case
   break;
   case match2:
     // Code to execute if condition matches case
   break;
   case match3:
     // Code to execute if condition matches case
   break;
   default:
     // Code to execute if condition matches case
}
```

The preceding code starts off with a switch statement and within the parenthesis of the `switch` statement, there is a variable named `var`. The code will attempt to match the value of the `var` variable with each case statement starting with the first one and once it finds a match it will execute the code.

The code within each `case` statement should end with a `break` statement. The `break` statement is needed because once the `switch` statement matches a case it will not only execute the code within that `case` statement but also the code in each subsequent `case` statement. This means that if we did not include the `break` statements and the `var` variable matched the value in the `match2` case, the code within the `match2` case, the `match3` case and default will all execute. The code encounters the `break` statement it immediately exits out of the `switch` statement preventing the code in the other `case` statements from executing.

Now that we have seen how to make decisions in the Arduino programming language, let's look at how to perform looping.

Looping

The Arduino programming language has three looping statements which are the `for`, `while` and `do/while` loops. We will start off by looking at the `for` loop.

The `for` loop is used to repeatedly execute a block of code. The `for` loop is usually used to execute a block of code a specific number of times or to access elements in an array. There are three parts to the `for` statement. These parts are the initialization, condition, and increment.

In the initialization portion of the `for` statement, we initialize any variables that need to be initialized. There can be multiple initializations separated by commas, but I would recommend avoiding any initialization here that is not directly related to the `for` loop.

The condition portion of the `for` statement, expect a statement that will return either a `true` or `false` and it usually contains a conditional statement. This portion of the loop determines when the loop will end. While the conditional statement returns `true`, the `for` loop will continue to execute the block of code. Once the conditional statement returns `false` the loop will exit.

The increment portion of the `for` statement is used to change the value of a variable. This change is performed each time the loop is executed. The following code shows the syntax for the `for` statement:

```
for (initialization; condition; change) { }
```

To see how this would look with actual code, the following shows how we would create a `for` statement that will loop ten times:

```
for (int i = 0; i < 10; i++) {
  // Code to execute
}
```

In the preceding code, the for statement initializes the `i` variable to zero in the initialization portion. In the condition portion, the `for` statements checks to see if the `i` variable is less than ten and if it is, the code will continue to loop. In the change portion, the `for` loop increments the `i` variable by one each time the loop is executed. In the example, the `for` loop will initially assign the value of `0` to the `i` variable and then increment it each loop until the `i` variable is equal to `9`.

The next loop that we will look at is the `while` loop. The `while` loop will repeatedly execute a block of code until the condition defined in the `while` statement returns `false`. This can be a dangerous loop to use because if the condition never returns `false` then the loop will continue indefinitely. The `while` statement takes the following syntax:

```
while (condition) {
   // code to execute
}
```

The condition within the `while` statement should return either `true` or `false`. This condition is usually a comparison statement. The following code shows an example of the `while` statement:

```
int x = 0;
while (x < 200) {
   // code to execute
   x++;
}
```

In the preceding code, the block of code is executed while the x variable is less than `200`. At the end of the code block, the x variable is incremented by 1. If we had forgotten to put the line that incremented x in the code block then the `while` loop would loop indefinitely. It is very important to make sure you put the change statement within the code block, otherwise the loop will never exit.

With the `while` loop, the condition is checked prior to the block of code being executed. That means that if the conditions return `false` when the `while` statement is first called then the code block would never be executed. If we require that the block of code be executed once, prior to the condition being check, we can use the `do/while` loop.

The `do/while` loop is exactly like the `while` loop except that the condition is checked after the block of code is executed rather than before. The following code shows the syntax for this loop:

```
do {
   // code to execute
} while (condition);
```

As with the `while` loop, the condition within the `while` statement should return either a `true` or `false` and is usually a comparison statement. The following codes show an example of the `do/while` statement:

```
int x = 0;
do {
   // code to execute
```

```
    x++;
} while (x < 200);
```

The preceding code will execute the block of code 200 times, exactly like the code in the previous `while` loop. The only difference is, in the `while` loop, the condition is checked prior to executing the block of code and in the `do/while` loop the condition is checked after.

Functions

A function is a named block of code that performs a specific task. When a new sketch is created, the IDE or Web Editor automatically creates two functions for us as we saw in the previous chapter; however, we are not limited to only those two functions, we also have the ability to declare custom functions ourselves. The following code shows the syntax for creating a function:

```
type name (parameters) { }
```

To declare a function, we need to declare what type the function is. The function type is the value that is returned by the function. If the function is not going to return a value, as with the `setup()` and `loop()` functions, then the function type would be `void`.

Once the function type is declared we define the name of the function. The function name should be something that describes what the function does. For example, if we are creating a sketch that will turn a LED on or off, then we may have functions named `ledOff()` and `ledOn()`. It is good practice to use camel case when naming a function as with variables.

After the name of the function, we put the parameters of the function within parentheses. Parameters are data that are passed to the function by the code that calls it. The function usually relies on the data to perform it's required logic. You may have multiple parameters within the parentheses by separating them with commas.

We use curly brackets to define the start and end of the code block for the function. The left curly bracket indicates the start of the function while the right curly bracket indicates the end of the function. The following examples show different examples of functions:

```
void myFunction() {
  // Function code
}

void myFunction(int param) {
  // Function code
}
```

```
int myFunction() {
  // Function code
}

int myFunction(int param) {
  // Function Code
}
```

The first function has a return type of void which means it does not return any value. It also does not have any parameters. This type of function would be used to perform a task that does not need to return any information back to the code that called it and does not require any additional information to perform its required task.

The second function also has a return type of void, but it does accept one parameter. This type of function would be used if the function needs some information, from the code that called it, to perform its task. The first part of the parameter is the parameter type. In this example, the type is an int, which means the data will be of the integer type. The second part of the parameter is the name of the parameter. This would mean that the parameter in this example is named param and is of the integer type. To declare multiple parameters, we would separate them with commas like this: (int param1, int param2, float param3).

The third function has an int return type, which means it must return an integer; however, it does not take any parameters. This type of function would be used if we wanted to pass information from the function back to the code that called it.

The fourth function returns an integer and accepts a parameter. This type of function would be used if we wanted to pass information back to the code that called it and it needed information from that code to perform its task.

We use the return statement to return a value from a function. The following code shows how we would do this:

```
int myFunction() {
  var x = 1;
  var y = 2;
  return x + y;
}
```

When a variable is created within a function, as we saw in the last example, the variable is only accessible within that function. The following code illustrates this:

```
int g = 1;
void function myFunction1() {
  int x1 = 2;
```

```
}
void function myFunction2() {
  int x2 = 3;
}
```

In the preceding code, the g variable, since it is declared outside of the functions, is accessible by any of the functions. When you declare a variable outside of the functions like this it is considered to be a global variable. The x1 variable is only accessible within the myFunction1() function and the x2 variable is accessible only within the myFunction2() function.

Summary

In this chapter, we covered the basics of the Arduino programming language. The material in this chapter lays the groundwork for everything else that is covered in this book, therefore, it is important to understand the items presented here.

In the next chapter, we will look at some more advanced features of the Arduino programming language and the Arduino development environments.

7
Programming the Arduino - Beyond the Basics

One of the things that I learned early on in my development career is that I can write some pretty amazing applications even if I only know the basics of the programming language that I am using; however, it usually makes the code hard to maintain and read while also adding significant development time to the project. I always tell people that are learning a language to take the time to understand some of the more advanced features of the language they are learning prior to using it for serious projects.

In this chapter, we will learn:

- How to set the pin mode on an Arduino digital pin
- How to get and set the values of an Arduino digital pin
- How to get and set the values of an Arduino analog pin
- How to use structures and unions
- How to use additional tabs
- How to use classes and objects

In the previous chapter, we looked at the basics of the Arduino programming language. In this chapter, we are going to go beyond the basics of the language itself. We will start off by looking at how we can interact with the digital pins on the Arduino.

 For the samples in this chapter, we will be using the prototype that we created at the end of Chapter 4, *Basic Prototyping*.

Setting digital pin mode

In Chapter 1, *The Arduino*, we saw that the Arduino has several digital pins that we can connect external sensors and other devices to. Before we use these pins, we should configure them for either input or output depending on what we are using them for. To do this, we use the pinMode() function that is built into the Arduino programming language. Usually for smaller sketches we call the pinMode() function within the setup() function; however, this is not required. The following code shows the syntax for the pinMode() function:

```
pinMode(pin, mode);
```

This function is called with two parameters. The first is the number of the pin that we are setting and the second is the mode for the pin. The mode for the pin can be either INPUT, to read the value from the pin (external sensor writes a value to the pin), or OUTPUT, to set the value for the pin. The following code shows how to use this command to set the pin mode for two pins:

```
pinMode( 11 , INPUT);
pinMode( 12 , OUTPUT);
```

In the preceding code, we set pin 11 to input and pin 12 for output. Therefore, we would write values to pin 11 and read values from pin 12.

It is good practice never to use the pin numbers themselves, as shown in the last example, to access the pin on the Arduino. Instead of using the pin numbers like this, we should set a variable or constant with the number of the pin and then use that variable or constant when accessing the pin. This will prevent us from typing in the wrong number within the code.

 My personal preference is to use #define to define the pin numbers that I am using when the pin number will not change. This allows me to separate my pin definitions from the other constants within my sketch. If you wish to use constants instead of #define, that is perfectly acceptable, and some people would say that it is preferable.

The following code shows how we should use the pinMode() function within a sketch:

```
#define BUTTON_ONE 12
#define LED_ONE 11

void setup() {
  pinMode(BUTTON_ONE, INPUT);
  pinMode(LED_ONE, OUTPUT);
}
```

In the preceding code, we defined constants that represented two pins. The first line defines BUTTON_ONE to the number (pin) 12 and the second line defines LED_ONE to the number (pin) 11. We then set the BUTTON_ONE pin to input mode and LED_ONE pin to output mode within the setup() function.

The pinMode() function can also be used to configure the internal pull-up resistor by setting the mode of the pin to INPUT_PULLUP. This will invert the behavior of the pin when it is in input mode.

These digital pins may have one of two values: HIGH or LOW. Let's see how we can set the value of a digital pin.

Digital write

To set the value of a digital pin in the Arduino programming language, we use the digitalWrite() function. This function takes the following syntax:

```
digitalWrite(pin, value);
```

The digitalWrite() function accepts two parameters, where the first one is the pin number and the second is the value to set. We should use either HIGH or LOW when setting the value of a digital pin. The following code shows how to do this:

```
digitalWrite(LED_ONE, HIGH);
delay(500);
digitalWrite(LED_ONE, LOW);
delay(500);
```

In the preceding code, we set the pin defined by the LED_ONE constant too HIGH and then pause for half a second. The delay() function in the Arduino programming language pauses the execution of the sketch for a certain amount of time. The time for this function is in milliseconds. After the delay() function we then set the pin defined by the LED_ONE constant too LOW and wait another half a second before looping back to the beginning.

The previous code can be used in the loop() function to blink an LED; however, before we do that we need to define the LED_ONE constant and also set the pin mode. Let's look at the full sketch required to blink an LED.

```
#define LED_ONE 11

void setup() {
  pinMode(LED_ONE, OUTPUT);
}
```

```
void loop() {
  digitalWrite(LED_ONE, HIGH);
  delay(500);
  digitalWrite(LED_ONE, LOW);
  delay(500);
}
```

This code starts off by defining the LED_ONE constant and setting to 11. The pin mode for the LED_ONE pin is then set in the setup() function. Finally, the code that will cause the LED to blink is added to the loop() function. If you connect the prototype that we developed in Chapter 4, *Basic Prototyping* and ran this code, you should see one of the LEDs blinking.

Now that we know how to write to a digital pin, let's see how we can read the value of one.

Digital read

To read the value of a digital pin in the Arduino programming language, we use the digitalRead() function. This function takes the following syntax:

```
digitalRead(pin);
```

The digitalRead() function takes one parameter, which is the number of the digital pin to read, and will return an integer value. The following code shows how we can use the digitalRead() function to read one of the digital pins on the Arduino:

```
int val = digitalRead(BUTTON_ONE);
```

With this code, the digitalRead() function will return the value of the pin defined by the BUTTON_ONE constant and put that value into the variable named val. The val variable is defined to be an integer. However, the digitalRead() function will only return a 0 or a 1. We can use the same HIGH and LOW constants that we saw in the *Digital write* section to see if the pin is either high or low. Using these constants are preferred and makes your code more readable.

Now let's see how we can use the digitalRead() function to read the status of a button. The following code will read the status of the button from the prototype that we built in Chapter 4, *Basic Prototyping*:

```
#define BUTTON_ONE 12

void setup() {
  Serial.begin(9600);
```

```
  pinMode(BUTTON_ONE, INPUT);
}

void loop() {
  int val = digitalRead(BUTTON_ONE);
  if (val == HIGH) {
    Serial.println("Button HIGH");
  } else {
    Serial.println("Button LOW");
  }
}
```

This code starts off by defining the BUTTON_ONE constant and setting it to 12. The serial monitor and the pin mode for the pin that the button is connected to are both configured in the setup() function. Within the loop button, the digitalRead() function is used to read the pin and the if statement is used to compare the value that was returned with the HIGH constant. If they are equal, then the message Button HIGH is sent to the serial monitor otherwise the message Button LOW is sent.

If this code is run on the prototype that was created in Chapter 4, *Basic Prototyping*, then you should see one of the two messages being printed to the serial monitor depending if the button is pressed or not.

Now let's see how we can write to an analog pin on the Arduino.

Analog write

Analog values are written to the Arduino with the **Pulse-Width Modulation** (**PWM**) pins. In Chapter 1, *The Arduino*, we looked at what PWM is and how they work. On most Arduino boards the PWM pins are configured for pins 3, 5, 6, 9, 10, and 11; however, the Arduino Mega has significantly more pins available for PWM functionality.

To perform an analog write, we use the analogWrite() function, which takes the following syntax:

```
analogWrite(pin, value);
```

The analogWrite() function accepts two parameters, where the first one is the pin number and the second is the value to set. The value for the analogWrite() function can range from 0 to 255.

Let's look at a sample sketch to see how we can use the `analogWrite()` function to fade a led in and out:

```
#define LED_ONE 11

int val = 0;
int change = 5;

void setup()
{
  pinMode(LED_ONE, OUTPUT);
}

void loop()
{
  val += change;
  if (val > 250 || val < 5) {
    change *= -1;
  }
  analogWrite(LED_ONE, val);
  delay(100);
}
```

This code starts off by defining a `LED_ONE` constant with a value of `11`. This will be the pin that the LED is connected to. There are also two global variables defined, both of the integer type, named `val` and `change`. The `val` integer will store the current value of the analog pin, and the `change` integer will store how much the `val` integer should change each loop.

The pin defined by the `LED_ONE` constant is set to output mode within the `setup()` function. This will enable us to write to the pin and change the brightness of the LED connected to the pin.

The `loop()` function starts off by adding the `change` variable to the `val` variable, and the result is stored in the `val` variable. If the value of the `val` variable is greater than 250 or less than 5 we multiple the `change` variable by -1. This causes the `change` variable to rotate between 5 and -5, which causes the `val` variable to increase or decrease each loop. Finally, the value of the `val` variable is written to the pin defined by the `LED_ONE` constant, and then there is a short delay before looping back.

If this code is run on the prototype that was created in `Chapter 4`, *Basic Prototyping*, then you should see LED fade in and out. Now let's look at how we can read an analog pin.

Analog read

We read the value from an analog pin using the `analogRead()` function. This function will return a value between 0 and 1023. This means that if the sensor is returning the full voltage of 5V, then the `analogRead()` function will return a value 1023, which results in a value of 0.0049V per unit (we will use this number in the sample code). The following code shows the syntax for the `analogRead()` function:

```
analogRead(pin);
```

The `analogRead()` function takes one parameter which is the pin to read from. The following code uses the `analogRead()` function with a tmp36 temperature sensor to determine the current temperature:

```
#define TEMP_PIN 5

void setup() {
  Serial.begin(9600);
}

void loop() {
  int pinValue = analogRead(TEMP_PIN);
  double voltage = pinValue * 0.0049;
  double tempC = (voltage - .5) * 100.0;
  double tempF = (tempC * 1.8) + 32;
  Serial.print(tempC);
  Serial.print(" -  ");
  Serial.println(tempF);
  delay(2000);
}
```

The preceding code starts off by defining the pin that the temperature sensor is attached to which is the analog pin 5. The `setup()` function configures the serial monitor so the application can print the temperature to it.

The `loop()` function begins by reading the analog pin and storing the value in the `pinValue` variable. To convert this value to the actual voltage, we multiply it by the 0.0049V value that we saw earlier in this section. If we look at the datasheet for the tmp36 temperature sensor, we will determine that the `(voltage - .5) *100.0` is the correct formula to calculate the temperature in Celsius. We can then use the standard formula `(celsiusTemp *1.8) + 32` to determine the temperature in Fahrenheit. Finally, we print these values to the serial monitor and delay for two seconds before beginning the loop again.

We will be using the `digitalRead()`, `digitalWrite()`, `analogRead()` and `analogWrite()` functions a lot in this book so you will be getting familiar with them.

Now let's look at structures.

Structures

A structure is a user-defined a composite data type that is used to group multiple variables together. The variables in a structure may be of different types enabling us to store related data, of different types, together. The following code shows the syntax of how we would define a structure:

```
struct name {
   variable list
   .
   .
};
```

When a structure is defined, the `struct` keyword is used followed by the name of the structure. The variable list is then defined between the curly brackets.

Let's take a look at how we can create and use a structure by changing the previous sketch, which used the `analogRead()` function to read the TMP36 temperature, to use a structure. The first thing we need to do is to define a structure that will store the temperature information from the sensor. We will name this structure `tmp36_reading`, and it will contain three variables all of the double type. The following code shows how to define this structure:

```
struct tmp36_reading {
   double voltage;
   double tempC;
   double tempF;
};
```

The preceding code defines a structure named `tmp36_reading` that contains three variables all of the double type. Keep in mind that the variables in a structure do not have to be of the same type, it just worked out that all of the individual variables in this structure were of the double type.

The following code shows how we would create a variable of the `tmp36_reading` type:

```
struct tmp36_reading temp;
```

The preceding code creates a variable named `temp` that is of the `tmp36_reading` type. We can then assign or retrieve values by using the dot syntax as shown in the following code:

```
temp.voltage = pinValue * 0.0049;
temp.tempC = (temp.voltage - .5) * 100.0;
temp.tempF = (temp.tempC * 1.8) + 32;
```

In the preceding code we assign values to the `voltage`, `tempC` and `tempF` variables of the `tmp36_reading` structure. Now let's see how we can integrate this code into a sketch that reads the TMP36 temperature sensor. The following is the complete code for the new sketch:

```
#define TEMP_PIN 5

struct tmp36_reading {
    double voltage;
    double tempC;
    double tempF;
};

void setup() {
    Serial.begin(9600);
}

void loop() {
    struct tmp36_reading temp;
    int pinValue = analogRead(TEMP_PIN);
    temp.voltage = pinValue * 0.0049;
    temp.tempC = (temp.voltage - .5) * 100.0;
    temp.tempF = (temp.tempC * 1.8) + 32;

    showTemp(temp);
    delay(2000);
}

void showTemp(struct tmp36_reading temp) {
    Serial.print(temp.tempC);
    Serial.print(" - ");
    Serial.println(temp.tempF);
}
```

This sketch functions exactly like the previous sketch that read the TMP36 temperature sensor, except now we use a structure to store the values from the sensor rather than variables.

If you have multiple values that you can group together like this, it is recommended that we use a structure rather than variables because all of the values are grouped together in one structure.

Now let's look at another special data type that may look similar to a structure; however, the functionality is significantly different.

Unions

A union is a special data type that enables us to store different data types in a single definition, similar to the structure; however, only one of the members may contain data at any one time. The following shows the syntax for defining a union:

```
union name {
   variable list
   .
   .
   .
};
```

If the syntax looks a lot like the syntax for a structure. In fact, it is the same syntax except for the struct/union keywords.

Let's see how we would use a union. The following code defines a new union:

```
union some_data {
   int i;
   double d;
   char s[20];
};
```

The preceding code defines a union named some_data that can contain an integer, double or a character string. The keyword in that last sentence is the *or*. Unlike the structure, which can store several different values, a union can only store one value at a time. The following code will illustrate this:

```
union some_data {
   int i;
   double d;
   char s[20];
};

void setup() {
   Serial.begin(9600);
   union some_data myData;
   myData.i = 42;
```

```
    myData.d = 3.14;
    strcpy( myData.s,  "Arduino");
    Serial.println(myData.s);
    Serial.println(myData.d);
    Serial.println(myData.i);
}
```

In the preceding code, we define a union named some_data. Then in the setup() function we create an instance of the some_data union type named myData. We then assign values to each member of the union type. The integer member is set to 42, the double member is set to 3.14 and the character string is set to Arduino. When this code is run, we will see that the Arduino character string is correctly printed to the serial monitor; however, when the integer and double members are printed to the serial monitor the information is not correct.

In the previous example, when the some_data.i member is set to 42, the some_data union will contain the integer 42. Then when we set the some_data.d member to 3.14, the integer value of 42 is overwritten, and the some_data union would now contain 3.14. Finally when we set the some_data.s member to Arduino it overwrites the some_data.d member, so the some_data union now contains the string Arduino.

Before we look at more features of the Arduino programming language, let's look at another feature of the Arduino IDE and the Web Editor.

Adding tabs

As you begin to work with larger and more complex projects, it quickly becomes important to divide your code up into separate workspaces because it makes your code easier to manage. To do this, in both the Arduino IDE and the Web Editor, we can add new tabs to a sketch.

To add a new tab to the Arduino IDE, click on the button with an upside-down triangle in it that is located at the upper right side of the IDE window, as shown in the following screenshot:

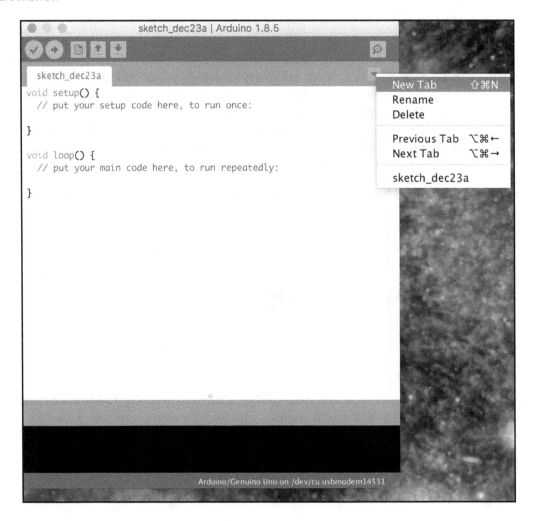

In the window that pops up, click on the **New Tab** option, and you will see an orange bar below the code section of the Arduino IDE windows. In this orange bar, you can name the new tab and then press the **OK** button to create the tab. The following screenshot shows how to name the new tab:

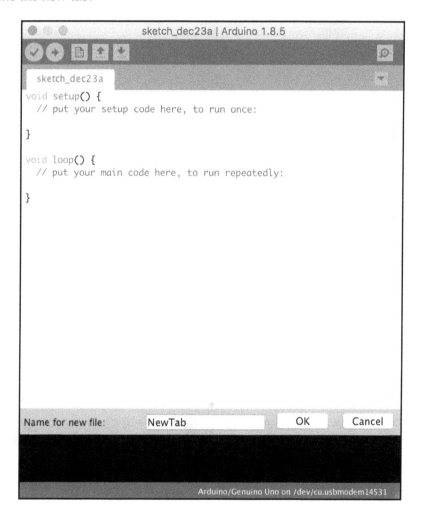

Once you click **OK** a new tab is created, with the name you gave it, as shown in the following screenshot:

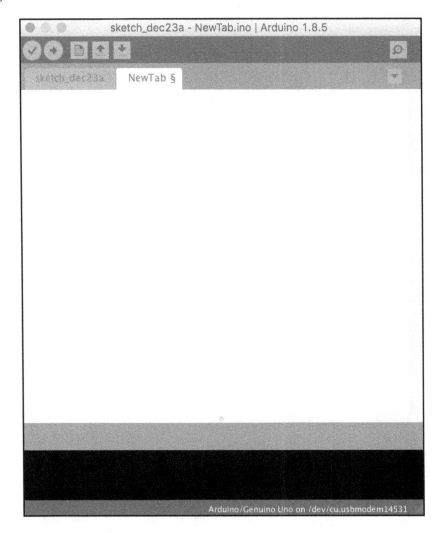

We can create a new tab in the Web Editor exactly as we did in the Arduino IDE. In the Web Editor, there is a similar button with an upside-down triangle. When that button is clicked a menu will appear, and you can select the **New Tab** option. Once you name the new tab, it will appear in the Web Editor.

Before we start adding tabs to our projects, we need to have a plan on how we want to separate the code. I find that for large projects it is good practice to only have the setup() and loop() functions in the main tab. I then create a tab for each functional area of the project. For example, if I made a weather station that had both temperature rain sensors, then I would have my main tab with the setup() and loop() functions and then have two additional tabs; one for the temperature sensor functionality and one for the rain sensor functionality.

In addition to using additional tabs for code, it is also good practice, for larger projects and libraries, to have tabs that define constants that need to be used in multiple tabs. These constants are usually put into header files. A header file should be named with a .h extension. Now let's see how to work with tabs.

Working with tabs

When creating a new tab, the first thing we need to decide is what is going to the tab. For example in this section, we will create two new tabs. One will be named led.h and the other led. The led.h file will contain the constant definition, and the led file will contain code.

When we create a tab with the .h extension we are creating, what is known in the C language, a header file. A header file is a file that contains declarations and macro definitions. These tabs can then be included in the normal code tabs. In the next section, we will see another type of tab which is the cpp tab.

Once the new tabs are created, add the following code to the led.h tab:

```
#ifndef LED_H
#define LED_H

#define LED_ONE 3
#define LED_TWO 11
#endif
```

This code will define two constants, which are the pin header numbers for the two LEDs on the prototype that we built in Chapter 4, *Basic Prototyping*. The #ifndef and #endif ensure that the header file is imported only once within any tab. The #ifndef looks to see if the LED_H constant is defined, and if not then it includes the code between the #ifndef and #endif.

Now in the led tab add the following code:

```
void blink_led(int led) {
   digitalWrite(led, HIGH);
   delay(500);
   digitalWrite(led, LOW);
   delay(500);
}
```

The blink_led() function contains a single parameter, which will be the pin for the LED that we wish to blink. The function itself will turn the LED on for 1/2 a second and then turn it off.

Now in the main tab, we will need to include an #include statement at the top of the tab to include the led.h header file. The following code shows how to do this:

```
#include "led.h"
```

The #include statement will take a header file and includes it in the tab, allowing us to use the definitions within our code. If we attempted to use one of the constants within our code but forgot to include the header file, we would receive an error that the constant was not declared in this scope meaning the compiler was unable to find the declarations for the constant.

If we are adding a header file from the sketch, we are working in, the name of the header file is surrounded by double quotes. If we include a header file from a separate library the name will be surrounded by the less than and greater than signs. We will see this later in this book as we use third-party libraries.

In the loop() function, we will want to call the blink_led() function from the led tab. One thing to note here is we only need to include the #include statement for the header file and not for the tab that contains the code. The following shows the code for the main tab:

```
#include "led.h"
void setup() {
   // put your setup code here, to run once:
   pinMode(LED_ONE, OUTPUT);
   pinMode(LED_TWO, OUTPUT);
```

```
}

void loop() {
  // put your main code here, to run repeatedly:
  blink_led(LED_ONE);
  delay(1000);
  blink_led(LED_TWO);
}
```

Now if you connect the prototype that we created in Chapter 4, *Basic Prototyping*, you should see the LEDs blink one after the other.

Dividing your code between separate tabs is a great way to organize it when working with larger projects. This makes it a lot easier to maintain and organize your code.

Classes are usually used when creating libraries for the Arduino. While creating libraries is beyond the scope of this book, it is good to know what classes are and how to use them because we will be using libraries in certain sections of this book.

Object-oriented programming

Object-oriented programming (**OOP**) is a programming paradigm that helps us divide our code into reusable components using classes and objects. An object is designed to model something. For example, we could create an LED object that will contain the properties and functionality we want for a LED; however, before we can create an object we need to have a blueprint for it. This blueprint is called a **class**. Let's see how this works by creating a class that will help us control a LED.

We will start off by creating two new tabs named led.cpp and led.h. The led.h file will contain the definition for the class, and the led.cpp file will contain the code. Let's start off by adding the following code to the led.h file:

```
#ifndef LED_H
#define LED_H

#dcfine LED_ONE 3
#define LED_TWO 11

class Led{
  int ledPin;
  long onTime;
  long offTime;
  public:
    Led(int pin, long on, long off);
```

```
        void blinkLed();
        void turnOn();
        void turnOff();
};

#endif
```

The code is similar to the `led.h` file in the working with tabs section except the `Led` class definition is added. The `Led` class definition defines three properties (variables) for the class: `ledPin`, `onTime`, and `offTime`. Previous to this example, all of the variables we used have been either global variables or defined within a function. Class properties are variables that are defined within a class and usually define something about the object. In this example, the `ledPin` property defines what pin the LED is connected to; the `onTime` property defines the amount of time to keep the LED on and the `offTime` property defines how long to keep the LED off.

After the properties, a constructor for the class is defined. A constructor is used to create an instance of a class, and we will see how to use this later in this section. After the constructor, three methods (functions) for the class. A class method is simply a function that is part of a class and usually defines the functionality of an object.

Where the `led.h` tab contains the definition for the `Led` class, the `led.cpp` tab contains the code for the class. Let's add the following code to the `led.cpp` tab:

```
#include "led.h"
#include "Arduino.h"

Led::Led(int pin, long on, long off) {
    ledPin = pin;
    pinMode(ledPin, OUTPUT);
    onTime = on;
    offTime = off;
}

void Led::turnOn() {
    digitalWrite(ledPin, HIGH);
}

void Led::turnOff(){
    digitalWrite(ledPin, LOW);
}

void Led::blinkLed() {
    this->turnOn();
    delay(onTime);
    this->turnOff();
```

```
    delay(offTime);
}
```

This code starts off by importing two header files. The first header file is the `led.h` file that we just created and the second is the `Arduino.h` header file. The `Arduino.h` header file contains the definitions for all of the custom Arduino functions. It is automatically added to the main tab; however, if you wish to use the Arduino custom functions in other tabs, as is needed here, we need to import this file.

Following the imports is the implementation of the constructor for the `Led` class that was defined in the `led.h` tab. When we implement a constructor or a method for a class we prefix the name of it with the name of the class followed by two colons (::). The name of a constructor for a class is required to be the same as the class name. Therefore, the implementation for the constructor is `Led::Led`. Within the constructor, we set the class properties and the pin mode for the pin that the LED is connected too.

The next two class methods, `Led::turnOn` and `Led::turnOff`, use the `digitalWrite()` method to turn the LED on or off. Notice how these two methods us the `ledPin` property within the `digitalWrite()` method. This property is set within the constructor when the class is created.

Finally the implementation for the `Led::blinkLed()` method is defined. This method uses the `Led::turnOn` and `Led::turnOff` methods defined previously to blink the LED on and OFF. When we call a method of a class we use the dash/greater than signs together (->) as shown in the `blinkLed()` method. The `this` keyword is used to refer to the current instance.

Now let's see how we would use the `Led` class. Within the main tab, the first thing we need to do is to include the `led.h` file. Add the following line to the top of the tab:

```
#include "led.h"
```

Next, we need to create a global instance of the `Led` class and give it a name of `led`. To do this, we use the constructor that we created for the class. The following code will create an instance of the `Led` class:

```
Led led(LED_ONE, 1000, 500);
```

Within the `Led` class the constructor is defined like this:

```
Led::Led(int pin, long on, long off)
```

Notice that the definition for the Led class has three parameters (pin, on and off). These three parameters match the three values that we are passing into the constructor when we create an instance of the Led class.

We can now use the class to make the LED blink by calling the blinkLed() method of the class. The following code shows how to do this:

```
led.blinkLed();
```

The following code shows the code within the main tab that will use the Led class to blink an LED:

```
#include "led.h"
Led led(LED_ONE, 1000, 500);
void setup() {
}
void loop() {
    led.blinkLed();
}
```

If you run this code on the prototype that we created in Chapter 4, *Basic Prototyping*, you will see one of the LEDs blink.

In this section, we only gave a very brief introduction to OOP enabling you to understand how most professional Arduino libraries are created and how to use them. There are whole books written about OOP, and if you wish to create libraries for the Arduino, I would recommend reading more object-oriented design in general and OOP for the Arduino.

Now let's look at how we can use the built-in String library for the Arduino.

String library

The String library, which is part of the Arduino core libraries, enables us to use and manipulate text easier and in a more complex way then character arrays do. It does take more memory to use the String library than it does to use character arrays but it is easier to use the String library

There are numerous ways to create an instance of the String type. Let's look at a few examples here:

```
String str1 = "Arduino";
String str2 = String("Arduino");
String str3 = String('B');
String str4 = String(str2 + " is Cool");
```

Both of the first two lines create a simple string with the word Arduino in it. In the third line, a new String instance is created from a single constant character. In this line, notice that the single quote is used. The last example concatenates two Strings. There are several more constructors that enable us to create instances of the String class from a number. Here are a few examples:

```
String strNum1 = String(42);
String strNum2 = String(42, HEX);
String strNum3 = String(42, BIN);
```

In the preceding code, the strNum1 String instance would contain the text 42, which is the decimal version of the number 42. The strNum2 String instance would contain the text 2a which is the hex version of the number 42. The strNum3 String instance would contain the text 101010, which is the binary version of the number 42.

There are also numerous methods that can be used in instances of the String class. Some of these methods are:

- concat(string): Concatenates one string to the end of the original string.
- endsWith(string): Returns true if the original string ends with the characters of the other string.
- equals(): Will compare two strings and return true if the strings contain the same text. When comparing the strings, this method is case sensitive.
- equalsIgnoreCase(): Will compare two strings and returns true if the strings contain the same text. When comparing strings, this method is case insensitive.
- length(): Returns the length of the strings. The length will not include the trailing null character.
- replace(substring1, substring2): This method will replace all instances of one substring with another substring.
- startsWith(string): Returns true if the original string starts with the characters of the other string.
- toLowerCase(): Returns the lower case version of the original string.
- toUpperCase(): Returns the upper case version of the original string.

The String library can be used as a replacement for the character array; however, you will find that most sample code on the internet uses character arrays mainly because they take up less memory and they execute faster than the String library.

Summary

This ends the introduction to the Arduino programming language. You can refer to the Arduino quick reference pages for additional information about the Arduino programming language.

You can find the reference pages here: `https://www.arduino.cc/reference/en/`. On this page, you will find links to information about the built-in Arduino functions and variables. That are also links to information about the operators and other Arduino language elements.

Don't worry if you do not feel comfortable writing your own Arduino programs right now because we will be writing a lot of code in the remaining chapters of this book, and by the end you should feel comfortable writing your own Arduino applications.

8
Motion Sensor

In this chapter, we will look at how to use the HC-SR501 motion sensor. It is a very easy sensor to connected to the Arduino and program, which is why it is usually one of the first sensors that people experiment with when they start working with microcontrollers. It is also very inexpensive and often comes with most starter kits.

In this chapter you will learn:

- How to connect an HC-SR501 motion sensor to the Arduino
- How to read the output of the HC-SR501 motion sensor
- Read the Fritzing diagram of the motion sensor project

Introduction

PIR sensors, also known as **Passive Infrared sensors**, are used by a microcontroller to sense motion usually by a human being, but they will detect any motion within the range of the sensor. These sensors are small, inexpensive, low-power and easy to use, which makes them perfect for beginners to experiment with, but industrial versions of these sensors can also be found in many consumer and military products as well.

PIR sensors are made of pyroelectric sensors that can detect infrared radiation levels. Every object that has a temperature above absolute zero emits some low-level infrared radiation that the pyroelectric sensor can detect. The passive part of the name means that the sensor does not generate or radiate energy that can be detected by other devices. Instead, it works by detecting the infrared radiation emitted by other objects.

The pyroelectric sensor in a motion sensor is usually split into two sides, which enables the motion sensor to detect changes in the infrared levels. When the sensor is not detecting any motion, both sides detect the same amount of infrared radiation and cancel each other out. When something starts to move within range of the sensor, one half of the sensor detects more of the infrared radiation than the other half, causing the sensor to trigger a motion alert.

PIR sensors come in many sizes and strengths. These sensors are used in numerous commercial products like burglar alarms, automatic lights and holiday decorations that talk or light up when someone approaches it.

In this chapter, we will be using the HC-SR501 motion sensor, which is shown in the following photograph with a stand that I designed and printed out for it. The downloadable code for this book includes an STL file that you can use to print out a stand for your own use:

The following image shows the connectors and adjustment screws on the bottom of the HC-SR501 motion sensor:

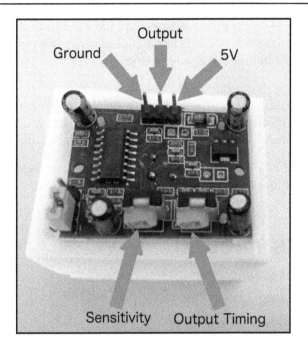

The **Sensitivity** adjustment screw adjusts the detection range of the sensor. The detection range can be set from 3 meters to 7 meters. Turning the sensitivity screw clockwise decreases the sensitivity of the sensor.

The **Output Timing** adjustment screw sets how long the output will remain high once motion is detected. The output timing can range from 5 seconds to 5 minutes. Turning the output timing adjustment screw clockwise will increase the time delay.

The **Ground** pin should be connected to the ground rail on the breadboard or directly to the ground pin on the Arduino. The **5V** pin should be connected to the power rail on the breadboard or directly to the 5V out on the Arduino. Finally, the middle pin is the **Output** pin for the sensor. If the sensor detects motion this pin will go high for the amount of time defined with the output timing adjustment screw.

NOTE: Some compatible sensors may have a different pin configuration than the ones shown in this book; please verify the pin configuration for your sensor before doing any wiring.

Before you look at the circuit diagram section of this chapter, think about how you would connect the HC-SR5012 motion sensor to an Arduino. One hint, you will not need anything but the motion sensor, an Arduino and jumper wire. Using a breadboard in this particular project is optional.

Now let's look at the components needed for this chapter's project.

Components needed

We will need the following components for this chapter's project:

- One Arduino Uno or compatible board
- One HC-SR501 motion sensor
- Jumper wires
- For the challenge, you will need an LED
- One breadboard

 The breadboard is optional because you may connect the HC-SR501 motion sensor directly to the Arduino. You will need a breadboard to complete the challenge section of this chapter.

Circuit diagrams

The following diagram shows the Fritzing diagram for this project:

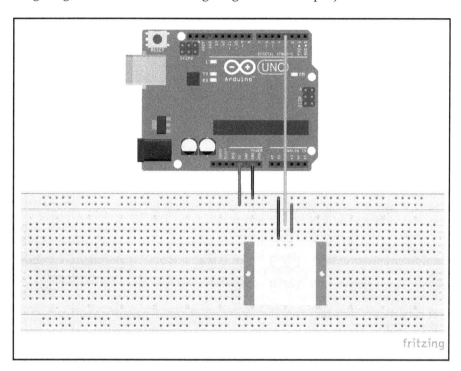

With the diagram, we can see that the ground pin on the HC-SR501 motion sensor is connected to the ground rail on the breadboard and the 5V input on the motion sensor is connected to the power rail on the breadboard. The power and ground rails of the breadboard are connected to the 5V power and ground pins on the Arduino.

The output pin on the motion sensor is a digital output (either HIGH or LOW), therefore we can connect the output pin directly to any of the digital pins on the Arduino. In this case, we are connecting the output pin from the sensor to pin three on the Arduino.

Here is the schematic diagram of the same circuit:

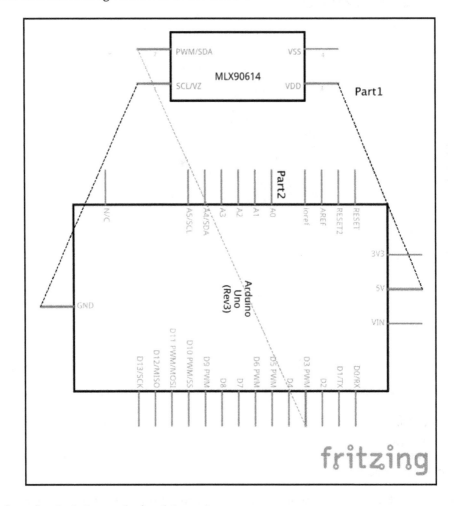

Let's look at the Arduino code for this project.

Code

To use the HC-SR501 motion sensor all we need to do is read the digital output from the sensor. If the output is HIGH, then the sensor detected motion and if it is LOW, then it did not. The output from the sensor will stay HIGH for the length of time defined by the output time adjustment screw. I usually keep the output time low, usually a couple oof seconds.

For this project, we will output the status of the sensor to the serial console. The output will get a little fancier in the challenge section.

The following is the code to read the HC-SR501 motion sensor:

```
#define MOTION_SENSOR 3

void setup() {
 pinMode(MOTION_SENSOR, INPUT);
  Serial.begin(9600);
}

void loop() {
  int sensorValue = digitalRead(MOTION_SENSOR);
  if (sensorValue == HIGH) {
    Serial.println("Motion Detected");
  }
  delay(500);
}
```

This code starts off by using the `#define` directive to create the MOTION_SENSOR macro and setting it to 3. In the `setup()` function we set the pin mode for pin 3 for input because we will be reading the digital output pin from the motion sensor. We are also initiating the serial console in the `setup()` function as well.

The `loop()` function begins by calling the `digitalRead()` function to read the output from the motion sensor and assigning the value to the sensorValue variable. If the sensorValue variable is equal to HIGH, we send the message Motion Detected to the serial console. If no motion is detected, we do not print anything. At the end of the `loop()` function, there is a half-second delay before looping back.

Now let's upload and run the code.

Running the project

We will need to have the serial console open when we run the code to see the output.

Once the code is uploaded and running, wave your hand near the sensor, and you should see the `Motion Detected` message is printed to the console, as shown in the following screenshot:

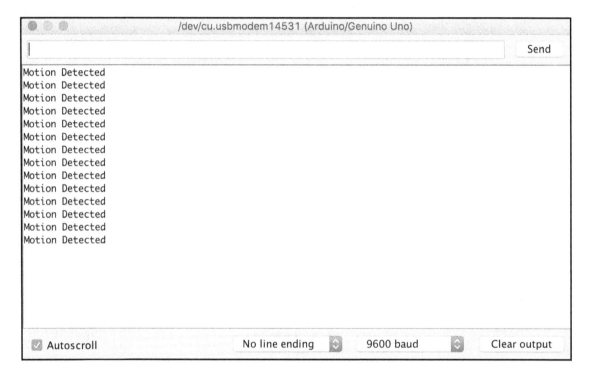

Now on to the challenge section of this chapter.

Challenge

The challenge, if you choose to accept it, is to add an LED to this project and have the LED light up when the motion sensor detects motion. In the first few chapters, we will give either the code or circuit diagram for the challenges to make it easier to troubleshoot any issues if the project does not work when first built.

For this challenge, we will give the code and let you figure out how to connect the LED to the project. One hint, do not forget about the resistor for the LED.

The following is the code that will light up an LED connected to pin 5 of the Arduino when the motion sensor detects nearby motion:

```
#define MOTION_SENSOR 3
#define LED 5

void setup() {
  pinMode(MOTION_SENSOR, INPUT);
  pinMode(LED, OUTPUT);

  digitalWrite(LED, LOW);
  Serial.begin(9600);
}

void loop() {
  int sensorValue = digitalRead(MOTION_SENSOR);
  if (sensorValue == HIGH) {
    Serial.println("Motion Detected");
  }

  digitalWrite(LED, sensorValue);
  delay(500);
}
```

Now it is up to you to complete this challenge.

Summary

In this chapter, we learned about the HC-SR501 motion sensor and how it works. We saw how we could wire it to an Arduino where the Arduino provided power for the sensor and also read the output pin of the sensor.

In the next chapter, we will see how we can sense the weather around us.

Environment Sensors

9

In this chapter, we will look at building a really simple weather station using the DHT11 temperature/humidity sensor and a raindrop sensor. While the previous chapter used the basic digital input, the DHT11 temperature sensor will give us the opportunity to use a third-party library, and the raindrop sensor will use an analog pin. We will also introduce a couple of handy functions that we can use.

In this chapter, you will learn:

- How to add third-party libraries to a sketch
- How to use the `isnan()` function
- How to use the `map()` function
- How to use the DHT11 temperature and humidity sensor
- How to use a rain sensor

Introduction

The DHT11 is a low-cost temperature and humidity sensor. This sensor uses a thermistor to measure the temperature. The word **thermistor** is a combination of thermal (temperature) and resistor because it is a type of resistor where the resistance is highly sensitive to temperature even more so than a normal resistor. The current temperature can be determined based on the output voltage of the thermistor.

When working with a thermistor, the first thing we need to do is to determine how to calculate the temperature based on the output voltage. With the TMP36 temperature sensor that we used with the prototype that was created in `Chapter 4`, *Basic Prototyping*, we could easily calculate the temperature based on the output voltage of the sensor with a basic formula of *(voltage - 0.5) * 100.0* because it uses a solid-state technique to determine the temperature. This is not the case with a thermistor. While a linear approximation, similar to how we calculated the temperature with the TMP36 sensor, may work for a small temperature range, to get an accurate temperature measurement from a thermistor we need to determine a resistance/temperature curve for the device.

Luckily there are several libraries for the Arduino that are written to help us get an accurate temperature from the DHT11 temperature and humidity sensor. In this chapter, we will be using the **Adafruit** library. The DHT11 sensor will look similar to the following photograph:

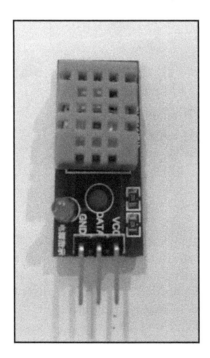

With most DHT11 sensors, the pins are clearly marked as shown in the preceding photograph. The **VCC** pin will connect to the power rail on the breadboard, which should be connected to the 5V out pin on the Arduino. The **GND** pin will connect to the ground rail on the breadboard, which should be connected to the ground out pin on the Arduino. The **DATA** pin will connect to one of the digital pins on the Arduino.

Some DHT temperature sensors come with a pull-up resistor built in, while others require an external one. Please look at the documentation for your sensor to verify if you need to add an external pull-up resistor or not. In the project for this chapter, we will show the external pull up resistor.

For the project in this chapter, we will also be using a generic raindrop sensor. This sensor has two parts. The first part is the rain sensor board, which detects the rain when the water completes the circuits on the board's printed leads. This sensor board acts as a variable resistor where the amount of current increases as the board gets wetter. The second part of the raindrop sensor is the electronic printed circuit board that will determine the amount water based on the current from the sensor board.

The following photograph shows what the raindrop sensor looks like:

The +/- pins on the printed circuit board connect to the pins on the rain sensor board. On the opposite side of the printed circuit board are four pins. The VCC and GND pins will connect to the power and ground rails of the breadboard respectively. For the project in this chapter, we will use the **A0** analog output pin as the output for the sensor. The A0 pin will connect directly to one of the analog in pins on the Arduino.

Components needed

We will need the following components for this chapter's project:

- One Arduino Uno or compatible board
- One DHT11 temperature/humidity sensor
- One MH-RD raindrop sensor
- One 4.7K resistor
- Jumper wires
- One breadboard

Circuit diagrams

The following diagram shows the Fritzing diagram for this project:

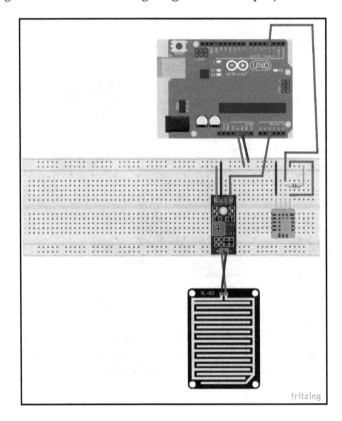

In this diagram, we can see that the VCC and ground pins on both sensors are connected to the power and ground rails on the breadboard. The power and ground rails on the breadboard are connected to the 5V out and the ground pins on the Arduino.

The image of the DHT11 sensor that we showed earlier in this chapter shows a DHT11 sensor with three pins; however, the sensor in the Fritzing library has four pins. It is safe to ignore the extra pin on the Fritzing diagram.

This diagram shows that the data pin on the DHT11 sensor is connected to the digital 3 pin on the Arduino and it also has a 4.7K pull-up resistor. If the DHT11 sensor that you are using does not have a built-in pull-up resistor, you will need to add this external one that is shown in this diagram. The analog out on the rain sensor is connected to the analog 2 input pin on the Arduino.

Code

Before we can start writing code, we will need to load in the DHT11 Adafruit library that we will be using to read the temperature and humidity readings. You can find the source code for this library on Adafruit's GitHub page here: `https://github.com/adafruit/DHT-sensor-library`.

Note: You will need to refer to this code for the challenge section of this chapter.

To install the library, if you are using the Arduino IDE, select the **Sketch** option in the menu bar and select **Include Library** and then **Manage Libraries** as shown in the following screenshot:

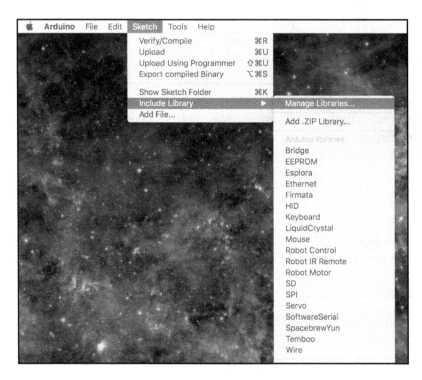

In the window that opens up, type dht11 in the search bar and you should see a couple different DHT11 sensor libraries. In this chapter, we will be using the one from Adafruit (In the following list, the first result). Click on this library, and you will see a button all the way to the right to install it as shown in the following screenshot:

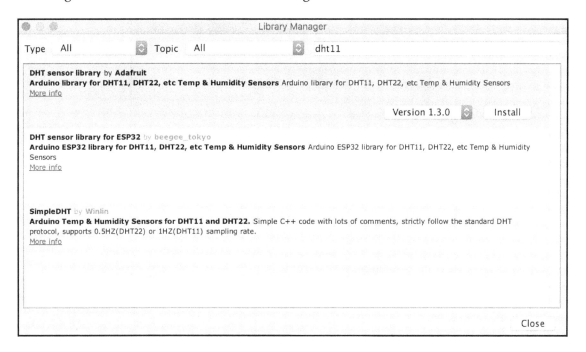

For the Arduino Web Editor, click on the **Libraries** option and then type dht11 in the search bar as shown in the following screenshot:

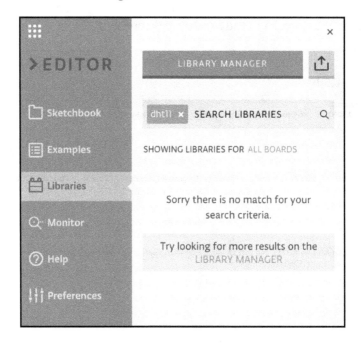

This probably will not return any results; therefore, we will need to click on the **LIBRARY MANAGER** link, which will bring up the library manager with results of the DHT11 search as shown in the following image:

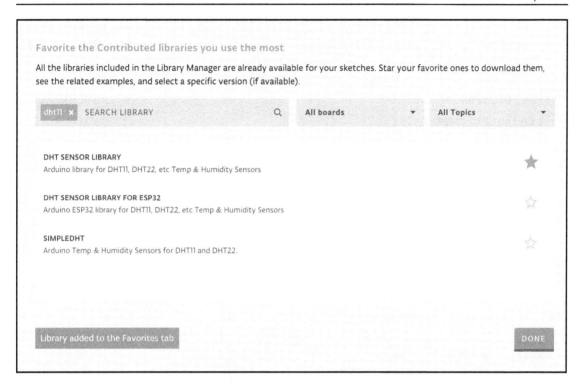

As the instructions at the top of this window tell us, we need to click on the star of the library we wish to include and then click on the **DONE** button. Unfortunately, the library manager in the Web Editor does not tell us who created the library; however, if you notice, the names from the three libraries match the library names we saw from the Arduino IDE. Therefore, we are able to tell which library is the Adafruit library by the title.

Now that we have the library installed it is time to start writing the code. The first thing we will need to do is to include the header file for the DHT sensor library. We can do this by adding the following `include` statement at the top of the sketch:

```
#include "DHT.h"
```

Next, we need to define some macros. We will start off by defining the Arduino pins that the DHT11 and the raindrop sensor are connected to:

```
#define DHT_PIN 3
#define RAIN_PIN A2
```

This code tells us that the DHT11 sensor is connected to the digital 3 pin and the rain sensor is connected to the analog 2 pin. The Adafruit DHT sensor library can read both the DHT11 and DHT22 sensors. Therefore, we will need to tell the library which sensor type we are using, and we should create a macro that contains this type. The following code defines the DHT sensor type:

```
#define DHT_TYPE DHT11
```

Finally, we will need to create four macros that will help us understand the readings from the rain sensor. If you recall, the Analog input pins will map the input voltage into integer values ranging from 0 to 1023. When we read the input from the rain sensor, a value of 1023 means that there is no rain while a value of 0 means a flood. This makes sense from a purely electronic point of view; however, it seems backwards from a logical point of view where a rain sensor should report a higher value when there is more rain.

We will use the Arduino map() function to change this for us. Therefore, we will need to define the min/max values for the analog readings and the min/max values for what we want to convert the analog values to. We will explain this some more when we look at the code for the map() function; for now here are the macros:

```
#define RAIN_SENSOR_MAX 1023
#define RAIN_SENSOR_MIN 0
#define RAIN_OUT_MAX 20
#define RAIN_OUT_MIN 0
```

Now we will want to create an instance of the DHT class using the DHT_PIN and DHT_TYPE macros we just defined. The following code will create an instance of the DHT class:

```
DHT dht(DHT_PIN, DHT_TYPE);
```

Now that we have defined the macros needed and created a global instance of the DHT class, we need to create the setup() function. In the setup() function we will need to initialize the serial monitor and the DHT class. The begin() method of the DHT class is used to initialize the instance of the class. The following code shows the setup() function:

```
void setup() {
  Serial.begin(9600);
  dht.begin();
}
```

Now that we have the `setup()` function let's look at how to read the DHT and rain sensors. The remainder of the code in this chapter will go into the `loop()` function of our sketch. The following code will read the humidity and temperature from the DHT sensor using the Adafruit library:

```
float humidity = dht.readHumidity();
float celsius = dht.readTemperature();
float fahrenheit = dht.readTemperature(true);

if (isnan(humidity) || isnan(celsius) || isnan(fahreheit)) {
  Serial.println("Read Failed");
  return;
}

Serial.print("Humidity: ");
Serial.println(humidity);
Serial.print("Temperature: ");
Serial.print(celsius);
Serial.println(" *C ");
Serial.print(fahreheit);
Serial.println(" *F");

delay(3000);
```

This code starts off by calling the `readHumidity()` method of the `DHT` class to read the humidity from the DHT sensor. The `readTemperature()` method is then called twice, once to read the temperature in Celsius and once to read the temperature in Fahrenheit. Notice that when the `readTemperature()` method is called without a parameter, we receive the temperature in Celsius and when we pass a Boolean parameter of `true` we receive the temperature in Fahrenheit. We could also pass a Boolean parameter of `false` to receive the temperature in Celsius.

After the temperature and humidity are read from the sensor, it is good practice to verify that the read was successful. To do this, we are using the `isnan()` function. The `isnan()` function will return `true` if the value passed in is not a number, therefore, the line `if (isnan(humidity) || isnan(celsius) || isnan(Fahrenheit))` reads "if humidity is not a number or Celsius is not a number or Fahrenheit is not a number then execute the code block". This code block will print an error message to the console and then execute a `return` statement to exit this loop.

If all of the variables are numbers, we print the humidity and temperatures to the serial console and then wait 3 seconds before exiting this loop and starting the loop function again.

Now let's look at how we would read the rain sensor. Put the following code between the final `Serial.println()` statement and the `delay()` function call of the DHT sensor code:

```
int rain = analogRead(RAIN_PIN);
if (isnan(rain)) {
  Serial.println("Read Failed");
  return;
}
int range = map(rain, RAIN_SENSOR_MIN, RAIN_SENSOR_MAX, RAIN_OUT_MAX,
RAIN_OUT_MIN);

Serial.print("Rain: ");
Serial.println(range);
Serial.println("-------------------------");
```

In this code, we call the `analogRead()` function to read the analog pin that the rain sensor's connected to and use the `isnan()` function to verify that the read was successful. After we verify that the `analogRead()` function was performed successfully, we call the `map()` function. The `map()` function will re-map a value from one range of numbers to a new range of numbers.

This function has five parameters, which are:

- `value`: The value to map
- `fromLow`: The lower limit of the value's current range
- `fromHigh`: The upper limit of the value's current range
- `toLow`: The lower limit of the value's new range
- `toHigh`: The upper limit of the value's new range

If we take the `map()` function call in the previous code and replace the macros with the actual values, the `map()` function would look like this:

```
int range = map(rain, 0, 1023, 20, 0);
```

The value for the rain variable comes from the `analogRead()` function, which we know will have a value ranging from 0 to 1023. Therefore, we set the current range to have a lower limit of 0 and an upper limit of 1023. If you recall from earlier in this chapter, a value of 1023 means there is no rain while a value of 0 means there is a flood. We will want to reverse this with the new range where the higher value will mean more rain and the lower value will mean less rain. Therefore, we set the lower limit of the new range to 20 and the upper limit to 0. This will map a value of 1023 from the old range to a value of 0 in the new range and a value of 0 in the old range to a value of 20 in the new range.

With this new range, a high value of 20 means that we have a flood and a low value of zero means there is no rain. A middle value from the old range (511 or 512) would map to the middle value in the new range (10). The map() function is very useful when we want to change a scale and/or reverse the order as we see in this example.

After the map() function is called we print the results to the serial console. Now let's see what happens when we run this project.

Running the project

When we run this project, we should see a result similar to the following screenshot:

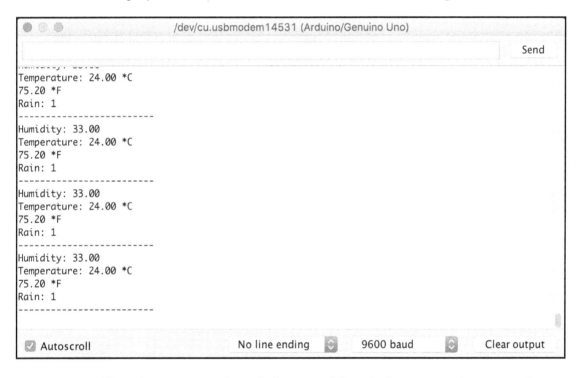

Now try sprinkling the rain sensor board (the part of the raindrop sensor that senses the rain) with water and see how it changes the rain output.

NOTE: Always use caution when using water around electronic projects. If you get your Arduino or other electronic component wet you will damage them. When working with AC power with relays, you also run the risk of electrocution.

Now let's look at the challenge.

Challenge

For this challenge, use the DHT library to compute the heat index. The heat index is the discomfort felt as the result of the temperature and humidity combined. There are methods within the DHT class that will do this for you.

At the beginning of this chapter, we gave a link to the GitHub repository that contained the code for the DHT sensor library. Look at the DHT.h file to see what methods are in the DHT class.

Summary

In this chapter, we used a third-party library for the first time. This was the Adafruit DHT sensor library. We also saw two new functions that we have not used before. These functions were the isnan() and map() functions.

In the next chapter, we will look at range and collision detection sensors.

10
Obstacle Avoidance and Collision Detection

If you are making an autonomous robot that needs to avoid obstacles, a remote-controlled car that needs to detect when it hits something or even a 3D printer that needs to know when the print heads have reached the limits of the print area, you will need to include some sort of obstacle avoidance or collision detection system in your project. In this chapter, we will look at several sensors that can be used for obstacle avoidance and collision detection systems.

Throughout this chapter, you will learn:

- How to use a crash sensor
- How to use an infrared obstacle avoidance sensor
- How to use an Ultrasonic rangefinder

Introduction

In this chapter, we will look at three sensors that we can use to add obstacle avoidance and/or collision detection to our projects. These sensors are:

- **Crash sensor**: Used to detect a crash and also used as limit switches for 3D printers
- **Infrared obstacle avoidance sensor**: Used for obstacle avoidance for robotics
- **Ultrasonic range finder**: Used for obstacle avoidance for robotics and has many other commercial and military uses

Crash sensor

A crash sensor is basically a simple switch that has some sort of extender on it that gives it a large area to detect a crash. The following photograph show what a basic crash sensor would look like:

The crash sensor shown in the preceding photograph takes a simple mechanical switch, like the types used for end stops on 3D printers, and attaches it to the end of a circuit board. This makes it easy to mount out a robot chassis or other surfaces. The concept behind a crash sensor is when the switch is triggered, the sensor has bumped into something.

The crash sensor has three pins that are clearly marked as **GND**, **VCC**, and **OUT**. The GND pin connects to the ground rail and the VCC connects to power rail on the breadboard. The OUT pin connects directly to a digital pin on the Arduino with a 4.7K pull-up resistor.

The infrared obstacle avoidance sensor consists of an infrared transmitter, an infrared receiver, and a potentiometer that adjusts the distance the sensor will detect obstacles at. The following photographs show the obstacle avoidance sensor that is used for the project in this chapter.

Obstacle avoidance sensor

The emitter on the infrared obstacle avoidance sensor emits infrared radiation and if an obstacle is in front of the sensor, some of the radiation is reflected back and picked up by the receiver. If no object is in front of the sensor then the radiation will dissipate, and the receiver will not receive anything back.

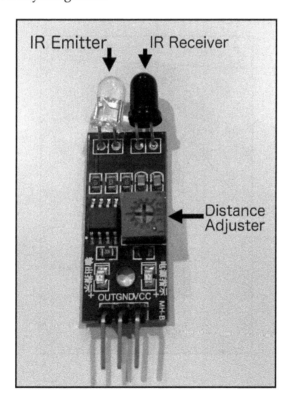

The pins on the sensor are clearly marked with **OUT**, **GND**, and **VCC**, from left to right. The GND pin is connected to the ground rail and the VCC pin is connected to the power rail of the breadboard. The OUT pin is connected directly to a digital pin on the Arduino. If the signal from the OUT pin is LOW, then an object was detected. If the output is HIGH, then no object was detected.

The distance adjuster will adjust the distance that the sensor detects objects. If the adjuster is turned counter-clockwise then the distance will be decreased, and if you turn it clockwise the distance will increase. The sensor will detect objects from 2 to 30 cm.

Ultrasonic range finder

The third sensor that we will be using is a **MaxSonar EZ1** Ultrasonic range finder. This sensor is one of my favorite sensors to use. I have used it in almost every autonomous robot that I have built to determine the distance to nearby objects. The following is an image of the EZ1 Ultrasonic range finder:

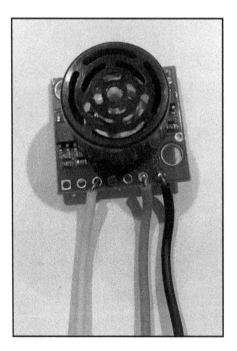

For the example, in this chapter, we will be using pins 3,6, and 7 on the sensor. Pin 3 is used for analog out, pin 6 is for VCC and pin 7 is for ground. Pins 4 and 5 are for serial RX/TX connection and pin 2 is for a pulse-width output, however, we will not be using those outputs in the example for this chapter.

An ultrasonic range finder works by sending an ultrasonic pulse in a particular direction. If there is an object in the path of the pulse when it is reflected back in the form of an echo. The sensor determines the distance to the object by measuring the time it takes for the echo to be received back.

The EZ1 ultrasonic sensor can detect and measure the distance to an object from 0 to 6.45 meters (254 inches). This sensor has virtually no dead zone and will detect objects right up to the front sensor face.

Components needed

We will need the following components for this chapter's project:

- One Arduino Uno or compatible board
- One crash sensor
- One obstacle avoidance sensor
- One EZ1 Ultrasonic sensor
- One 4.7K resistor
- Jumper wires
- One breadboard

Circuit diagrams

The following diagram shows the Fritzing diagram for this project:

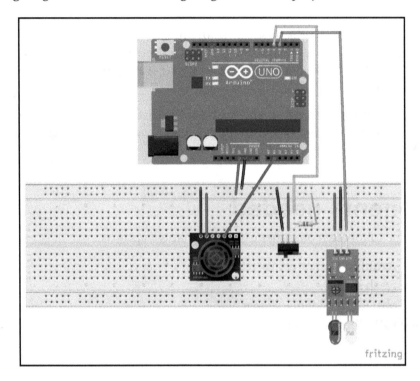

The middle sensor, shown in the diagram, represents the crash sensor because there isn't a Fritzing part for a crash sensor. The switch in the diagram has the same pin layout as the crash sensor shown earlier in this chapter.

In the diagram, we can see that all of the ground pins on the sensors are connected to the ground rail of the breadboard and all of the VCC pins on the sensors are connected to the power rail on the breadboard.

The analog out on the EZ1 Ultrasonic sonar sensor is connected to the A1 analog pin on the Arduino, the crash sensor is connected to digital pin 3 and the infrared sensor is connected to digital pin 2. The crash sensor also has a 4.7K pull-up resistor. Now that we have the sensors connected to the Arduino, let's look at the code for this project.

Code

We will begin the code with three macros that define the pins that the three sensors are connected to. The macros will look like this:

```
#define COLLISION_SWITCH 4
#define IR_SENSOR 3
#define RANGE_SENSOR A1
```

These macros show that the crash sensor is connected to digital pin 4, the infrared sensor is connected to digital pin 3 and the ultrasonic rangefinder is connected to analog pin 1. Now we need to set the mode for the two digital pins that we are using and also initiate the serial monitor. We can do this by adding the following code to the setup() function:

```
Serial.begin(9600);
pinMode(COLLISION_SWITCH, INPUT);
pinMode(IR_SENSOR, INPUT);
```

This starts off by initiating the serial monitor and then configures the crash and infrared sensor pins to input so we can read the values. Now we need to add the code to the loop() function that will read the sensors. Let's start off by looking at how we would read and interrupt the crash sensor:

```
int collisionValue = digitalRead(COLLISION_SWITCH);
if (isnan(collisionValue)) {
  Serial.println(" Failed to read collision sensor");
  return;
}
if (collisionValue == LOW) {
  Serial.println("Collision Detected");
}
```

This code starts off by using the digitalRead() function to read the pin that the crash sensor is connected to and then uses the isnan() function to verify that the digitalRead() function returned a correct value. If the value returned by the function is not valid (not a number) then an error message is printed to the serial console the return statement is called to exit this loop.

If the value returned by the digitalRead() function is valid, then we check to see if the value is LOW and if so then an obstacle was detected, and a message is printed to the serial console. Now let's add the code for the infrared sensor:

```
int irValue = digitalRead(IR_SENSOR);
if (isnan(irValue)) {
 Serial.println(" Failed to read infrared sensor");
```

```
    return;
  }
  if (irValue == LOW) {
    Serial.println("IR Detected");
  }
```

This code is exactly the same as the crash sensor except we read the infrared sensor pin and check that value. Now let's add the code for the Ultrasonic range finder:

```
int anVolt = analogRead(RANGE_SENSOR);
if (isnan(anVolt)) {
  Serial.println(" Failed to read range sensor");
  return;
}
int mm = anVolt*5;
float inch = mm/25.4;
Serial.println(mm);
Serial.print("MM:    ");
Serial.println(mm);
Serial.print("Inches: ");
Serial.println(inch);
Serial.println("-------------------------");
delay(1000);
```

This code starts by using the analogRead() function to read the pin that the ultrasonic range finder is connected too. We then use the isnan() function to verify that a correct value was returned.

The distance to the object is then calculated in both millimeters and inches. The numbers used in the calculations documented on the datasheet for the sensor and may be different depending on the model that you are using. Now we will want to put a short delay at the end of the loop() function to pause the execution.

Now let's run the project.

Running the project

When we run this project, the output should look similar to the following screenshot:

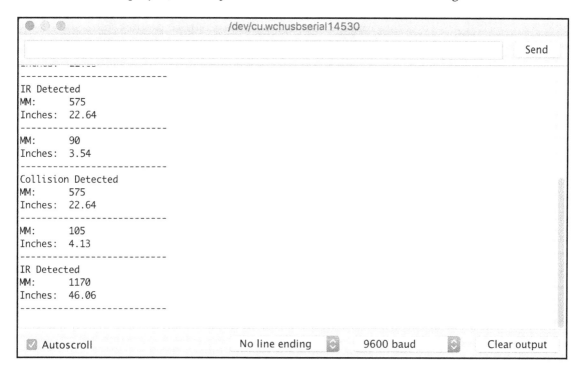

This screenshot shows that an object tripped the infrared sensor twice, where IR Detected is printed to the serial console and the crash sensor once, where Collision Detected was printed to the serial console. It also shows the distance that the rangefinder returned as the closest object.

Challenge

This challenge is going to be a little different than most. There isn't really a project to do; instead, it is a thinking challenge. The challenge is to think about how all three of these sensors work can work together to create an autonomous robot. To do this, think about how all three of the sensors work:

1. **Crash sensor**: A digital sensor that is tripped when the sensor bumps into something
2. **Infrared sensor**: A digital sensor that is tripped when something gets close
3. **Ultrasonic range finder**: Analog sensor used to detect how far an object is from the sensor

Here are the answers:

The Ultrasonic range finders are the most expensive by far, so I usually use only two of these sensors facing out form the front of the robot. These are used to by the robot to navigate around obstacles. With the ability to tell how far something is from the front of the robot, we can give the robot the logic it needs to decide when to turn and also, with two ultrasonic sensors, the logic to decide which way to turn. We can also use the Ultrasonic sensors to map a room.

The infrared sensors are very inexpensive and can be used on the sides and back to make sure the robot does not bump into anything when it is turning or backing up. Since they are a lot cheaper than the ultrasonic sensors, we can use multiple infrared sensors to make sure we have the full area around the robot covered. We could also use the infrared sensors, facing down, to make sure the robot does not drive off a ledge.

The crash sensors are also very inexpensive and can be used all around to the robot to detect if the robot crashes into anything that the ultrasonic or infrared sensors missed. The biggest problem with the ultrasonic and infrared sensors is how high they are on the robot. If they are too high, then they may miss obstacles that are low to the ground. A crash sensor can be used to detect these.

Summary

In this chapter, we saw how to use three sensors that can be used for obstacle avoidance and collision detection. The crash sensor is a digital sensor that can be used to tell when the sensor bumps into something. The infrared obstacle avoidance sensor is also a digital sensor that can tell when the sensor is within a certain distance of an obstacle. The Ultrasonic range finder is an analog sensor that can be used to tell how far an obstacle is from the sensor.

In the next chapter, we will look at some different types of LEDs and see how we can use them in our projects.

11
Fun with Lights

Most of the larger projects that we create will use one or more LEDs as indicators. These LEDs can indicate things such as power, receiving data, warnings or anything else that we may need visual feedback for. We have already seen how to use a basic, single-color LED but what if we need multiple LEDs or even multicolor LEDs? In this chapter, we will look at other ways to add LEDs to your project.

In this chapter, you will learn:

- What NeoPixels are
- How an RGB LED works
- How to use NeoPixels in your projects
- How to use an RGB LED in your projects

Introduction

In this chapter, we will look at how to use RGB LEDs and a **WS2812 40 RGB LED Pixel Arduino shield**. Let's start off by learning about the RGB LED.

A multicolor or RGB LED isn't really a single LED that can change color, it is actually three LEDs. An RGB LED contains three LEDs, which are red, green, and blue in color. The color that the LED produces is a combination of the colors produced by these three LEDs.

There are two types of RGB LEDs. These are the common anode and the common cathode LED. In a common cathode LED, the three LEDs share a common ground source, and in a common anode RGB LED, the three LEDs share a common power source.

The RGB LED has four pins, one for each color and the fourth one for the common cathode or anode connection. The following diagram shows the pins for both the common cathode and common anode RGB LED:

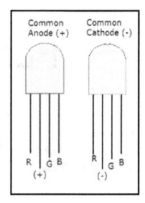

To produce the various colors, we can adjust the intensities of the three different LEDs using the PWM pins on the Arduino. The light will then mix together, because the LEDs are so close, producing the color we want. Now let's look at what a WS2812 integrated light source, or, as they are known on Adafruit's site, the **NeoPixel**. For most of this chapter, we will refer to the WS2812 integrated light source as a NeoPixel because it is shorter and also sounds cool.

As you can imagine, if we wanted to include 10 RGB LEDs in a project, where each LED required three input pins, the project would very quickly turn into a wired mess. Not to mention we would quickly run out of pins on the Arduino as well. One of the ways that we can solve this problem is to use the NeoPixel. The NeoPixel integrates red, green and blue LEDs alongside a driver chip on a tiny surface-mounted package. This package can be controlled through a single wire and can be used individually or as a group. NeoPixel's come in many form factors including strips, rings, Arduino shields and even on jewelry.

One nice thing about the NeoPixel is there is no inherent limit to the number of NeoPixels that can be chained together. However, there are some practical limits based on the RAM and power constraints of the controller you are using.

In this chapter, we will be using a NeoPixel shield. If you use individual NeoPixels, there are a couple of things you need to keep in mind:

- Before connecting the NeoPixels to a power source, you will want to add a 1000 microfarad, 6.3V or higher capacitor.
- You will also want to add a 470 ohm resistor between the Arduino data output and the input line on the first NeoPixel.
- If at all possible, avoid connecting/disconnecting NeoPixels when the circuit is live. If you must connect them to a live circuit, always connect the ground first. If you must disconnect them from a live circuit, always disconnect the 5V power first.
- NeoPixels should always be powered from a 5V power source.

In this chapter, we will be using the **Keyestudio 40 RGB LED 2812 Pixel Matrix shield**. This shield already contains the capacitor and resistor, so all we need to do is to place the shield on top of the Arduino Uno and we are good to go. The Keyestudio shield attaches to the Arduino as shown in the following photograph:

When using other NeoPixel form factors, always read the manufacturers' data sheet prior to connecting it to the Arduino. It is really easy to damage a NeoPixels so make sure you follow the manufacturers' recommendations.

Components needed

We will need the following components for this chapter's project:

- One Arduino Uno or compatible board
- One RGB LED either a common cathode or a common anode
- Three 330 ohm resistors
- One Keyestudio 40 RGB LED 2812 Pixel Matrix shield
- Jumper wires
- One breadboard

Circuit diagrams

The following diagram shows how we would connect a common anode RGB LED to the Arduino:

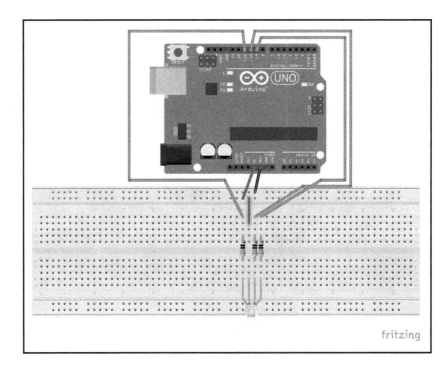

In this diagram, we show how to connect a common anode RGB LED. We can see this because the common pin is connected to the power rail on the breadboard. If the RBG LED that you are using is a common cathode LED, then connect the common pin, on the LEDs, to the ground rail instead of the power rail. Each of the RGB pins is connected to the Arduino PWM pins with a 330 ohm resistor.

We are not showing a circuit diagram for the NeoPixel shield because we only need to attach the shield to the Arduino. Now let's look at the code.

Code

Let's start off by looking at the code for the RGB LED.

RGB LED

We will start off by defining which pins on the Arduino are connected to the RGB pins on the LED:

```
#define REDPIN 11
#define BLUEPIN 10
#define GREENPIN 9
```

This code shows that the red pin is connected to the Arduino 11 PWM pin, the blue pin is connected to the Arduino 10 PWM pin and the green pin is connected to the Arduino 9 PWM pin. We are going to define an empty macro that will let the application code know whether we have a common anode or a common cathode RGB LED. The following code will do that:

```
#define COMMON_ANODE
```

If you are using a common cathode RGB LED, then comment or remove this line from your code. We will see how to use this when we look at the function that sets the colors of the LED. Now let's look at the setup() function.

```
void setup() {
  pinMode(REDPIN, OUTPUT);
  pinMode(GREENPIN, OUTPUT);
  pinMode(BLUEPIN, OUTPUT);
}
```

The `setup()` function will set the mode of the pins, that are connected to the RGB pins on the LED, to output. This will allow us to use the PWM pins to set the light intensity of the three-color LEDs that make up the RGB LED. Next, we will need to create a function that will set these colors. We will name this function `setColor()`, and it will take three parameters that will define the intensity of each RGB LED and contain the following code:

```
void setColor(int red, int green, int blue) {
  #ifdef COMMON_ANODE
  red = 255 - red;
  green = 255 - green;
  blue = 255 - blue;
  #endif
  analogWrite(REDPIN, red);
  analogWrite(GREENPIN, green);
  analogWrite(BLUEPIN, blue);
}
```

The code in this function starts off with a `#ifdef` statement. This statement says that if the COMMON_ANODE macro is defined, then execute the code between the `#ifdef` and the `#endif` statements; otherwise, skip that code. Therefore, if we define the COMMON_ANODE macro at the beginning of the code, then we subtract each parameter from 255 to get the correct intensity. We then use the `analogWrite()` function to write the values to the RGB pins.

At the beginning of this chapter, we explained that an RGB LED worked by adjusting the intensity of each of the three RGB LEDs that are inside of the RGB LED. If we write the value of 255 to a common cathode LED, then the LED will be at its brightest. For a common anode LED, we will need to write a value of 0 to make the LED its brightest. That is why we subtracted the value of each parameter by 255 if the COMMON_ANODE macro is defined.

In the `loop()` function, we loop through a couple colors to demonstrate how the LED displays different colors. The following shows the code for the `loop()` function:

```
void loop() {
  setColor(255, 0, 0); // Red
  delay(1000);
  setColor(0, 255, 0); // Green
  delay(1000);
  setColor(0, 0, 255); // Blue
  delay(1000);
  setColor(255, 255, 255); // White
  delay(1000);
  setColor(255, 0, 255); // Purple
  delay(1000);
}
```

In the `loop()` function, we call the `setColor()` function five times to change the LED's color. The colors that we display are red, green, blue, white and purple. Each time the color changes there will be a one-second pause before the next color is displayed. The pause is from the `delay()` function.

How we display the colors in an RGB LED is pretty similar to how we light a normal LED except that we define the light intensity (brightness) for the three colors. Now let's look at the code for the NeoPixel shield.

NeoPixel shield

Before we begin coding, we will need to install the **Adafruit NeoPixel** library. The following screenshot shows the library that should be installed by the library manager. If you do not remember the steps to install a library, refer back to `Chapter 9`, *Environment Sensors*:

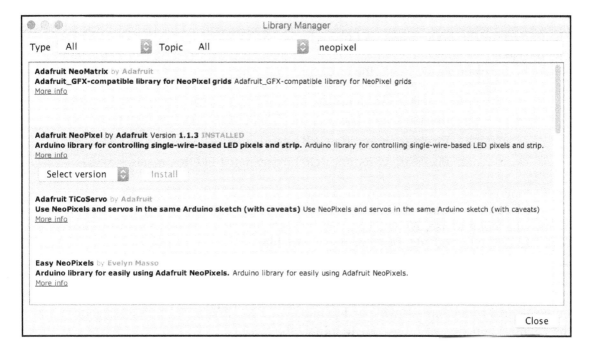

Sensors where we install the library for the DHT11 temperature and humidity sensor.

Once the library is installed, we will need to include it by putting the following line at the top of our code:

```
#include <Adafruit_NeoPixel.h>
```

When we use the Adafruit NeoPixel library, we need to tell it what pin the NeoPixels are connected to and how many NeoPixels are attached. Therefore, we will define macros that contain these values:

```
#define SHIELD_PIN 13
#define MAX_PIXELS 40
```

According to the datasheet for the Keyestudio shield, the shield is connected to pin 13 on the Arduino, and the shield contains 40 NeoPixels; therefore, we define those values in the macros. We will now use these values to initiate an instance of the Adafruit_NeoPixel class as shown in the following code:

```
Adafruit_NeoPixel pixels = Adafruit_NeoPixel(MAX_PIXELS, SHIELD_PIN,
NEO_GRB + NEO_KHZ800);
```

The first parameter is the number of pixels in the shield and the second parameter is the pin that the NeoPixels are connected to. The last parameter is the pixel type flag. The values shown in this example are by far the most common. The following are the possible values:

- NEO_KHZ800: 800 KHz bitstream (most NeoPixel products w/WS2812 LEDs)
- NEO_KHZ400: 400 KHz (classic v1 (not v2) FLORA pixels, WS2811 drivers)
- NEO_GRB: Pixels are wired for GRB bitstream (most NeoPixel products)
- NEO_RGB: Pixels are wired for RGB bitstream (v1 FLORA pixels, not v2)

In this example, we will be turning each pixel, one by one, to a certain color. Therefore, we will need a global variable to point to the pixel we are on and another global variable to define what color to use. We will be using two colors in this example and swap between the two. The following code defines this global variable:

```
int num = 0;
boolean color = 0;
```

In the setup() function, we will need to initiate the NeoPixels. The following code shows the setup() function with the code to initiate the NeoPixels:

```
void setup() {
  pixels.begin();
  pixels.show();
  pixels.setBrightness(50);
}
```

The `begin()` function prepares the data pin, on the Arduino, for output to the NeoPixels. The `show()` function pushes the data out to the NeoPixels and isn't absolutely necessary here; I find that it is good practice to include the function anytime we write anything to the NeoPixels for thoroughness. The third function controls the brightness of the pixels. I usually set this to 50% because the NeoPixels are very bright.

Now let's look at the `loop()` function that will set each pixel to a color one by one.

```
void loop() {
  num++;
  if (num > (MAX_PIXELS -1)) {
    num = 0;
    color = !color;
  }
  if (color) {
    pixels.setPixelColor(num, 170, 255, 10);
  } else {
    pixels.setPixelColor(num, 10, 255, 170);
  }
  pixels.show();
  delay(500);
}
```

In the `loop()` function, we start off by increasing the `num` variable by one and then checking to see whether we have reached the last pixel. If we have reached the last pixel, we set the `num` variable back to zero and swap the `color` variable. In the line `color = !color`, the `!` operator is the NOT operator, which causes the `color` variable to switch between true and false. This works because the NOT operator returns the opposite of the current value of the `color` variable. Therefore if, as an example, the `color` variable was currently false, then the `!color` operation would return true.

We then use the `setPixelColor()` function to set the current pixel to one of two colors depending on whether the `color` variable is true or false. The `setPixelColor()` function comes in two versions. The version that we see here uses the first parameter as the pixel number that we are setting and then the next three numbers define the intensity of the red, green and blue colors that make up the color we want. If we were using an RGBW NeoPixel, we would also need to define the white color. Therefore, this function would add an additional parameter like this:

```
setPixelColor(n, red, green, blue, white);
```

The second way to call the `setPixelColor()` function is to pass two arguments where the first one is the pixel number and the second is a 32-bit number that combines the red, green and blue values. This version of the function looks like this:

```
setPixelColor(n, color);
```

The color value can range from 0 to 16,777,216.

After we set the pixel's color, we then call the `show()` function to push the values out to the pixels and then use the delay function to put in a half-second pause in the code.

Running the project

If we run the sketch for the RBG LED, we would see the LED slowly cycle between the five colors. The code for the NeoPixels will flip the pixels, one by one, between two colors.

Challenge

This will be one of the hardest challenges in the book. The Keyestudio NeoPixel shield has eight columns of pixels where each column contains five pixels where the pixels are numbered like this:

1	2	3	4	5	6	7	8
9	10	11	12	13	14	15	16
17	18	19	20	21	22	23	24
25	26	27	28	29	30	31	32
33	34	35	36	37	38	39	40

For the challenge, set each column to a different color and have the colors rotate from left to right across the shield. Here are a couple of hints to get you started. The first is the Adafruit NeoPixel library, which has a function named `Color()` that will return the 32-bit color based on the three red, green and blue values. Therefore, you can use the following code to convert an 8-bit number to the 32-bit color.

```
uint32_t colorNum(int color) {
  colorPos = 255 - colorPos;
  if(colorPos < 85) {
    return pixels.Color(255 - colorPos * 3, 0, colorPos * 3);
  }
```

```
  if(colorPos < 170) {
    colorPos -= 85;
    return pixels.Color(0, colorPos * 3, 255 - colorPos * 3);
  }
  colorPos -= 170;
  return pixels.Color(colorPos * 3, 255 - colorPos * 3, 0);
}
```

We could then use the following code, which will set all of the pixels in a column to their color:

```
for (int j=0; j<5; j++) {
  int pixNum = (j*8) + i;
  pixels.setPixelColor(pixNum, colorNum((tmpColorMode * 30) & 255));
}
```

The `tmpColorMode` variable is a number from 1 to 8 that will be used to pick the color for that column. That should give you the basics to start this challenge. The answer is in the downloadable code for the book.

Summary

In this chapter, we learned how RGB LEDs work, how to use them and looked at the differences between a common anode and common cathode RGB LED. We also learned how the WS2812 (NeoPixel) works and how to use it. NeoPixels come in many different form factors and can be used almost anywhere that you need a large number of RGB LEDs.

In the next chapter, we will look at how to use a small buzzer with the Arduino to produce sound.

12
Fun with Sound

Adding sound to your robotic project can be the difference between a good robot and an awesome robot. Just think about how cute R2-D2, from the movie *Star Wars*, would have been if he did not make any sound. We can use sound for more than just robots. For example, we may want to add a loud alarm if a motion sensor detects motion or maybe we just want to play a melody when the temperature is just right outside.

In this chapter, you will learn:

- How to connect a piezo buzzer to the Arduino
- How to connect a speaker to the Arduino
- How to use the `tone()` function to generate a sound
- How to play music with the Arduino

Introduction

In this chapter, we will be doing several projects that can use either a **piezo buzzer** or a small 8-ohm speaker. By using both the buzzer and the speaker, you will be able to hear the difference between the two to help determine which is right for our project.

A piezo buzzer is compact, reliable and very inexpensive. They are easier to mount and use than a normal speaker in most electronic projects. These buzzers can emit a wide range of sounds, from soft hums to loud alerts.

A piezo buzzer, sometimes known as a piezo speaker, creates sounds a little differently than a normal speaker. The working component of these buzzers is a thin disc of piezoelectric material usually bonded to a metal diaphragm. As the voltage is applied to the piezoelectric material, it deforms. This causes the metal diaphragm to bend forward or backward. This deformation happens very rapidly, causing the ceramic/metal bending element to vibrate at the frequency of the applied voltage, which produces the audible sound.

The following photograph shows what a piezo buzzer looks like:

The shorter pin should be connected to ground while the longer pin should be connected to power.

The 8 ohm speaker is a typical speaker that contains an electromagnet, which is a metal coil that creates a magnetic field when electricity is applied. By reversing the direction of the coil, the poles of the magnet reverse. This electromagnet is placed in front of a normal magnet where the poles cannot be reversed. The current direction that is applied to the electromagnet is changed rapidly, causing the magnets to attract and repel each other creating sound from a cone that is connected to the electromagnet.

The following diagram shows what an 8 ohm speaker could look like:

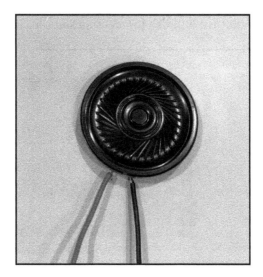

Now let's look at the components needed for this project.

Components needed

We will need the following components for this chapter's project:

- One Arduino Uno or compatible board
- One piezo buzzer
- One 8 ohm speaker
- Jumper wires
- One breadboard

Circuit diagrams

Here is the circuit diagram that we will use for all code samples in this chapter:

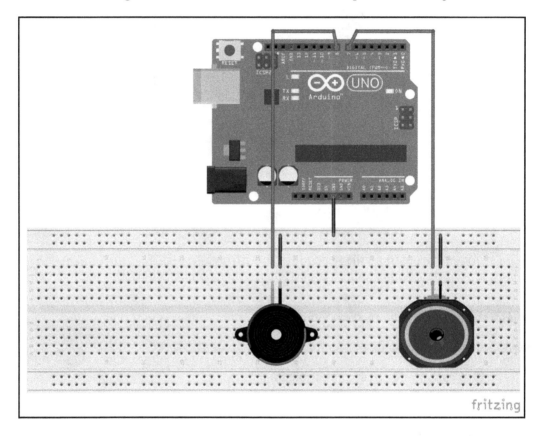

This diagram shows that the ground pins on both the speaker and piezo buzzer are connected to the ground rail on the breadboard. The power pin on the piezo buzzer is connected to pin 8 on the Arduino, and the power wire on the speaker is connected to pin 7 on the Arduino.

Code

Let's start off by using the tone() function.

Using the tone function

For the first few examples in this chapter, we will be using the Arduino `tone()` function. This function comes in two varieties. The first variety takes two arguments, where the first is the pin number that the buzzer or speaker is connected to and the second is the frequency in hertz to play the sound at. The function looks like this:

```
tone(pinNumber, frequency);
```

When this function is used with only two parameters, the sound is played indefinitely. The following code shows how we could use this function to play a note using the previous circuit diagram:

```
#define PIEZOPIN 7
#define SPEAKERPIN 8

int soundPin = PIEZOPIN;

void setup() {
  tone(soundPin, 1000);
}
```

With this code, the `tone()` function is used within the `setup()` function to play at 1000 Hz. We can set the sound pin to either the piezo buzzer or the speaker pin depending on which one you wish to play the sound. We would use this version of the `tone()` function if we wanted to play a sound continuously until some user interaction happens. An example of this would be playing an alert sound until the user acknowledged it.

The second variety of this function takes a third argument, which is the duration in milliseconds to play the sound. This function looks like this:

```
tone(pinNumber, frequency, duration);
```

This version of the `tone()` function can be used like this:

```
#define PIEZOPIN 7
#define SPEAKERPIN 8

int soundPin = PIEZOPIN;

void setup() {
  tone(soundPin, 1000, 1000);
}
```

This code is exactly like the previous code except the sound is only played for one second. We would use this version of the tone function if we wanted to play short notes with specific durations. An example of this would be playing a song, which we will see in the next example.

Before we can play a song with the Arduino, we need to define what frequency to play for different notes. The list of frequencies is quite large and can be downloaded with the downloadable code for this book. The file with the frequencies is called `pitches.h`, and the frequencies are defined like this:

```
#define NOTE_G6   1568
#define NOTE_GS6  1661
#define NOTE_A6   1760
#define NOTE_AS6  1865
#define NOTE_B6   1976
#define NOTE_C7   2093
```

Now let's look at how we can use these frequencies to play a song. The first thing we will need to do is to create a pitches header tab, named `pitches.h`, which will contain the frequencies and then include it in the main tab with the following line:

```
#include "pitches.h"
```

Now we need to define the notes or melody that makes up the song. These notes will be stored in an array named `melody`:

```
int melody[] = {
  NOTE_E5, NOTE_E5, NOTE_E5, NOTE_E5, NOTE_E5, NOTE_E5,
  NOTE_E5,
  NOTE_G5,
  NOTE_C5,
  NOTE_D5,
  NOTE_E5,
  NOTE_F5, NOTE_F5, NOTE_F5, NOTE_F5, NOTE_F5,
  NOTE_E5, NOTE_E5, NOTE_E5, NOTE_E5, NOTE_E5,
  NOTE_D5, NOTE_D5,
  NOTE_E5,
  NOTE_D5,
  NOTE_G5
};
```

Each note in the song should play for a certain duration. We can create another array that contains the duration of each note, and we will call that array `tempo`:

```
int tempo[] = {
  4, 4, 2, 4, 4, 2,
  4,
  4,
  4,
  4,
  1,
  4, 4, 4, 4, 4,
  4, 4, 8, 8, 4,
  4, 4,
  4,
  2,
  2
};
```

We will be using the `tone()` function to create the notes. With this function, we will not need to set up anything in the `setup()` function. The following code can be put in the `loop()` function to play the song defined by the `melody` and `tempo` arrays:

```
// Get the number of notes in the song
int songSize = sizeof(melody) / sizeof(melody[0]);

//Loop through each note
for (int note = 0; note < songSize; note++) {

  //Calculate how long to play the note
  int noteDuration = 1000 / tempo[note];

  //Play the note
  tone(soundPin, melody[note], noteDuration);

  //Calculate how long to pause before playing next note
  int pauseBetweenNotes = noteDuration * 1.20;
  delay(pauseBetweenNotes);
}
delay(3000);
```

This code starts off by calculating the number of notes in the `melody` array by dividing the size of the `melody` array by the size of the first element in the array. We use this logic to calculate the number of elements in an array because the `sizeof(melody)` code returns the number of bytes occupied by the array and the `sizeof(melody[0])` returns the number of bytes occupied by the first element in the array. It takes two bytes to store a single integer, and there are 26 notes in the melody array. Therefore, the `size of (melody)` code will return 52, and the `sizeof(melody[0])` code will return 2.

A `for` loop is used to loop through the `melody` and `temp` arrays. Within the `for` loop, the note duration is calculated by taking one second and dividing it by the note type (the elements in the `tempo` array) where a quarter note is equal to 1000 divided by 4 and an eighth note is equal to 1000 divided by 8.

The `tone` function is used to play the note from the `melody` array for the calculated duration. The `tone` function will not cause the application to pause while the note is playing. Therefore, we need to create our own pause. We will also want to pause slightly longer than the duration of the note to have a slight pause between the notes. For this, we multiply the note duration by 1.2 and then use the `delay()` function. After the `for` loop has completed, there is another delay for three seconds before starting over.

This last example shows how we can play a song using the `tone()` function with two arrays, one for the notes and one for the tempo. Now let's look at how we can use a library that will enable us to play music that is in the **RTTTL** (**Ring Tone Text Transfer Language**) format. The RTTTL format was developed by Nokia to transfer ringtones to cellphones.

Playing a ringtone in the RTTTL format

The Arduino library manager does not have a library that we can download to play RTTTL files at this time. Therefore, we will need to download and manually install a library. We will be using Arduino-rtttl-player that can be downloaded here: `https://github.com/ponty/arduino-rtttl-player`. We will need to create a ZIP file of the library to load it into the IDE. If you do not have access to a utility that can zip up the files, the downloadable code for this book contains the library already zipped.

When we create the ZIP file to load into the Arduino IDE, we do not want to zip up everything that is downloaded from the GitHub repository because the Arduino IDE will not recognize the ZIP file as a library file. We only want to zip up the directory that contains the code for the library, and in the case of the Arduino-rtttl-player library that would be the `rtttl` folder.

After we download the library and create a ZIP file that contains the `rtttl` folder from the library, we will want to load the library into the Arduino IDE. To do this, we will want to select **Sketch** | **Include Library** | **Add .ZIP Library...** from the main menu as shown in the following screenshot:

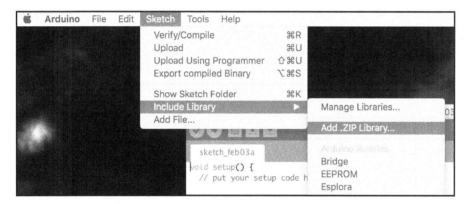

After you select the **Add .ZIP Library** option, you will be presented with a file picker where you can browse to the location of the ZIP file you created and select it. If the library was successfully imported, you will see a message in the message bar as shown in the following screenshot:

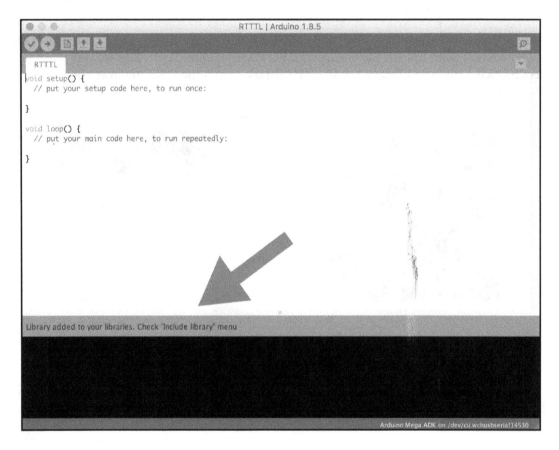

Now we are ready to play an RTTTL melody. The first thing we need to do is to include the library with the project by adding the following `include` statement to the sketch:

```
#include <rtttl.h>
```

We will want to include both the piezo buzzer and the speaker as we did in the earlier projects with the following code:

```
#define PIEZOPIN 7
#define SPEAKERPIN 8

int soundPin = PIEZOPIN;
```

We will need to define the song to play. There are plenty of RTTTL codes on the internet. To find some, do a search for `rtttl songs` and you should see plenty of RTTTL codes for a wide variety of songs. For this example, we will play the *Star Wars* theme. The following code contains the RTTTL code for this:

```
char *song = "Star
Wars:d=8,o=5,b=180:f5,f5,f5,2a#5.,2f.,d#,d,c,2a#.,4f.,d#,d,c,2a#.,4f.,d#,d,
d#,2c,4p,f5,f5,f5,2a#5.,2f.,d#,d,c,2a#.,4f.,d#,d,c,2a#.,4f.,d#,d,d#,2c";
```

To play this song, add the following code to the `setup()` function:

```
Rtttl player;
player.begin(soundPin);
player.play(song, 0);
```

We use the `begin` function from the Arduino-rtttl-player library to initiate the library, and define what pin the speaker is connected to and then the `play` function to play the song. The second parameter in the `play` function is the octave. The higher the octave is set to the higher pitch the song will play at. I usually leave this at zero.

When this code is run, you should recognize the *Star Wars* theme.

Challenge

For the challenge, we will stay with the *Star Wars* theme. Let's say that we wanted to build a robot that looks like R2-D2 from *Star Wars*. One of the features that we would put in would be to have it sound like R2-D2. How would you make the robot sound like R2-D2?

Summary

In this chapter, we saw how to connect both a speaker and a piezo buzzer to an Arduino. We then learned how to use the `tone()` function to create sounds and also play a song. We also saw how we could install and use a third-party library so we could play RTTTL files.

In the next chapter, we will look at how we can use LCD displays to display messages.

13
Using LCD Displays

There are times that we would like to have the ability to display data from the Arduino to the user. For this, we can use an LCD display. There are numerous types of LCD displays that we can use and probably the most popular is the 1602 display. Because they are so popular, you can find numerous tutorials on how to use them on the internet. While these displays are easy to use, you are limited by what you can do with them.

In this chapter, we will look at a display that we can do a lot more with. This display is the **Nokia 5110 LCD display**.

In this chapter, you will learn:

- How to connect a Nokia 5110 LCD to an Arduino
- How to print text to an LCD
- How to draw circles on an LCD
- How to draw rectangles on an LCD
- How to draw rounded rectangles on an LCD

Introduction

The Nokia 5110 LCD display is a basic monochrome graphics LCD screen that can be used in numerous projects. Nokia originally developed this display for use with cell phones in the late 1990's. This display uses the **PCD8544 LCD controller/driver**.

Having an LCD display greatly improves the user interface of any project because we have the ability to display messages directly to the user letting them know what is happening or giving them specific error messages if something goes wrong. The 5110 LCD allows us to display both text and graphics.

The 5110 LCD has a display area of approximately 4.2 cm with 84 × 48 individual pixels. The display is inexpensive and very easy to use with the Adafruit 5110 LCD library that we will be using in this chapter. The 5110 LCD that we will be using in this chapter looks like the following:

The 5110 LCD display comes mounted on a PCB board and has eight pins that are used to power the display and interface with it. These pins are, from left to right:

1. **RST**: Reset – Active low
2. **CE**: Chip Select – Active low
3. **DC**: Mode (data/instruction) selection – Select between command mode (low) or data mode (high)
4. **DIN**: Serial Data Inline
5. **CLK**: Serial Clock Line
6. **VCC**: Power input 3.3V
7. **BL**: Backlight LED control – 3.3V
8. **GND**: Ground

The reset pin will reset the 5110 LCD module and is active low, which means that the reset will be triggered if the pin goes to 0V. The chip select pin is used when more than one SPI peripheral is connected. The pin is also active low.

The DC pin is used to select between data or command mode. When the pin is high data mode is used, and when the pin is low command mode is used.

The DIN pin is the input pin where serial instructions are sent.

The CLK pin is the common clock used for the SPI modules. The clock source is supplied to the pin.

The BL pin powers the backlight display. This pin should never be above 3.3V. If the pin is low, then the backlight will be off.

VCC and GND are power and ground respectively. Power should never be above 3.3V.

Let's see what parts we will need for this chapter's project.

Components needed

- One Arduino Uno or compatible board
- One Nokia 5110 LCD
- Four 10K ohm resistors
- One 1K ohm resistor
- Jumper wires
- One breadboard

Circuit diagrams

The following diagram shows the circuit diagram for this chapter's project:

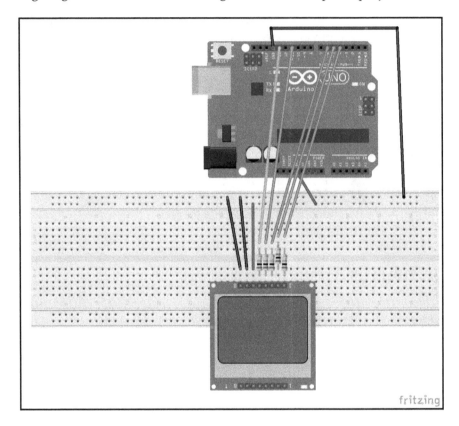

The Nokia 5110 LCD should use the 3.3V power out from the Arduino and not the 5V that we have used in the earlier projects. We use inline resistors to protect the 3.3V input lines on the LCD. The CE line uses a 1K ohm resistor and the remainder use 10K ohm resistors.

The following chart shows what pins on the 5110 LCD module are connected to what pins on the Arduino:

5110	Arduino
RST	3
CE	4
DC	5
DIN	11
CLK	13
VCC	3.3V out
BL	GND
GND	GND

The backlight is set to ground to turn it off. If you wish to use the backlight, you can connect the pin to the 3.3V power out that was used for the VCC pin.

Now let's see how we can display items on the LCD.

Code

We will need to start off by installing two Adafruit libraries. These are the **Adafruit GFX Library** and the **Adafruit PCD8544 Nokia 5110 LCD library**. These libraries are installed as we will need to include them and the SPI library. We can do this by adding the following include statements at the beginning of the sketch:

```
#include <SPI.h>
#include <Adafruit_GFX.h>
#include <Adafruit_PCD8544.h>
```

We will not want to initiate an instance of the Adafruit_PCD8544 type using the following code:

```
Adafruit_PCD8544 display = Adafruit_PCD8544(13, 11, 5, 4, 3);
```

The parameters are the Arduino pin numbers that the CLK, DIN, DC, CE and RST pins respectively are connected too.

In the setup() function, we will want to add the following code to set up the Adafruit_PCD8544 instance:

```
Serial.begin(9600);

display.begin();
```

```
display.setContrast(40);
```

Now the rest of the code can go in the `setup()` function for test purposes or in the `loop()` function. Let's start off by seeing how to light up a single pixel on the display. This can be accomplished by using the `drawPixel()` function as shown in the following code:

```
display.clearDisplay();
display.drawPixel(10, 10, BLACK);
display.display();
```

Before we draw anything to the screen, we will want to clear the display and buffer. We do this with the `clearDisplay()` function. Next, we use the `drawPixel()` function to light up a single pixel located at the X coordinate 10 and the Y coordinate 10. Before anything is displayed on the LCD, we need to run the `display()` function as shown in the preceding code. It is important to remember to run the `clearDisplay()` function before we draw anything to the LCD, and we run the `display()` function after we draw everything to the screen to display it.

Drawing a line

We could put several of the `drawPixel()` function calls together to draw a line, but it would be a lot easier to use the `drawLine()` function as shown in the following code:

```
// draw a line
display.drawLine(3,3,30,30, BLACK);
display.display();
```

The `drawLine()` function takes five parameters. The first two parameters are the X/Y coordinates of the starting point for the line. The next two parameters are the X/Y coordinates for the ending point of the line, and the final parameter is the color to draw the line. Since the Nokia 5110 LCD is a monochrome display, the only options here are BLACK or WHITE.

If we ran this code, we would see a line on the display like the one seen in the following photograph:

Displaying text

The Adafruit library also makes it very easy to display text to the Nokia 5110 LCD. The following code shows how we can display text:

```
// Display text
display.setTextSize(1);
display.setTextColor(BLACK);
display.setCursor(0,0);
display.println("Hello, world!");

// Display Reverse Text
display.setTextColor(WHITE, BLACK);
display.println(3.14);

// Display Larger Text
display.setTextSize(2);
display.setTextColor(BLACK);
display.print("This is larger text");
display.display();
```

The setTextSize() function sets the size of the text. In the first example, the text size is set to 1. The setTextColor() function will set the color of the text. Once again, since the Nokia 5110 LCD is a monochrome display, the two options are BLACK or WHITE. The setCursor() function sets the position of the cursor to the position on the screen to write the text too. In this case, the cursor is set to the upper left corner of the screen. Finally, the println() function is used to print the Hello World! message to the screen.

In the next example, we use the setTextColor() function to set the foreground color to WHITE and the background color to BLACK to reverse the text and then use the println() function to print the value of PI to the screen. Since we did not call the setTextSize() function, the text stays at the previously defined size, which is 1.

In the last example, the text size is set to 2, and the text color is set back to black. The following image shows what the screen will display when this code is run:

Rotating text

We can also rotate text. The following code shows how to do this:

```
display.setRotation(1);
display.setTextSize(1);
display.setTextColor(BLACK);
display.setCursor(0,0);
display.println("Hello, world!");
display.display();
```

The `setRotation()` function will rotate the text counterclockwise. A value of 1 will rotate the text 90 degrees counterclockwise. Values of 2 and 3 can also be used to rotate the text at 180 and 270 degrees. The following photograph shows how the text will look when this code is run:

Notice that the text will wrap to a new line if it is longer than what can be displayed on a single line.

Basic shapes

The Adafruit library also enables us to create basic shapes on the LCD. These include circles, rectangles and rounded rectangles. There are also functions that enable us to create these shapes and fill them in. The following code and screenshots show how to use the circle functions:

```
display.drawCircle(display.width()/2, display.height()/2, 6, BLACK);
```

Filled shape

```
display.fillCircle(display.width()/2, display.height()/2, 6, BLACK);
```

The circle functions take four parameters. The first two parameters are the *X/Y* coordinates for the center of the circle. In these two examples, the center of the circle is the center of the screen. The third parameter is the radius of the circle, and the last parameter is the color for the circle and also the color to fill the circle in the case of the `fillCircle()` function.

Rectangle

The next two examples show how to draw a rectangle and also a filled rectangle:

```
display.drawRect(15,15,30,15,BLACK);
```

Filled rectangle

```
display.fillRect(15,15,30,15,BLACK);
```

Rounded rectangle

The rectangle functions take five parameters. The first two are the *X/Y* coordinates of the upper left corner of the rectangle. The next two parameters are the *X/Y* coordinates of the lower right-hand corner of the rectangle, and the last parameter is the color to draw the rectangle and the color to fill the rectangle for the `fillRect()` function.

The next two examples show how we can draw rounded rectangles with the Adafruit library:

```
display.drawRoundRect(15,15,30,15,4,BLACK);
```

Filled rounded rectangle

```
display.fillRoundRect(15,15,30,15,8,BLACK);
```

The first four parameters for the round rectangle functions are the same as the regular rectangle functions, which are the coordinates for the upper left and lower right corners of the rectangle. The next parameter is how much to round the corners, and the last parameter is the color to draw the rounded rectangle and the color to fill it.

As we can see from the examples in this chapter, we can do a lot more than text with the Nokia 5110 LCD display, and the Adafruit library makes it very easy to use.

Challenge

For the challenge, take any of the previous projects in this book and add the Nokia 5110 LCD display to it. Then, rather than displaying the output to the serial console, display the output to the LCD display. An example would be to add the LCD display to the rangefinder project from Chapter 10, *Obstacle Avoidance and Collision Detection*, and use the LCD to display the distance.

Summary

In this chapter, we saw how we could add a Nokia 5110 LCD monochrome display to our projects. These displays can greatly enhance the user experience of almost any project because we are able to tell the users what is happening and what is wrong if there is an issue.

In the next chapter, we will see how we can add a voice synthesizer and voice recognition to our projects.

Speech Recognition and Voice Synthesizing

14

Anyone who has used Amazon's Echo, Google's Home speaker or even Apple's Siri knows how powerful and convenient speech recognition and voice synthesizing can be. Now imagine if we could add these features, at a smaller scale, to our smart devices? If we could, we would have the ability to speak directly to our coffee pot and tell it to start brewing our coffee in the morning or command the robots that we build.

In this chapter, we will look at how we can add voice recognition and voice synthesizing to any Arduino projects using the MOVI shield. Throughout this chapter, we will learn:

- How to use the MOVI shield for speech recognition
- How to use the MOVI shield for voice synthesizing
- How to create a voice-activated thermometer

Introduction

The name **MOVI** stands for **My Own Voice Interface**. The MOVI Arduino shield by Audeme is an extremely easy to use speech recognition and voice synthesizing shield. This shield will work directly with the **Uno R3**, **Duemilanove**, **Mega 2560**, or **Leonardo Arduinos**. However, you should not power the board through the USB connector while the MOVI shield is connected. The MOVI shield requires a minimum of 7V. Therefore, you may damage the MOVI and/or the Arduino if you attempt to power it from a USB connection.

 You can read about the MOVI shield and download the user manual from Audeme's website here: https://www.audeme.com.

When powering and programming the Arduino with the MOVI attached, you will want to power the Arduino through the DC supply input connector using an input of 9V. Once the boards are powered up, you can then connect the USB cable between the Arduino and your computer for programming. Since the board was originally powered by the DC supply input connector, it will continue drawing power from that source rather than the USB connection.

 Very important: Do not power the Arduino, when the MOVI shield is connected, from the USB connector.

While programming the MOVI, it is recommended to attach an external microphone, to get better voice recognition, and headphone, so you can hear the MOVI's responses. The following photograph shows the MOVI attached to an Arduino with an external microphone and earphones attached to the MOVI:

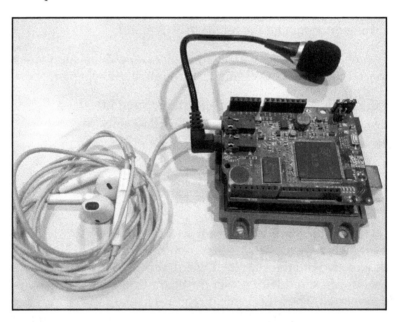

There is a built-in microphone on the MOVI shield that can be used rather than an external one. However, there is no built-in speaker. To receive audio feedback, which includes errors and system messages, you must connect headphones or an external speaker to the MOVI shield. The speaker impedance should be 32 ohms, which is the standard for headphones. You should not connect a 4- or 8-ohm speaker to the external speaker jack.

The MOVI can be used as a replacement for buttons, remote controls or any other control input. As we will see in the sample project for this chapter, we can use the MOVI to issue voice commands that the Arduino can respond to.

One of the best features with the MOVI shield is that no internet connection is required. This alleviates any privacy concerns that are normally associated with other voice control devices such as the Amazon Echo and Google Home speaker, since no data is sent to external servers.

There is an LED on the MOVI shield, which indicates the state that the shield is in. The following list shows the different states the MOVI shield can be in and the associated LED state:

- **LED off**: Indicates that the shield is turned off or there is not enough power for the MOVI to operate
- **LED blinking faster and faster**: The MOVI is booting
- **LED blinking randomly**: The MOVI is writing to the SD card
- **LED blinking with constant frequency**: There may be an issue with the SD card
- **LED on**: Indicates that the MOVI is on and ready

The MOVI shield is one of the most interesting and fun boards that you can use with the Arduino. If you are interested in some of the more advanced things you can do with it, you should look at the examples that come with the MOVI library.

In this chapter, we will create a voice-activated thermometer using the DHT-11 temperature sensor that we used in `Chapter 9`, *Environment Sensors*, and the MOVI shield. To connect the temperature sensor and the MOVI shield to the Arduino, we will want to attach the MOVI shield to the Arduino first and then connect the DHT-11 temperature sensor to the pin headers on the MOVI shield.

Let's look at the components that we will need for this project.

Components needed

In this chapter, you will need the following components.

- One Arduino Uno or compatible board
- 9V power source such as a wall outlet adapter
- One MOVI shield
- One DHT-11 temperature/humidity sensor

- One 4.7K resistor
- Jumper wires
- One breadboard

Circuit diagrams

The following diagram shows how to connect the DHT-11 temperature sensor for this project. Remember to attach the MOVI shield to the Arduino prior to connecting the temperature sensor. The resistor shown in the following diagram is a 4.7K- ohm resistor:

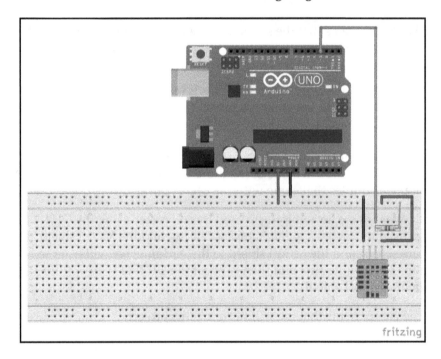

Now let's look at the code for our voice-activated temperature sensor.

Code

You should already have the DHT-11 library downloaded from the example in Chapter 9, *Environment Sensors*, but you will need to download the MOVI library. If you go to the library manager and do a search for Movi, you will find several libraries that match that term. Look for the **MOVI Voice Dialog Shield library by Audeme LLC** and download it.

We will begin the sketch by including both the MOVI and the DHT libraries. The following code shows how to include both:

```
#include <DHT.h>
#include <MOVIShield.h>
```

Next, we will define the DHT pin/type and create an instance of the DHT type as we did in Chapter 9, *Environment Sensors*:

```
#define DHT_PIN 3
#define DHT_TYPE DHT11
DHT dht(DHT_PIN, DHT_TYPE);
```

Now we will want to create an instance of the MOVI type as shown in the following line of code. The Boolean `false` value indicates that we do not want serial debugging turned on:

```
MOVI movi(false);
```

Finally, we will need a character array that will be used to create the sentence that contains the current temperature so the MOVI shield can tell us the temperature when we ask for it.

```
char answer[21];
```

Within the `setup()` function we will need to initialize both the DHT temperature sensor and also the MOVI shield. The following code shows the `setup()` function:

```
void setup() {
  dht.begin();
  movi.init();
  movi.callSign("buddy");
  movi.addSentence("temp");
  movi.train();
}
```

This function starts off by initializing the DHT temperature sensor by calling the `begin()` function from the `dht` type. Next, we initiate the `movi` type by calling the `init()` function. This function must be called first to initialize the `movi` type.

Most voice-activated devices like Amazon Echo are activated by a call sign. For Amazon's devices, the call sign is "Alexa." In our example, the MOVI shield will also use a call sign that will activate it. A call sign can be set up using the `callSign()` method, where the call sign to use is passed in as a string. In this example, the call sign will be "buddy".

Next, we will want to add a sentence or words that the MOVI will match. We do this with the addSentence() function. For this example, we will try to match the word "temp." We do have the option of training the MOVI shield with complete sentences or words. If you wish for the MOVI shield to recognize a sentence, it is recommended to add the complete sentence even if you need to add multiple versions of the same sentence. By adding the complete sentence, the MOVI's algorithm can be used to identify the sentence. This gives greater accuracy. It is also recommended that all trained sentences be close to the same size. A single long sentence will be favored over much smaller ones if a lot of words are spoken.

Finally, the train() method is called to tell the MOVI shield that we have added all of the sentences and the call sign. The first time you add a sentence or call sign the MOVI shield will take some time to train, but if the call sign and sentence stay the same between builds of your application, then the MOVI shield will start up very quickly.

Now that the setup() function is complete, let's look at the loop() function. The following code shows the loop() function:

```
void loop() {
  signed int res=movi.poll();
  if (res == 1) {
    float fahreheit = dht.readTemperature(true);
    int tmp = (int)fahreheit;
    sprintf(answer, "The temperature is %02d", tmp);
    movi.say(answer);
  }
}
```

In the first line, we use the poll() function from the movi instance. This function will poll for any match to the trained sentences. This function would return zero (0) if no event happened or a positive number if it matches a sentence. The number that is returned is the number of the sentence that it matched. In our example, we only have one sentence. Therefore, the only possible match is to sentence number 1.

If a match to the sentence is found, the current temperature is read from the DHT-11 temperature sensor and then it is converted from a float value to an integer value by typecasting.

To construct the string that we wish for the MOVI shield to say, the sprintf() function is used. This function can be used to construct a character array. In this example, we start with the sentence The temperature is and then add the temperature value using the %02d format. This tells the sprintf() function to add a two-digit integer to the string. The character array that is created is stored in the answer array that was created at the beginning of this sketch.

We use the `say()` function from the `movi` instance to have the MOVI shield tell us the current temperature through the connected headphones or speaker.

Now let's run the project.

Running the project

The first time the project is run, it will take a little time to train the MOVI shield. Wait for the shield to say that it is ready and then use the call sign to activate it. Once you say the call sign, you will hear a beep if the MOVI shield recognizes it. If MOVI recognizes the call sign say the sentence "temp." The MOVI shield should respond back by telling you the current temperature that was read by the DHT-11 temperature sensor.

This example only touches the very basics of what you can do with the MOVI shield and gives you enough to get started with it.

Challenge

There are other very useful functions that we can use with the MOVI instance. Here are a few additional functions that you can try to add to the project:

- **isReady()**: Will return a Boolean value of true if the MOVI is ready or false if it is not ready.
- **setVolume(int volume)**: Will set the volume of the MOVI's output from 0 (muted) to 100 (full volume).
- **setVoiceGender(bool female)**: Will set the gender for the MOVI's voice. A true value will set it to a female voice, and a false value will set it to a male voice.
- **setThreshold(int threshold)**: Sets the noise threshold for the speech recognizer. Values can range from 2 to 95. A value of 15 is good for a noisy environment while a value of 30 is good for a very noisy environment.
- **welcomeMessage(bool on)**: Will set the MOVI welcome message on or off.
- **beeps(bool on)**: Turns the recognition beep on or off.
- **ask() and ask(string question)**: Directly listens without waiting for a call sign. If a string is passed in, then the MOVI will ask the question first before listening.

The challenge is to try to add some of these functions in the sample project and see what else you can do with the MOVI shield. Also, try adding additional sentences for MOVI to listen for.

Summary

In this chapter, we saw how we could use the MOVI shield for both speech recognition and also for voice synthesizing. We used the speech recognition to listen for a specific command and the voice synthesizing to respond to the command.

In the next chapter, we will look at how we can use DC motors and motor controllers.

15
DC Motors and Motor Controllers

So far, in this book, all of the projects have been stationary projects. By stationary projects I mean the projects had no way to move on their own. In this chapter, we will look at how we can add DC motors to any project, giving it the ability to move on its own. When using DC motors, I would recommend using a motor controller to control them. Motor controllers enable us to very easily connect an external power supply to the motor and control the direction and speed of the motor.

In this chapter, you will learn:

- How a brushed DC motor works
- How an H-bridge works
- How to use the L298 and L293D motor controllers

Introduction

A DC motor is a class of rotary electrical device that converts electrical energy into physical motion. There are numerous types of DC motors; however, in this chapter, we will look at one specific type, which is the **brushed DC motor**.

Brushed DC motors are used in a wide variety of applications, ranging from toys and robotics to powered windows and power tools. Some advantages of brushed DC motors are their initial low cost, simple control, and low-speed torque. The disadvantages of these motors are their high maintenance costs and low lifespan in high-intensity environments. For the prototyping and robotic projects that we normally do with the Arduino, the disadvantages of the brushed DC motors are normally not a concern.

At the center of a brushed DC motor is a spinning armature, which contains an electromagnet. To the outside of the spinning armature is a permanent, stationary magnet. When the electromagnet in the armature is powered, a magnetic field is created that attracts and repels the permanent stationary magnets. This causes the armature to begin spinning.

To keep the armature spinning, the polarity of the electromagnet needs to be reversed. To do this a segmented copper sleeve called a **commutator** is used, which resides on the axle of the motor. As the motor turns, brushes slide over the commutator, coming in to contact with different parts of the commutator, causing the polarity of the magnet to switch.

The following diagram illustrates the parts of the brushed DC motor:

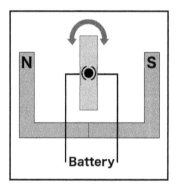

Brushed DC motors come in numerous shapes and sizes. Some of these motors have built-in gearboxes that can change the torque and speed that the motor will spin at. The following photograph shows some examples of brushed DC motors:

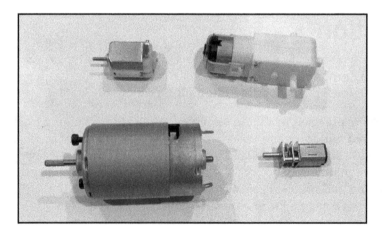

Powering a DC motor directly from the Arduino for anything other than demonstration purposes, is usually not a good idea because the voltage and current provided from the pin headers are pretty limited. We can use a motor controller to control the direction and speed of a DC motor from the Arduino while still providing an external power source to power it. In this chapter, we will look at how we can use the L298 dual H-bridge motor driver, shown in the following photograph, and also how to use the L293D chip:

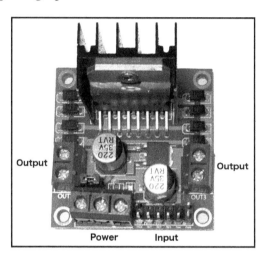

The L298 motor driver enables us to control the direction and speed of two motors. This driver allows us to control motors from 5V all the way up to 35V with a maximum current of 2A. If the supply voltage is 12V or less, we can also use the 5V output to power the Arduino. The L298 motor driver has several inputs, outputs and power connectors that are labeled. These inputs from left to right are:

- **ENA**: Enables motor A and controls the speed of the motor
- **IN1 and IN2**: Controls the direction of motor A
- **IN3 and IN4**: Controls the direction of motor B
- **ENB**: Enables motor B and controls the speed of the motor

ENA and ENB normally have jumpers across the pins. In order to control brushed DC motors, we will need to remove these jumpers and connect the pin to a PWM port. The outputs are:

- **OUT1 and OUT2**: Output power to motor A
- **OUT3 and OUT4**: Output power to motor B

The power inputs, from left to right, are:

- **Vmotor**: Power from an external source that will be used to power the motors
- **GND**: Ground
- **Vout**: 5V output that can be used to power the Arduino

If we are building a project where we have limited space, rather than using a motor controller such as the L298 dual H-bridge motor driver, we can use an integrated chip such as the **L293D H-bridge IC**. The L293D chip can drive two motors, similar, to the L298 motor driver, and can power motors up to 35V with 600mA of steady current with a maximum of 1.2A. The following diagram shows the pinout for the L293D IC:

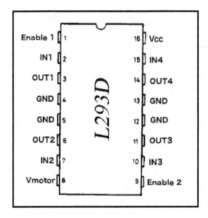

Both the L298 motor controller and the L293D chip are H-bridges. Let's take a quick look at how an H-bridge works. An H-bridge is an electric circuit that allows us to apply a voltage to our motors in either direction allowing the motor to run forwards or backwards. The term H-bridge comes from the typical graphic representation of the circuit, which looks like a capital H. The following diagram shows how an H-bridge works:

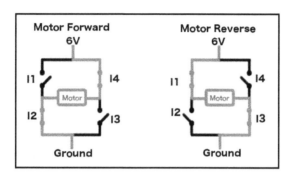

An H-bridge is usually built with four solid state switches. As we see in the preceding image, when switches 1 and 3 (**I1** and **I3**) are open and switches 2 and 4 (**I2** and **I4**) are closed, the right side of the motor is connected to the power supply while the left side is connected to ground, spinning the motor in one direction. If switches 1 and 3 (**I1** and **I3**) are closed and switches 2 and 4 (**I2** and **I4**) are open, then the left side of the motor is connected to the power supply while the right side is connected to ground, spinning the motor in the other direction.

Let's look at the parts that we will need for our projects in this chapter.

Components needed

In this chapter, you will need the following components.

- One Arduino Uno or compatible board
- One L298 motor driver
- One L293D H-bridge chip
- Two brushed DC motors
- One external 12V battery (or other external DC power source such as a 9V battery)
- Jumper wires
- One breadboard

Circuit diagrams

In this chapter, we will create two projects. The first project will use the L298 motor driver to control a single motor and the second project will use the L293D chip to control a single motor. Here is the circuit diagram for the L298 motor driver project:

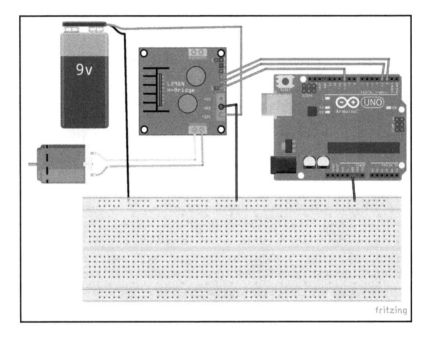

Before we explain this diagram, let's look at the circuit diagram for the L293D chip circuit as well because there are a lot of similarities between these two diagrams:

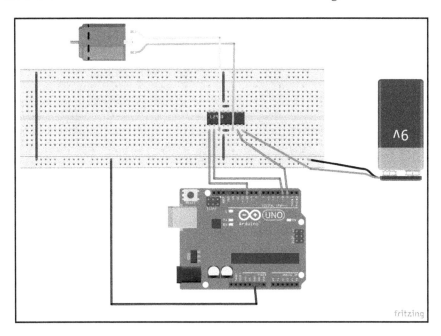

The first thing to note with these two diagrams is the circuits contain a common ground. What this means is the ground connectors on the Arduino, battery and the motor controllers (both the L298 and L293D) are all connected together. In projects like these, which include multiple power sources, we must have a common ground between all devices and power sources.

In both circuits, the PWM out of 10 pins on the Arduino are connected to the enable pin on the motor controller. Also, in both circuits, the digital 2 and 3 pins are connected to the IN1 and IN2 pins on the motor controllers. This enables us to use the same code for both projects.

Now let's look at the code for these projects.

Code

The code to control the motors only needs to use the standard `digitalWrite()` and `analogWrite()` functions from the Arduino standard library, so no external libraries are needed for this code. Therefore, our code will start off by defining the pins on the Arduino that are connected to the motor controllers. This following code does this:

```
#define MC_IN_1 3
#define MC_IN_2 2
#define MC_ENABLE 10
```

Now we will need to configure the pins for output in the `setup()` function as shown in the following code:

```
void setup() {
  pinMode(MC_ENABLE, OUTPUT);
  pinMode(MC_IN_1, OUTPUT);
  pinMode(MC_IN_2, OUTPUT);
}
```

Now we are ready to power the motors. Let's put the following code into the `loop()` function:

```
void loop() {
  digitalWrite(MC_IN_1, HIGH);
  digitalWrite(MC_IN_2, LOW);
  analogWrite(MC_ENABLE, 250);
  delay(2000);
  analogWrite(MC_ENABLE, 0);
  delay(1000);
  digitalWrite(MC_IN_1, LOW);
  digitalWrite(MC_IN_2, HIGH);
  analogWrite(MC_ENABLE, 125);
  delay(2000);
  analogWrite(MC_ENABLE, 0);
  delay(1000);
}
```

The `loop()` function starts off by using the `digitalWrite()` function to set input 1 on the motor controller to `HIGH` and input 2 to `LOW`. The `analogWrite()` function is then used to create a duty cycle of 250 to the enable pin on the motor controller. Remember the PWM pins have a maximum duty cycle of 255; therefore, once the `analogWrite()` function is performed, the motor should start spinning at almost full speed.

In order for a brushed DC motor to spin, one input must be HIGH, and the other must be LOW. If the inputs are both HIGH, both LOW or the duty cycle on the enable pin is 0, the motor will not spin. The following chart shows this:

IN1	IN2	Enable Duty Cycle	Result
HIGH	LOW	>0	Motor spins on direction
LOW	HIGH	>0	The motor spins other direction
HIGH	HIGH		Motor stopped
LOW	LOW		Motor stopped
		0	Motor stopped

After the `analogWrite()` function is called, the `delay` function is used to pause the execution of the application for two seconds to let the motor run. The `analogWrite()` function is then called again to set the duty cycle to 0, which will stop the motor from spinning and delay for one second to give the motor a chance to stop.

The `digitalWrite()` functions are then used to input 1 pin `LOW` and the input 2 pin `HIGH` which is the opposite of how they were originally set which will spin the motor in the opposite direction. The `analogWrite()` function is then called to set the duty cycle to 125, which will start spinning the motor at half speed. The `delay` function is then used to pause the execution of the application for two seconds, and then we stop the motor again.

Running the project

When this code is run, the motor should spin in one direction for two seconds, stop for one second, spin in the other direction for two seconds, stop for one second and then start over.

Challenge

For this chapter's challenge, try to add second motors to both projects and then change the code so both motors will spin at the same time. You could also try to wire the motors so they will spin in the same direction if you apply a `HIGH` value to the IN1 and IN3 pins with a `LOW` value to the IN2 and IN4 pins.

Summary

In this chapter, we learned the basics of how a brushed DC motor works and how we can use both the L298 motor driver and the L293D chip to control a brushed DC motor. We also learned how an H-bridge works.

In the next chapter, we will look at a different kind of DC motor. This motor is called a servo motor and is used in projects where precise positioning is needed, such as with robotic arms.

16
Servo Motors

When power is supplied to a brushed DC motor, it will begin to continuously spin until the power is cut off. This makes brushed DC motors very good for such items as turning the wheels on a robot or the blades on a fan. There are times when we need more precise control over how much the motor turns. For example, to control a robotic arm, we would need the motors to turn at a precise amount to put the arm where it needs to be. For applications like this, we can use a servo motor.

In this chapter, you will learn:

- How to control a servo motor
- How to use the Arduino servo library
- How to power a servo motor

Introduction

The types of servo motors that we will use with the Arduino are pretty small, but most have fairly high torque and are very energy efficient. This allows us to use these motors for industrial-grade applications such as robotic arms, conveyor belts, autofocus lenses in cameras and even solar-tracking systems for solar panels.

A servo motor is made up of a DC motor, which does the actual work; a potentiometer, which controls the amount of power going to the motor; control circuitry, which controls the movement of the motor and gears. The following photograph shows a servo motor connected to a robotic claw:

A servo motor contains three wires for the control signal, power and ground. The signal wire is usually orange or yellow. The power is the usual red, and the ground wire is usually brown or black.

Some smaller servo motors can use the 5V out on the Arduino; however, in this chapter, I will be using the **MG996R high torque motor**, which can handle up to 7.2V and has a running current of 500mA to 900mA. Therefore, we will be connecting it to an external 6V battery pack that contains 4 AA batteries. I would recommend referring to the datasheet for your servo motor to determine the correct power input for your servo motor.

NOTE: While some of the smaller motors can be powered by the 5V out, I would recommend using an external power source anytime you are powering motors.

The ground wire should be connected to a common ground that is shared with the battery pack and also the Arduino ground. The signal wire should be connected to a PWM out pin on the Arduino.

The duty cycle from the PWM pin determines the position of the servo shaft. When the shaft of the servo motor is at the desired position, the power supplied to the motor is cut off. The speed that the motor will spin at is proportional to the difference in the actual position and the desired position, which means the further the desired position is from the actual position, the faster the motor will spin. This makes the servo motor very efficient because it only works as hard as it needs to.

Different servo motors have different maximum turn radiuses. The turn radius of most servo motors is either 120 degrees (60 degrees each direction) or 180 degrees (90 degrees each direction). The MG996R servo motor that I will be using in this chapter has a maximum turn radius of 120 degrees. Once a servo motor rotates to the desired position, it will attempt to hold that position and will resist any attempt to push it out of position.

Let's look at the components we will need for this chapter's project.

Components needed

In this chapter, you will need the following components:

- One Arduino Uno or compatible board
- One servo motor (the code has been tested with the MG996R servo. However, any standard servo should work)
- One potentiometer
- One 4 AA battery holder with batteries to power the servo motor
- Jumper wires
- One breadboard

Circuit diagrams

The following diagram shows how to connect the servo motor with the Arduino:

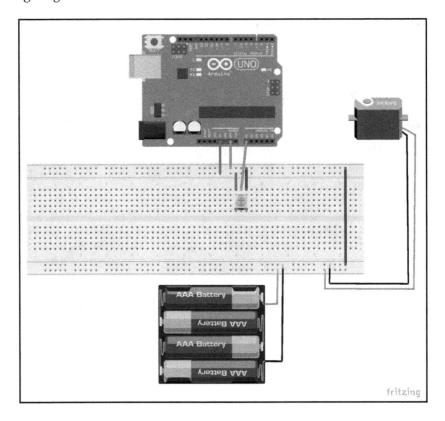

In this project, we will use the potentiometer to control the position of the servo motor. Notice that the potentiometer uses the 5V power source from the Arduino while the servo motor uses 6V (4 × 1.5V) from the batteries; however, the two power sources share a common ground. Now let's look at the code to control the servo motor.

Code

Both the Arduino IDE and Web Editor come with a servo library that we can use simply by including the header file. The following code will do this:

```
#include <Servo.h>
```

Next, we need to define the pin that the servo motor and the potentiometer are connected to. The following code will connect the signal wire to the digital 3 pin and the potentiometer to the analog 0 pin on the Arduino:

```
#define SERVO0_POT 0
#define SERVO0_OUT 3
```

Now we need to define an instance of the Servo type as shown in the following line:

```
Servo servo0;
```

Within the setup function, we need to call the attach() method from the servo instance to initialize the instance and to tell it what pin the servo is attached to. The following code shows this:

```
void setup() {
   servo0.attach(SERVO0_OUT);
}
```

We will want to define a function that will read the potentiometer and set the position of the servo position based on how much the potentiometer is turned.

```
void setServo(int pot, Servo out) {
   int servo = analogRead(pot);
   long int servo_val = map(servo, 0, 1023, 0, 120);
   out.write(servo_val);
}
```

This function will accept an integer, which is the pin that the potentiometer is connected to. The analogRead() function is called to read the pin that the potentiometer is connected to. We use the map() function to map the value that was read from the analog pin (values from 0-1023) with the 120 degrees that the servo motor can move. The write() function from the servo type is then used to write that value to the servo, causing the servo to adjust its position.

The setServo() function is then called from the loop() function to read the potentiometer and set the servo as shown in the following code:

```
setServo(SERVO0_POT, servo0);
delay(15);
```

The reason we created the setServo() function, rather than putting that code directly in the loop() function, is it makes it a lot easier to add multiple servo motors. For example, if we want to create a robotic arm with five servos, we could very easily do it by setting up the servos as we did with the first one and then using the following code in the setup() function:

```
setServo(SERVO0_POT, servo0);
setServo(SERVO1_POT, servo1);
setServo(SERVO2_POT, servo2);
setServo(SERVO3_POT, servo3);
setServo(SERVO4_POT, servo4);
delay(15);
```

If we have the code, like the code in the setServo() function that may be used multiple times, it is always a good idea to put that code in a separate function like this.

If this project is run, the position of the servo will change as the potentiometer is turned.

Challenge

For the challenge in this chapter, you will need a 6 **DOF** (**Degree of Freedom**) robotic arm. The following image show what a 6 DOF robotic arm looks like:

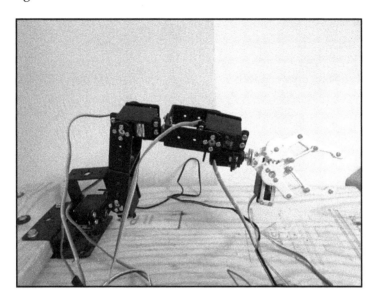

For this challenge, you will need to figure out how to wire the remaining servo motors to the Arduino and the correct power configuration. You can order 6 DOF robotic arm kits from Amazon or eBay. Go to their site and do a search for 6 DOF robotic arm. Prices for these kits varies greatly depending on the size and power of the arm/claw. You can get the robotic arms prebuilt, or as a kit that you need to build yourself.

Summary

In this chapter, we learned how a servo motor works and how we can control them with an Arduino. We also saw what components make up a servo motor. In the next chapter, we will see how to use a relay board.

17
Using a Relay

There are times where we want to control higher voltage items such as a light, fan or any other household appliance. However, the Arduino and every project so far in this book uses **direct current** (**DC**) while your household appliances use **alternating current** (**AC**). There are significant differences between AC and DC. In this chapter, we will look at how we can use a relay with an Arduino to control a lamp that runs on AC.

In this chapter, you will learn:

- What a relay is
- How to use a relay to control an AC-powered device
- How to use a relay to control a DC-powered device
- How to isolate circuits using a relay

Introduction

WARNING: In this chapter, we will be using 120V or 240V AC depending on what country you live in, which is significantly more powerful than anything else we have used in this book.

Mishandling, incorrect or improper use of the relay or the power cables can result in serious injury and even death. Make sure that you have read and understood how your relay board works, the voltage and current it is rated for, and the risks involved when using AC power before you attempt the project in this chapter.

Do not be afraid to seek professional help if you are uncertain about anything. AC power is significantly more dangerous than the DC power that we have used previously in this book.

If you do not feel comfortable using AC power in a project or if you are not familiar enough with it, there will be two circuit diagrams for this chapter. One diagram will show how to connect an AC-powered lamp to the relay and the other shows how to connect a motor and a 9V power source with a relay. The code for this chapter will work with either project and will turn the lamp or motor off and on.

 When working on an AC-powered device, *always* make sure the device is unplugged prior to doing any work on it. An electrical shock from a wall socket can cause serious injury and even death.

A relay can be thought of as an electric switch. Many relays use electromagnets to mechanically operate the switch. However, there are other ways to control a relay. An example of this is a solid-state relay, which uses no mechanical parts. Most relays that we would use with the Arduino use electromagnets to operate the switch.

Relays are used when there is a need to isolate two or more circuits from each other while still having the ability for a component from one of the circuits (the Arduino) to control a component in the other circuits. When you are using DC power for all components in the project, there usually isn't a need to isolate the circuits; however, when you want to control an AC-powered device, such as a desk lamp, then a device like a relay is needed.

As we mentioned earlier, if you are not familiar with working on AC-powered devices, then use the DC motor project rather than the lamp project. The same concepts are used in both projects; however, one is powered by AC, and the other is powered by DC.

The plug for the AC-powered devices contains two wires. In order to connect this device to a relay, we will need to cut one of the wires and connect one end to the COM connection on the relay and the other to the NO connection on the relay. The other cable is left intact. The following photograph illustrates this:

The **NO** label on the relay stands for **Normally Open** while the **NC** label stands for **Normally Closed**. The COM connection, which is usually between the NO and NC connections is the common connection. When the relay is off, power runs through the NC connection, which means that if the AC-powered device should be on when the relay is off, then it should be connected to the COM and NC connections. If the AC-powered device should be on only when the relay is turned on, then it should be connected to the COM and NO connections as we are doing here.

Relays are typically rated with a maximum voltage of 230 VAC to 250 VAC or 30 VDC at 10A. You will want to verify that the relay in your project can handle the voltage and current that you are running.

The following diagram shows how a relay works:

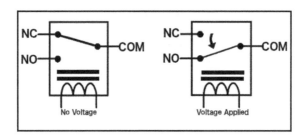

In the preceding images, we see that when no voltage is applied to the relay, (image on the left) the NC pin is connected to the COM terminal, thereby completing that circuit. When a voltage is applied, the armature is pulled to the NO pin connecting it to the COM terminal, completing that circuit.

In the preceding photograph, a board with a single relay was used. However, there are boards that contain multiple relays, which give us the ability to control components in multiple circuits. The following photograph shows a board with four relays:

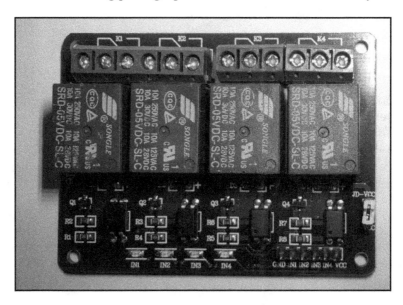

The relays that were shown in this chapter are rated for both AC and DC circuits. Therefore, they can be used for either project in this chapter. You could even attempt to do both projects if you would like.

Let's look at the components that we will need for this chapter's projects.

Components needed

- One Arduino Uno or compatible board
- One relay board
- Jumper wires
- One AC-powered device that you would like to control with the Arduino, such as a desk lamp, or if you wish to use a DC power device rather than an AC powered one
- One 9V battery adapter with a battery with a DC motor

Circuit diagrams

The following diagrams show how we would connect an AC-powered device and an Arduino to a relay:

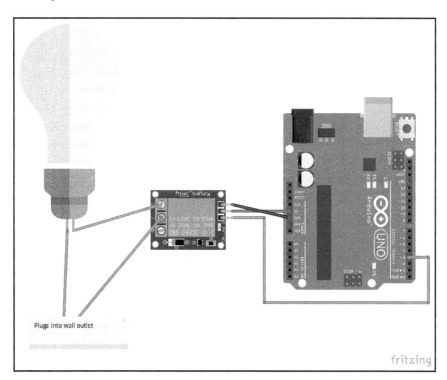

The AC-powered device is connected to the relay as described in the *Introduction* section. The **VCC** pin on the relay is connected to the **5V** out on the Arduino, and the **GND** pin on the relay is connected to the **GND** pin on the Arduino. We connect the digital 3 pin on the Arduino to the pin labeled **IN** on the relay. The digital 3 pin will be used to control the relay.

The following diagram shows how we would use a relay to control a DC motor and 9V power source with the Arduino:

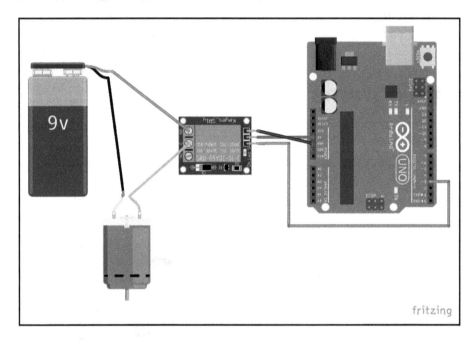

In preceding circuits, we stressed the need to have a common ground between the various components; however, in this circuit, you will notice that there is not a common ground between the Arduino and the motor/9V battery circuit. When using a relay, the circuits on opposite sides of the relay are isolated from each other; therefore, we do not want a common ground between them. If you wish to have a common ground between the two circuits, then a relay is not necessary because a relay is used to isolate two circuits.

Now let's look at the code for these circuits.

Code

The following is the code for the projects in this chapter:

```
#define RELAY 3

void setup() {
  pinMode(RELAY, OUTPUT);
}

void loop() {
  digitalWrite(RELAY, HIGH);
  delay(3000);
  digitalWrite(RELAY, LOW);
  delay(3000);
}
```

This code should look pretty familiar by now. This code starts off by defining that the relay is connected to the digital 3 pin on the Arduino. In the setup() function, we enable the relay pin for output because we want to use the digitalWrite() function to turn the relay on and off.

In the loop() function, we use the digitalWrite() function to set the relay pin to high, pause three seconds, use the digitalWrite() function again to set the relay pin to low and finally pause three seconds again. This will turn the components connected to the relay on and off every three seconds. This code will work with either the AC circuit or the DC circuit shown previously in this chapter.

Challenge

For this chapter's challenge, use a board with four relays and try connecting a component to each relay that can be controlled by the Arduino. Keep in mind that each circuit needs its own isolated power source.

Summary

In this chapter, we saw how we could use a relay to control both AC and DC components. We also saw that the circuits on either side of the relay need their own isolated power source.

In the next chapter, we will see how we can use radio frequencies to remotely control the Arduino.

18
Remotely Controlling the Arduino

When I was a kid, my parents used to use both myself and my sister as the remote control for the television sets because back then, television sets did not come with remote controls. Fortunately, Eugene Polley, an engineer at *Zenith*, came up with the idea to control television with remote controls, saving millions of kids from having to change the channels for their parents. The remote control greatly enhanced how we interacted with the television set and can do the same for your Arduino project.

In this chapter, you will learn:

- How to connect a radio frequency remote control to an Arduino
- How to determine what button is pressed on a radio frequency remote
- How to connect an infrared remote control to an Arduino
- How to determine what button is pressed on an infrared remote

Introduction

In this chapter, we will look at a couple of ways that we can control our Arduino project remotely. For the first project, we will use the Keyestudio IR (infrared) receiver, which uses the **HX1838 infrared control module**. The HX1838 infrared control module is used in numerous IR receivers that can be used by the Arduino. Therefore, you do not need to specifically get the Keyestudio one that we use here.

An infrared transmitter has an LED that emits infrared radiation, which is picked up by the infrared receiver. When a button is pressed on the remote control, the LED on the transmitter will blink very quickly for a fraction of a second and the receiver will read the pattern of blinks and interpret it.

The Keyestudio IR receiver that we will be using in this chapter looks like the following photograph:

The pin marked with the **S** is the signal pin and should be connected to one of the digital pins on the Arduino. The pin marked with the + sign should be connected to 5V and the pin with the - sign should be connected to ground.

One of the really nice things about using an IR receiver as the remote control for your project is you can use pretty much any IR remote controller as the transmitter. For example, I can use this remote that came with one of my IR receivers:

Or I could use any of my spare TV remotes that use infrared such as the one shown in the following photograph:

Some remotes, however, do not use infrared technologies such as the Apple TV remote, which uses Bluetooth 4.0. Therefore, they cannot be used with the infrared receiver.

Infrared remotes do have a couple drawbacks, the biggest being that they must have a line of sight to communicate with the receiver. What this means is the transmitter must be pointed directly at the receiver; otherwise, the receiver will not be able to read the transmission. Another drawback with infrared remotes is they are only really useful up to 30 feet (10 meters).

Rather than using an infrared transmitter/receiver we could use a **radio frequency** (**RF**) transmitter and receiver. In this chapter, we will look at how to use a basic four-button keyfob RF transmitter and a receiver like the ones shown in the following photograph:

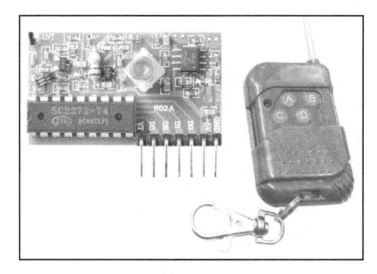

The two biggest advantages of using an RF transmitter and receiver is that the RF signal can travel further, and they can go through normal walls, which means it does not need line of sight. Unlike the infrared receiver, which can work with almost any infrared transmitter, if the RF transmitter and receiver are not designed to work together, and are set to the same frequencies, they will not be able to communicate. RF transmitters such as the one shown in the preceding photograph, also have far fewer buttons than infrared remotes.

Let's look at the parts we will need for these projects.

Components needed

For these projects, you will need the following items:

- One Arduino Uno or compatible board
- One infrared receiver
- One or more infrared transmitter(s)
- One RF transmitter and receiver pair
- Jumper wires
- Breadboard

Circuit diagrams

The following diagram shows how we connect the infrared receiver to the Arduino:

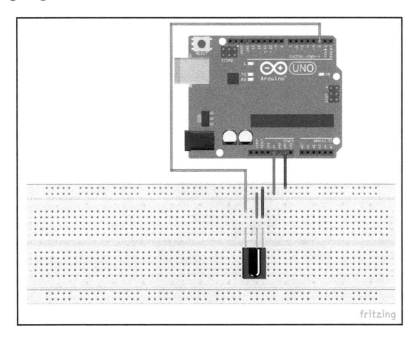

The 5V in and the ground pins on the IR receiver are connected to the appropriate rails on the breadboard. The signal pin is connected to the digital 2 pin on the Arduino. Now let's look at how we would connect the radio frequency receiver to the Arduino:

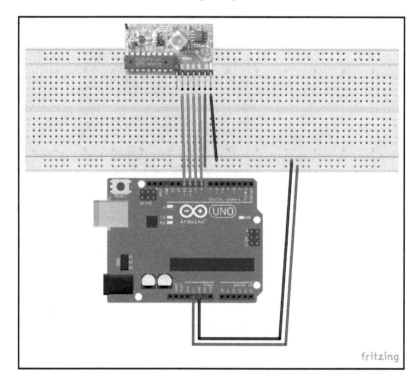

The 5V in and the ground pins on the RF receiver are connected to the appropriate rails on the breadboard. The four output pins on the receiver are connected to the 8, 9, 10 and 11 digital pins on the Arduino. When a button is pressed on the transmitter, the corresponding output pin on the receiver goes to HIGH.

Now let's look at the code for our projects.

Code

Before we can start writing the code that will read the input from the infrared receiver, we will need to load the **IRremote library** by shirriff. The following screenshot shows the library and version that we will use:

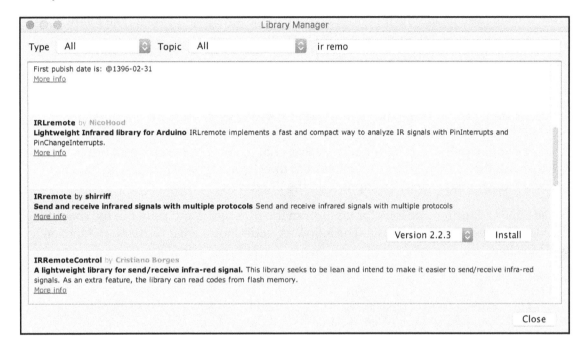

Once the library is loaded, we will need to start by importing the header file for the IRremote library and creating the global variables and directives. The following code shows how to do that:

```
#include <IRremote.h>

#define IR_PIN 2
IRrecv ir(IR_PIN);
decode_results irCode;
```

In the preceding code, we start off by including the `IRrremote.h` header file into our project. We then define that the infrared receiver is connected to pin 2 on the Arduino. Next, we create an instance of the `IRrecv` type, which is used to read the input from the IR receiver. Finally, we create an instance of the `decode_results` type, which is used to store the values from the IR receiver.

Now we will need to add the initialization code to the `setup()` function. The following codes shows the `setup()` function for this example:

```
void setup()
{
  Serial.begin(9600);
  ir.enableIRIn();
}
```

In this example, we start off by initializing the serial monitor so we can print out the results. We then call the `enableIRIn()` function from the `IRrecv` type instance, which will prepare the Arduino to read the input from the IR receiver.

In the `loop()` function, we look for input from the IR receiver and print out the codes for the buttons pressed on the remote. The following code shows what the `loop()` function will look like:

```
void loop()
{
  if (ir.decode(&irCode))
  {
    Serial.println(irCode.value, HEX);
    ir.resume();
  }
  delay(100);
}
```

In the `loop()` function, we use the `decode()` function, passing in the instance of the `decode_results` type, to read the code of the button that was pressed. Once a code has been received, the `Serial.println()` function is used to print out the code to the serial console. We delay the execution of the application for 100 milliseconds to give the user a chance to release the button before a repeat code is sent. Finally, the `resume()` function is called to begin listening for results again.

The results of the code should look something like the following screenshot:

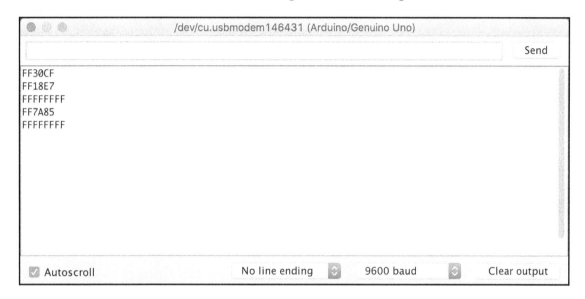

The Car mp3 remote, shown earlier in this chapter, was used to get the results shown in the preceding screenshot. `FF30CF` is the code for button number 1, the `FF18E7` code is the number 2 button, and the `ff7A85` code is the number 3 button. The `FFFFFFFF` results mean that the button is being held down; therefore, the last valid code should be used again.

You will probably want to save this project somewhere because it is very useful for getting valid codes for buttons on your remotes. Once you have the codes, you can then use the IRremote library in your other projects and perform whatever activities are needed depending on the codes returned from the receiver.

The RF receiver is a little easier to read because we do not need an external library to read it because there is one pin per button on the transmitter. When a user presses the button, the corresponding pin on the receiver will be pulled HIGH.

We will start the RF code by defining what pins on the Arduino are connected to the pins on the RF receiver. If you connected the RF receiver as shown in the Fritzing diagram, the buttons would be defined like this:

```
#define BUTTON_A 10
#define BUTTON_B 8
#define BUTTON_C 11
#define BUTTON_D 9
```

We then need to set up these pins for input within the setup() function and also initialize the serial monitor. The following code shows the setup() function for this project:

```
void setup() {
  pinMode(BUTTON_A, INPUT);
  pinMode(BUTTON_B, INPUT);
  pinMode(BUTTON_C, INPUT);
  pinMode(BUTTON_D, INPUT);
  Serial.begin(9600);
}
```

In the loop() function, we need to read each of the pins, check whether it is HIGH, and if so, perform what function is needed within your project. For this project, we simply print out that the pin was pressed. The following shows the loop() function for this project:

```
void loop() {
  int valA = digitalRead(BUTTON_A);
  if (valA == HIGH) {
    Serial.println("Button A");
  }

  int valB = digitalRead(BUTTON_B);
  if (valB == HIGH) {
    Serial.println("Button B");
  }

  int valC = digitalRead(BUTTON_C);
  if (valC == HIGH) {
    Serial.println("Button C");
  }

  int valD = digitalRead(BUTTON_D);
  if (valD == HIGH) {
    Serial.println("Button D");
  }
  delay(100);
}
```

When this code is run, you will be able to see which buttons were pressed within the serial monitor. Adding a remote control to your project may seem like simply a *nice to have;* however, it can really enhance the usability of your project and also save you from constantly getting up to interact with it. Now let's look at our challenge for this chapter.

Challenge

In this chapter, we saw two types of remote control devices. The first was the IR control, which needs a line of sight to the project and can have a lot of different buttons. The radio frequency remote is good when the remote needs to work over greater distances from the device or even in a different room.

There are numerous other ways to create remote controls using wireless signals, such as **Zigbee** radios or even Wi-Fi; however, for this challenge, we want you to think outside the box and to begin to expand your own horizons. The challenge for this chapter is to think of ways to remotely control your device without using a wireless signal.

You may be shaking your head right now wondering what we mean by remotely controlling a project without using a wireless signal. One example of this would be the clapper. The clapper is a sound-activated electrical switch. You clap once, and the switch will turn on, you clap again, and the switch will turn off. Another example is a motion sensor that controls your outside lights. If the motion sensor detects motion, it will turn on the light. Now try to think outside the box and come up with other ways that you can control your device without using a wireless signal.

Summary

In this chapter, we saw how to use an IR remote and an RF remote with an Arduino. You were also challenged to think outside of the box and think of other ways that you could remotely control your project without using a wireless signal. The reason this challenge was in this last project chapter was to get you to start thinking outside of the box when designing your projects because thinking outside of the box and creating new and improved ways to do something is what gets people excited about these types of projects. It can also make you a lot of money if you are able to monopolize your project.

In the next chapter, we will talk about how you can use the knowledge you gained from previous project chapters to create a simple robot. We will not be writing the code or designing the circuits for you. Instead we will show you how to put the pieces you have learned in the book together, so you can design your own robot or create other projects.

19
Creating a Robot

When I first started working with development boards like the Arduino, my initial goal was to build a robot. However, I had no idea where to start. I had so many questions, what is a good body style for the robot? What motors should I use? How do I power the robot? Do I need a separate power source for the motors? How does object avoidance work? This chapter is written to help answer a lot of these question for you and to show you that after reading the previous chapters in this book, you now have enough knowledge to design and build your own robot.

In this chapter, we will discuss:

- How we can use what we learned in this book to create a fully-working robot
- A range of additional tips and hints that will help you with your projects
- What are the other projects we can build with the Arduino beyond this book

We will finish the chapter by challenging you to create your own project and then share it with us.

Introduction

In this chapter, unlike previous project chapters, we will not be designing and building a specific project. Instead, we will show you how you can take the knowledge that you gained in previous chapters and use it to design your own robot. We will also give you various tips and hints to help you avoid some of the mistakes that people make when they first started building robots.

When we started designing our first robot, the first thing that we did was to decide what the robot should do because we thought the whole robot design should revolve around the robot's purpose. That was a BIG mistake because the list of items for the robot to do was extensive. It was going to be a cross between R2-D2, Wall-E and Commander Data. It was going to be the most awesome robot ever and then, as you can probably guess, we got really overwhelmed and had to scale everything way back.

When initially designing your first few robots, you should start with either designing/buying the robot chassis (body) or figuring how the robot should move. It really is a chicken and egg dilemma here because what chassis you use really defines how the robot will move, but on the other hand, how the robot should move (or even not move at all) defines what type of chassis you need; therefore, I usually try to take both into account when designing robots.

Chassis and movement

One of the easiest ways to get started building a robot is to purchase an off-the-shelf tank chassis. Some of these chassis even have the motors and motor controllers built in, or they are designed to work together, which makes it even easier to get started. The first robot that I built used the Rover 5 Tank Chassis and the Rover 5 Motor Controller Board, designed and manufactured by Dagu Electronics. Here is a photograph of my first robot:

All of the parts for this robot were bought including the top plate that the boards are connected too. Purchasing all of these parts can quickly get expensive, especially as you begin to add additional sensors and equipment to the robot.

If you are planning on building numerous robots, or even doing a lot of other prototyping with the Arduino, it is worth the money to purchase a 3D printer because rather than buying premade parts for the chassis, you can design and print your own. As an example, a little while ago I took the Rover 5 chassis back out and created another robot with it that I named BuddyBot. It was created using parts that I designed and printed, which enabled me to get the BuddyBot the look I wanted it to have. The following photograph show the front of the BuddyBot:

You can even print the entire chassis if you want. The following photograph shows two robot chassis that I designed and printed with my 3D printer. The chassis on the left is one where I printed the entire chassis, and the one on the right is an experimental chassis that I am designing. I also printed the Omni wheels for the chassis on the right:

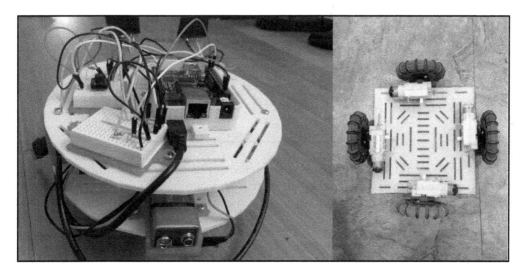

Chassis come in all shapes and sizes. Finding or designing the perfect one is usually one of the easiest parts of building your robot. The key is to make sure you have a chassis that can be expanded. If you notice, in the preceding photograph, the plates have long and narrow rectangular groves in them. These are designed so we can remove and add new parts very easily. You will notice that the little breadboards, on the left-hand robot in the preceding photograph, can be unscrewed and removed or moved to a different part of the robot very easily.

By designing the robot in a modular way, we can very quickly expand its functionality. You will want to avoid chassis that have limited expandability because, unless you are designing a robot for a particular function, you will always be thinking of new components and functionality that you would like to add to it.

We have talked a lot about chassis so far but what about defining how the robot will move? The Rover 5 chassis that I showed earlier in this chapter uses tank treads to move. The yellow robot that was in the previous photograph uses the standard and very cheap Arduino car motor and wheels (which is shown in the following photograph) while the experimental chassis uses Omni wheels that I printed.

Using tank treads to move your robot gives you the ability to move on almost any terrain. However, they are more expensive than standard wheels/motors, and the chassis has to be designed for them as well. You also tend to need motors with higher torque, but we will talk about motors in the next section.

Using the Arduino car motor and wheel is a much cheaper option than the tank treads, however you are limiting your robot to indoor use unless you have a high-end chassis like the Bogie Runt Rover shown in the following photograph:

Bogie Runt Rover is a very nice chassis to work with, but I would definitely recommend having a 3D printer so you can print your own expansion parts for it.

Omni wheels are a very particular type of wheels that have small discs around the wheel that allow them to be pushed laterally because the small discs will spin, which reduces the friction. If you ask people that have used Omni wheels their opinion of them, the answers you receive will range the entire spectrum as some people absolutely hate them and think they are useless, while others love them.

You can also make robots that walk. These types of robots are beyond an introductory book like this, and I would recommend for your first couple of robots you stick with something that uses tank treads or wheels.

Now let's look at motors and how we would power them.

Motors and power

Deciding what motor to use and how to power them can be one of the hardest decisions you make when you start building robots because there are so many choices. The following photograph shows some of the motors that I have used in my projects:

It can save you a lot of money to get used motors, and there are a number of ways that you can acquire them. I have bought numerous used remote-controlled cars and other electronics like old DVD players and removed the motors from them. That is where the two smallest motors shown in the preceding photograph came from; however, if you want more powerful motors, look at removing the motors from power drills. The largest motor in the preceding photograph came from an old Ryobi 12V drill.

When you first start building robots, I would recommend starting with the Arduino car motor. They are very easy to use and are designed to power robotic cars. They can also be powered by a wide range of power sources because they can handle voltages as low as 3V and as high as 12V. The recommended voltage range is 6V to 8V. However, I often use a 12V battery that has a maximum current of 1.3A to power these motors. When you purchase motors, make sure you read the specifications carefully to ensure the motor is rated for the power source you are using in your project.

To control the motors, you will want to use a motor controller. The L298 motor controller that we showed in `Chapter 15`, *DC Motors and Motor Controllers*, is a perfect motor controller to start with. It handles a wide range of voltages from 5V up to 46V and current up to 2A. You can refer back to `Chapter 15`, *DC Motors and Motor Controllers*, to see how to use this controller.

Powering the motors can be confusing at first especially when purchasing batteries. To begin with, you do not want to power the motors from the Arduino's 5V power source. For small robotic projects, you can use AA batteries or a 9V battery. For chassis that can handle a larger battery, I would recommend getting a small 12V battery like the Duracell Ultra 12V 1.3Ah one shown in the following photograph:

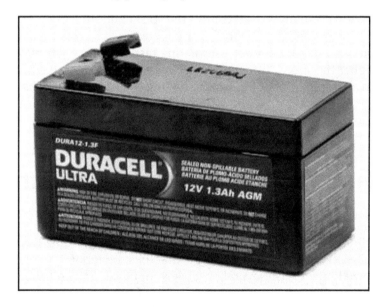

One critical factor when picking out the battery is the specifications of the motors and how many you will have. When you connect the motors, through the motor controllers, to the battery, you will be connecting them in parallel to each other. If you recall the comparison between series and parallel circuits in `Chapter 3`, *Circuit Diagrams*, you will remember that in a parallel circuit each branch will have the maximum voltage that is output from the power source. However, the current will be divided up between the branches. This means that if our battery can produce 12V and 1.2A and we are attempting to power 6 motors, then each motor will have 12V and can draw 200mA (1.2A divided by 6) if each motor is rotating at the same speed. Therefore, the Duracell Ultra that was previously shown will be fine to power six Arduino car motors, but if you are looking at using larger motors you may need a battery with a larger capacity.

You may have noticed that the Duracell battery was rated at 12V and 1.3Ah. Do not confuse the Ah rating with Amps. A battery is rated by the capacity, and 1.3Ah means that it can continuously supply 1.3A for 1 hour before you need to recharge it.

One good rule to use when picking up the battery that will power your robotic project is; it is better to have more power rather than less. This rule works great unless you take it to the extreme and try to use a 12V battery to power a little RC car that has two small motors.

With the L298 motor controller, we can control the speed and direction of the wheels, which enables us to steer robots with wheels or tank tracks. The robot will turn if the wheels or track on one side of the robot are rotating faster than the wheels or track on the other side. The higher the speed difference is between the two sides, the faster the robot will turn. You can also spin a robot in place by having the wheels or tracks on one side of the robot rotating in a forward direction while the wheels or track on the other is rotating in the reverse direction.

Autonomous robot–obstacle avoidance and collision detection

If you want to build an autonomous robot, you will need to have some form of obstacle avoidance and collision detection with the logic that tells the robot how to move around obstacles. We showed how to use several obstacle avoidances and collision detection sensors in `Chapter 10`, *Obstacle Avoidance and Collision Detection*, but the question may be how we develop logic to go around or avoid objects that are detected.

Before we start to discuss the logic of obstacle avoidance, let's take a look at the BuddyBot robot again:

If you look closely at the "eyes" on the BuddyBot, you may recognize them as the MaxSonar EZ1 Ultrasonic range finder that was discussed in `Chapter 10`, *Obstacle Avoidance and Collision Detection*. To refresh your memory, the MaxSonar EZ1 works by sending an ultrasonic pulse in a particular direction. If there is an object in the path of the pulse, then it is reflected back in the form of an echo. The sensor determines the distance to the object by measuring the time it takes for the echo to be received. The following photograph shows what the MaxSonar EZ1 looks like:

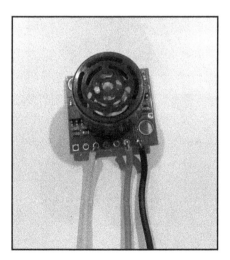

The BuddyBot uses two MaxSonar range finders to help with the obstacle avoidance logic. Let's see how this works. The first thing we need to do is to determine at what distance we want to start the obstacle avoidance logic. For example, we probably do not have to worry about avoiding obstacles that are five feet away if we are building a small robot that is moving around in a house. If we have a large robot that is moving around in a factory maybe five feet is a reasonable distance to start the obstacle avoidance logic at. The environment that the robot will be moving in plays a big part in designing the obstacle avoidance logic.

Once the correct distance to start the obstacle avoidance logic at is determined, we can then start building the logic. By using two sensors, we are able to determine at what angle the robot is approaching the object at. This next diagram shows the robot approaching an object at a slight angle:

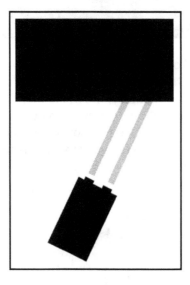

When the robot approaches an object at an angle like this, we can compare the distance being reported by both range finders and determine that the object is closer to the left side of the robot. By determining that the left side of the robot is closer to the object, we can use some fundamental logic to tell the robot to turn right until the object is out of range, as shown in the following diagram:

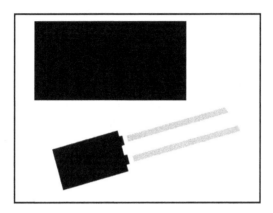

Once the object is out of range, we can start moving forward again. This is very basic obstacle avoidance and does require constant polling of the rangefinder. For a cheaper option, because the MaxSonar rangefinders are fairly expensive as compared to other sensors, we could use the infrared obstacle avoidance sensor that is also described in Chapter 10, *Obstacle Avoidance and Collision Detection*. The reason that I prefer the MaxSonar rangefinder is that the infrared radiation beam that is emitted from the IR sensor is a much narrower beam than the sound wave that is emitted from the MaxSonar rangefinder. With the wider beam from the rangefinder, it is less likely that we will miss objects that are slightly to the left/right or higher/lower than the sensor.

You will also want to put crash sensors around the robot as well; these can be used to detect when the robot bumps into something. These work very well on the back of the robot to detect if the robot bumps into something while it is reversing. Obstacle avoidance can be a very complicated subject, one that is easy to get started in, as shown here, but can because very complex.

Now let's look at how we can control a robot remotely.

Remotely controlling a robot

The RF remote that we saw in `Chapter 18`, *Remotely Controlling the Arduino*, is a much better choice for remotely controlling a robot than the IR remote because the RF remote does not need line of sight for the signal. The only issue with the RF remote is there usually is not enough buttons for everything we want our robots to do. This lack of buttons can be overcome by making the robot an autonomous robot where it can use object avoidance to move around on its own but then use the remote to tell the robot to perform a specific task. These tasks can include things like telling the robot to start/stop moving, play music through a speaker or to bring you a drink from the refrigerator.

At the end of `Chapter 18`, *Remotely Controlling the Arduino*, you were challenged to think outside the box for ways to remotely control a project other than using a wireless signal. Think about your answers to that challenge and see if you can use them to control a robot.

One of my favorite ways to control a robot is through voice recognition using the MOVI shield that we saw in `Chapter 14`, *Speech Recognition and Voice Synthesizer*. With the MOVI shield, we can program in commands such as *turn right*, *turn left*, *stop*, or anything else you want your robot to do.

Another sensor that we can use is a sound sensor where we put three or four in a circular or square pattern around the robot, so it can detect the direction that the sound is coming from and then move in that direction. We could also use a single sound sensor to start or stop the robot when we clap or make some other loud noise.

Let's look at how we can provide feedback to the user of the robot.

User feedback

We always want to provide some way to provide feedback to let us know what is going on with the robot. This is very handy when we are programming the robot for debugging purposes. If you recall the image of the BuddyBot from earlier in this chapter, the nose was lit up by a multicolor LEDs. The LED color indicated what the robot was supposed to be doing and if it detected obstacles on the left or right side. By seeing what color the LED was, I knew what the robot was supposed to be doing, and if it wasn't doing it, I knew something was wrong with the programming or hardware.

Using multicolor LEDs is one of the easiest and quickest ways to add feedback from our robot. We can very quickly set different colors to indicate different activities. If we need to indicate multiple activities at the same time, we could add multiple LEDs without it costing much. I prefer multicolor LEDs to single-color ones because we can use different colors to indicate different things, while the single-color LEDs are either on or off, and therefore they can only indicate one item.

Another way to provide feedback is with sounds. In Chapter 12, *Fun with Sound*, we saw how the Arduino could produce sound using various speakers. If you have ever used the Roomba or another autonomous robot vacuum, you are aware that when something is wrong, like the vacuum is stuck on something, it makes a sound to let the owner know that it is stuck. Playing a sound is another easy way to add feedback from the robot.

In Chapter 12, *Using LCD Displays*, we say how we could use LCD displays to relay messages from our project. Adding an LCD display enables your project to give precise information to the user. These can be in the form of words or images.

User feedback should be one of the first things you put into your project because it can be used to help with troubleshooting while you are developing your project. Now let's talk about how we can make things rotate.

Making things rotate

In Chapter 16, *Servo Motors*, we saw how we could use a servo motor to open and close a robotic claw; however, a servo motor can do so much more than that. With a servo motor, as we saw with the robotic claw, we can rotate the motor to a specific angle. In the past, I have attached a MaxSonar Range Finder to a servo motor and pointed the sensor straight ahead. Then when the rangefinder detected an object in front of the robot, the servo would turn the rangefinder in different directions, so it could determine the best direction to move in. This enabled me to build an autonomous robot, with obstacle avoidance, using only a single rangefinder.

We could also attach a light source to a servo motor to make a rotating searchlight that will enable you to see where the robot is in the dark, or equally it is just a really cool addition to your robot with really no functional purpose.

An essential piece of advice I recommend is that when you first start creating robots you avoid attempting to attach a robotic arm to your robot. Robotic arms usually weigh too much for most small to medium robot chassis, and it takes a lot of programming to get them to move precisely where you want them to. I am not saying that you should not think about adding a robotic arm to your robot. However, it is a really advanced project that will take a lot of time to perfect.

Non-robotic projects

If you are not into robots, there are still a lot of other projects that you can do with the Arduino. Let's take a look at a few of these.

Weather station

In Chapter 9, *Environment Sensors*, we saw how to use numerous environmental sensors like the DHT-11 temperature/humid sensor and the rain sensor. We could use these sensors with any additional ones, like a wind speed sensor to develop a weather station. Just remember that you will need to put the Arduino and other electronic parts in a weatherproof container.

Smart thermostat

In Chapter 9, *Environment Sensors*, we saw how an Arduino could read the temperature and humidity with the DHT-11 temperature/humidity sensor. If we connected a window or portable air conditioning unit or a humidifier to a relay board, as described in Chapter 17, *Using a Relay*, we can tune the air conditioning unit and/or humidifier on or off automatically.

In fact, using a relay board, you can turn almost any AC, powered device on or off depending on what various sensors read. For example, we could very easily create our own clapper clone by connecting a sound sensor to the Arduino and using the Arduino to turn a relay on or off each time it detects a loud sound.

Proximity sensor

In Chapter 10, *Obstacle Avoidance and Collision Detection*, we saw how to use the MaxSonar rangefinder. If we attached the rangefinder to a servo motor, which we saw in Chapter 16, *Servo Motors*, we could create a proximity sensor that could rotate up to 180 degrees to monitor a large portion of a room. When the proximity first starts up, it would need to run through an initial cycle to map where the objects are, to begin with, and then monitor if anything changes after the initial run. If the proximity sensor does detect that something is closer than it should be, it could play an alarm through a speaker as described in Chapter 12, *Fun with Sound*.

These are just some of the projects that you can create with the Arduino. Now for your last challenge.

Challenge

I started learning how to use prototyping boards, like the Arduino, so I could build robots. You may want to build other projects like a weather station using the temperature, humidity and rain sensors, or maybe a security system using the motion sensor that is described in Chapter 8, *Motion Sensor*.

Whatever you are interested in, I challenge you to make some super cool projects with the Arduino. Once you have finished, I would love to see pictures with descriptions of your project and will even post some of them on my blog giving the submitter credit for their project. If you have a video on YouTube of your project, I would love to see that as well. You can send your pictures, and descriptions to: mastering.arduino@gmail.com.

Summary

In the first part of this book, we learned about the Arduino and basic electronics. These chapters were designed to give you, the reader, a basic understanding of how the Arduino worked and how you can safely attach electronic components to your Arduino without damaging yourself or the electronic components.

Next, we learned about the development tools that we can use with the Arduino and how to program the Arduino. These chapters gave you a basic understanding of the development tools and also the Arduino programming language.

In the last chapter, we combined what we learned earlier in the book and showed how to connect various different components to the Arduino. These chapters were designed to show you a wide range of different components that interface with the Arduino in different ways. This will hopefully give you enough variety that when you purchase various sensors for your own project, you will understand how they interface with the Arduino even though they were not explicitly cover in this book.

In the next two chapters, we will take a look at Bluetooth radios to see how we can implement two-way communication in our projects.

20
Bluetooth LE

In this book so far, all external communication with our Arduino projects has been in a closed environment. By closed environment, we mean that our project simply received information or direction from a remote control and no information was transmitted out from the project. There are numerous use cases where we need to transmit information from our Arduino project to an external device such as a smartphone or other IoT device. When there is a need such as this, one of the first technologies that is brought up is **Bluetooth Low Energy**, also known as **Bluetooth LE** or Bluetooth Smart.

In this chapter, you will learn:

- What Bluetooth LE is
- How the Bluetooth LE radio works
- What the GAP profile is
- What the GATT profile is
- How to use the HM-10 Bluetooth LE radio module with the Arduino

Introduction

One of the most common misunderstandings of Bluetooth LE by people that are not familiar with the technology is that Bluetooth LE is a lightweight subset of **Bluetooth Classic**. This is not true, as Bluetooth Classic and Bluetooth LE are two fundamentally different protocols with different design goals.

Most wireless technologies, such as Wi-Fi and Bluetooth Classic, were designed to satisfy a wide range of use cases; however, the design of Bluetooth LE is a bit different. Originally created by Nokia and known as **Wibree**, the primary design focus of Bluetooth LE was to create a radio standard with the lowest possible power consumption and optimized for low cost, low complexity, and low bandwidth.

Bluetooth LE specifications were released as part of the Bluetooth 4.0 Core specifications in June of 2010. The Bluetooth Core Specifications are overseen and updated by the Bluetooth **Special Interest Group (SIG)**.

 You can find information about Bluetooth and download the specifications from their site at https://www.bluetooth.com; however, at over 2500 pages, I would recommend that you read this chapter instead of the Bluetooth specifications unless you are looking for help with insomnia.

The adoption rate of Bluetooth LE has been much faster than most other wireless technologies. The reason for this is the adoption of the Bluetooth LE standard in the mobile industry where Apple and Google have put significant effort into including reliable Bluetooth LE stacks with the iOS and Android operating systems and developing easy-to-use-and-understand Bluetooth LE APIs for developers. This makes it very easy for developers to create and interact with devices that have Bluetooth LE radios.

The reason that the mobile industry has been pushing for the adoption of Bluetooth LE is that devices that connect using Bluetooth LE consume far less power, hence the name Bluetooth Low Energy, as compared to other wireless technologies such as Bluetooth Classic and Wi-Fi. This leads to longer battery life for their phones, which leads to happier customers.

Bluetooth devices come in three types, where each type supports either Bluetooth Classic, Bluetooth LE or both. The following chart shows what each type supports:

Device Type	Bluetooth Classic Support	Bluetooth LE Support
Pre-4.0 Bluetooth	Yes	No
Single-Mode	No	Yes
Dual-Mode	Yes	Yes

While the Bluetooth 5.0 specifications were released in June of 2016, at the time this book is being written, there are very few Bluetooth modules for the Arduino that support this new specification. In fact, at this time, there is very little support for the Bluetooth 4.1 or 4.2 specifications either; therefore, in this book, we are going to focus on the Bluetooth 4.0 specifications, knowing that Bluetooth 5.0, 4.2 and 4.1 are all backward compatible with this standard.

In order to design IoT devices that use Bluetooth LE we really need to understand the technology so we know when actually to use it. Therefore, we will delve into this technology a lot further than we have with other technologies in this book. We will start off by looking at the radio specifications.

Bluetooth LE radio

Since we will be using Bluetooth LE 4.0 for all the projects in this book, the following specifications are for this standard:

Range	Up to 100 meters
Radio Frequency	2.402 - 2.481 GHz
Radio Channels	40 (37 data and 3 advertising)
Maximum OTA Data Rate	1 Mbit/s
Application Data Throughput	0.125 Mbit/s
Network Topologies	Point-to-Point
Network Standard	IEEE 802.15.1

Bluetooth LE has a maximum range of 100 meters, but this is very dependent on the surroundings. When the connected devices are indoors, the range will be dramatically reduced due to walls and other obstacles that the radio signal needs to go through. Generally, we will not see a range close to 100 meters unless we are outside in an open field. Even then it is rare to get a range of 100 meters.

The Bluetooth LE radio operates on over 40 channels, ranging from 2.402 GHz to 2.481 GHz. Of these channels, 37 are reserved for data and three are reserved for advertising. The reason for the multiple channels is Bluetooth LE uses frequency hopping to mitigate interference. The three advertising channels are used for discovery of devices. Once a device is discovered, the same channel is used to exchange initial connection parameters. Once the connection parameters have been exchanged, the regular data channels are used for communication.

The following figure shows the channels used by Bluetooth LE:

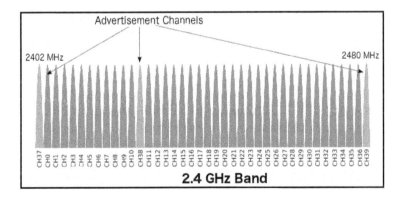

Bluetooth LE is designed to operate at low power, and the best way to avoid using power is to turn the radio off as often as possible and for as long as possible. For Bluetooth LE, this is achieved by sending short bursts of packets at a certain frequency, and in between those radio bursts, the radio is powered off. This is often referred to as **Racing to Idle**, since the radio is essentially sending out information as fast as it can and then shutting down for a short period of time.

The biggest sacrifice that we make for the low power usage of Bluetooth LE is the application data throughput. In the previous chart, we saw that the Bluetooth LE radio has a maximum over-the-air data rate of 1 Mbit/s. However, we also listed the application data throughput as only 0.125 Mbit/s. This means that the radio can theoretically transfer 1 Mbit per second; however, with the limitations put on the radio to conserve power, we only have a maximum transfer rate of 0.125 Mbit per second. In a real-world application, we will actually never see anything close to this data transfer rate.

Let's examine the race to idle and the limitations put on by the Bluetooth LE standards to understand why the data throughput is so low. To start off with, the Bluetooth LE specifications define that the connection interval, which is the time interval between two consecutive connection events (when the two devices exchange data), to be between 7.5 ms and 4 s. This means that if we set the connection interval to the shortest time possible (7.5 ms), we will have a maximum of 133 connection events per second.

The radio can transmit up to six data packets per connection event, where each data packet can contain a maximum of 20 bytes of user data. This gives up a maximum of 120 bytes for each connection event.

If we put all of the information together, we get the following formula:

133 connection events per second * 120 bytes per event = 15960 bytes/second
or ~ .125 Mbit/second

This shows that the maximum data throughput would be 0.125 Mbit/second; however, as we mentioned earlier, even that number will never be reached because we generally will never max out the bytes per packet or have 133 connection events in one second. Devices themselves can add further limitations to the connection interval and data packets per connection. In the best case, we will generally see around 5-10 KB per second for the data throughput. This means that we generally only want to use Bluetooth LE technology when we are exchanging short bursts of data and avoid it when we wish to exchange large amounts or even stream data.

Now let's look at the network topology for Bluetooth LE connections.

Network topology

Bluetooth LE devices can communicate with other Bluetooth LE devices through broadcasting or an established connection. Each of these methods have their own advantages and disadvantages. We will begin by looking at the network topology when the devices communicate by broadcasting. For the projects in this chapter, we will focus on exchanging data over established connections, but it is good to have a knowledge of how data can be exchanged by broadcasting. Therefore, we will cover it in this introduction section.

Bluetooth LE broadcasting

The following diagram shows the network topology for a broadcast network:

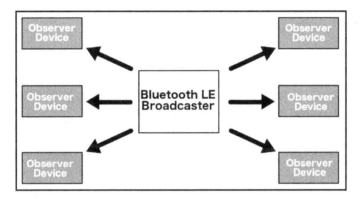

There are two roles defined when broadcasting:

- **Broadcaster**: This device sends non-connectable advertising packets at set time intervals to any other device that is listening
- **Observer**: This device scans the advertising frequencies to receive the non-connectable advertising packets that the broadcaster is sending out

Broadcasting data is the only way that a device can send data to multiple devices. The standard broadcasting packet can have a payload of 31 bytes of data, which is usually used to describe the broadcaster and its capabilities. However, it can also include any custom information that we wish to broadcast to other devices. Bluetooth LE also supports an optional second advertising payload called the **scan response**, which can include an additional 31 bytes of data.

Broadcasting is fast and easy if we wish to transmit small amounts of data to multiple devices; however, there is no security or privacy on the data. The security is usually the biggest reason to avoid using broadcast packets. However, another big reason to avoid using broadcast packets is the observer does not have the ability to send any data back to the broadcaster.

Now let's look at Bluetooth LE connections

Bluetooth LE connections

The following diagram shows how Bluetooth connections work:

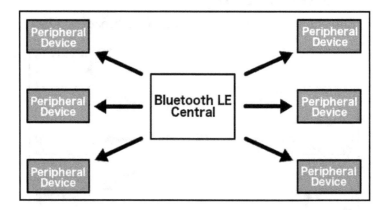

As with the Bluetooth LE broadcasting topology, the connection topology also defines two roles:

- **Central**: The central is usually a device such as, a laptop, tablet or phone. These devices will scan the advertising channels and listen for connectable advertising packets. When a device is found, the central may attempt to establish a connection to the device. After the connection is established the central manages the timing and initiates the data exchanges. The central device can connect to more than one peripheral.
- **Peripheral**: The peripheral is usually a device such as a smartwatch, a weather station or medical device. These devices send out periodic connectable advertising packets and accept incoming connections. Once a connection is established, the peripheral will generally follow the central's timing and exchange data when the central requests it. A peripheral can connect to only one central device.

A peripheral will generally advertise until a central device discovers it and requests a connection. Once the connection is established, the peripheral will stop advertising and then the two devices can exchange data. The data exchange in this topology can go both ways, where the peripheral and central can both send and receive data.

When a central and a peripheral establish a connection, the data that is transmitted and received is organized in units called **services and characteristics**. We will look at this more when we look at the **Generic Attribute Profile** (**GATT**) a little later in this chapter. The thing to understand now is that a Bluetooth LE peripheral can have multiple characteristics, which are used to send and receive data. These characteristics are organized or grouped into services.

The biggest advantage with establishing a Bluetooth LE connection is you can have multiple characteristics to organize your data, and each of these characteristics may have their own access rights and descriptive metadata. Another advantage is the ability to establish secure encrypted connections.

With Bluetooth 4.0, a device can act as a central or a peripheral but not both. Starting with Bluetooth 4.1, this restriction was removed and with newer versions of Bluetooth LE, a device can act as a peripheral, a central or both.

Now let's look at the Bluetooth LE profiles.

Bluetooth LE profiles

Bluetooth LE defines two types of profiles. These are profiles that define the basic mode of operations required by all Bluetooth LE devices to ensure interoperability (Generic Access Profile and GATT) or profiles that are used for specific use cases (health device profile and proximity profile). In this chapter, we will not go into the specific use cases of these profiles; however, we do want to look at both the **Generic Access Profile** (**GAP**) and the Generic Attribute Profile (GATT). We will start off by looking at the GAP.

Generic access profile (GAP)

The GAP defines how devices interact with each other to ensure device interoperability. It defines how Bluetooth LE devices discover each other, establish secure connections, terminate connections, broadcast data and device configuration. This is the lowest level of the Bluetooth LE stack that we will cover in this chapter.

Earlier in this chapter, we saw that a Bluetooth LE device could be in one of two states. In the broadcasting topology, a device can be either the broadcaster (slave) or observer (master). If a connection between the two devices is established, then the devices become either a central (master) or peripheral (slave). We introduced the terms master and slave here to illustrate the states that the devices can be in. The following diagram shows the different states:

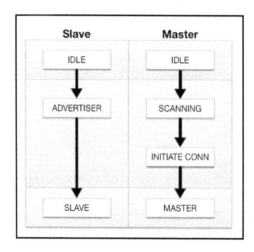

Both types of devices start in an idle or standby state. This is the initial state when the device is reset. A slave device will then become an advertiser, where it is advertising specific data, letting any master device know that it is a connectable device and what services it offers. After the idle state, a master device will begin scanning for slaves that are advertising. When a master receives an advertisement, it will send a scan request to the advertiser, and the slave will respond back with a scan response. This is the device discovery process.

After the device discovery process, if the master wishes to connect to the advertising device, it will initiate a connection. When initiating the connection, the master will specify the connection parameters. Once the connection is made the devices will assume their roles as master and slave. With Bluetooth LE 4.0, the slave device can have only one master. Also, with Bluetooth LE 4.0, the devices can act as either a master or a slave but not both. With later revisions of the Bluetooth specifications, these limitations have been removed. I know we have mentioned that a couple of times so far in this book, but it is important to keep in mind when developing your devices.

We mentioned that the master specifies the number of connection parameters when initiating the connection. Some of these parameters are:

- **Connection Interval**: With Bluetooth LE uses a frequency hopping scheme the two devices that are communicating most know which channel to transmit/receive on, when to switch channels and when to make the connection. The time interval between the connection attempts is known as the connection interval.
- **Slave Latency**: The slave latency gives the slave device the option to skip a certain number of connection events. The slave device must not skip more than the number of connection events defined by this parameter.
- **Supervision Time-out**: The supervision time-out is the maximum amount of time between two successful connection events. If this time is exceeded, the device will terminate the connection, and the slave device will go back to an unconnected state.

There are a number of considerations when deciding what to set these parameters to. The main consideration is power consumption and data throughput. As the throughput increases, the device will use more power. For example, if we lower the connection interval, thereby increasing the number of connection attempts per second, the power consumption of the device will increase because the radio will be on more of the time. By reducing the slave latency, once again the radio will be on more. Therefore, it will also increase the power consumption. When working with a Bluetooth LE radio, you need to balance the power consumption with the data throughput needs for your project. There is no magic ratio that will work for all types of devices; it is something you will need to look at on a project-by-project basis.

In the example projects for this chapter, we will show how to AT commands to adjust the various settings for the Bluetooth LE module. Now let's look at the GATT profile.

Generic attribute (GATT) profile

While the GAP profile defines the low-level (advertising and connection) interactions of Bluetooth LE devices, the GATT profile defines the details on how the devices exchange data. The GATT is also the reference framework for all attribute-based profiles that define specific use cases, such as heart rate and blood pressure profiles.

As with the GAP profile, the GATT profile defines two roles. These roles are the client and the server. When you look at the diagram on how this works, the roles may seem a little odd at first; however, once we see how Bluetooth LE devices exchange data it will make more sense. The client role in the GATT profile corresponds to the master role in the GAP profile and the server role in the GATT profile corresponds to the slave role. The following diagram illustrates this:

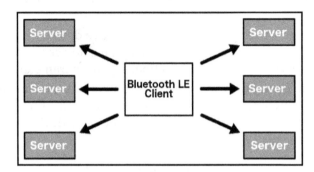

In this diagram, we can see that one client can have multiple servers; however, each server can have only one client. In the GATT profile, the client (central role in the GAP) requests information from the server (peripheral in the GAP). While we are showing the relationship between the GATT and GAP roles, it is worth noting that the GATT and GAP roles are actually independent of each other, and in later versions of the Bluetooth LE specifications, a device can act as both a central and a peripheral.

The smallest data entity defined by the GATT profile is the attribute. An attribute is an addressable piece of information that is located on the server, which can be accessed and potentially modified by the client. Each attribute is uniquely identified by a **UUID** (**universally unique identifier**), which can be either a 16-bit or 128-bit number. This identifier is known as the handle.

The GATT profile defines a set of permissions that are associated with all attributes. Permissions specify which operations can be performed on each attribute. These permissions are:

- **Access Permissions**: Access permissions specify which actions can be performed on the attribute. Each attribute will have one of the following permissions:
    - **None**: The attribute cannot be read or written by the client
    - **Readable**: The attribute can be read by the client
    - **Writable**: The attribute can be written to by the client
    - **Readable and Writable**: The attribute can be read and written to by the client

- **Encryption**: Encryption permission determines the level of encryption that is required for a client to access the attribute
    - **No Encryption** (Security Mode 1, Level 1): No encryption is required
    - **Unauthenticated Encryption** (Security Mode 1, Level 2): The connection must be encrypted; however, the encryption keys do not need to be authenticated
    - **Authenticated Encryption** (Security Mode 2, Level 2): The connection must be encrypted, and the encryption keys must be authenticated
- **Authorization**: Authorization permission determines whether the user needs to be authorized to access the attribute
    - **No Authorization**: No authorization is required to access the attribute
    - **Authorization Required**: Authorization is required to access the attribute

The GATT defines a strict hierarchy, which organizes the attributes. The attributes are grouped into services, where each service may contain zero or more characteristics. These characteristics can include zero or more descriptors. Services, characteristics and descriptors are all attributes within the GATT server.

The following diagram shows the hierarchy:

Services are used to group related attributes into a common entity. Each service is identified by a unique UUID, which can be either 16-bit for officially adopted service types or 128-bit for custom service types.

 You can see a list of officially adopted services on the Bluetooth SIG site here: `https://www.bluetooth.com/api/silentlogin/login?return=` `http%3a%2f%2fwww.bluetooth.` `com%2fspecifications%2fgatt%2fservices`.

If you look at the Heart Rate service, you can see that this service contains three characteristics.

Characteristics are containers for the data, where each characteristic encapsulates a single data point. As with the services, a characteristic is identified by either a 16-bit or 128-bit UUID. Characteristics are the main entry point that a Bluetooth LE client interacts with a server.

 You can find a list of officially adopted characteristics on the Bluetooth SIG site here: `https://www.bluetooth.com/specifications/gatt/` `characteristics`.

Access permissions for each characteristic should be either read-only or write-only. It is very rare to have a characteristic that has both read and write permission. As an example, if we wanted to create a simple serial interface for our Bluetooth LE device, we would create a TX characteristic to transmit data with read-only permission for the client and an RX characteristic to receive data with write-only permission for the client. We would not want to create a single characteristic that had both read and write permission because as the client writes data to it, the server could overwrite it.

The descriptors are used to provide the client devices with additional information about the characteristics and their values.

 You can find a list of officially adopted descriptors on the Bluetooth SIG site here: `https://www.bluetooth.com/specifications/gatt/` `descriptors`.

Generally, the server simply responds to a client's request for data from a characteristic; however, it is possible for a server to initiate the communication by using server-initiated updates. There are two types of server initiated updates, which are:

- **Notification**: Characteristic value change notifications are used when the server is configured to notify the client that the value of the characteristic has changed but does not expect the client to acknowledge the notification. Notification is turned on for all projects in this chapter; however, it is only used in the first and third projects.
- **Indication**: Characteristic value change indications are used when the server is configured to indicate to the client that the value of the characteristic has changed and expects the client to acknowledge that it has received the indication.

Now that we have a very basic understanding of Bluetooth LE and how it works, let's look at the HM-10 Bluetooth module that we will be using in this chapter.

HM-10 Bluetooth module

The HM-10 is a Bluetooth 4.0 module that is based on the TI CC2530 or CC2541 Bluetooth **SOC** (**System-on-Chip**). The HM-10 is a very popular Bluetooth 4 module for the Arduino, mostly due to its cheap cost and ease of use. The HM-10 provides a standard serial connection to the Bluetooth layer. This allows for a very straightforward interface; however, it does hide the actual Bluetooth LE layer.

In `Chapter 21`, *Bluetooth Classic*, when we look at the HC-05 Bluetooth module, you will notice that the interface between the HC-05 and HM-10 use the same serial interface; however, understanding the difference between Bluetooth LE and Bluetooth Classic technologies will help you decide which to use in your project.

We can control the module using AT commands, and we will look at how to do that in the project section of this chapter. The following photograph shows what the HM-10 Bluetooth module looks like:

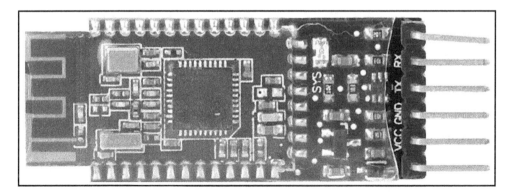

The HM-10 has six pins. However, we are only interested in the middle four, which are:

- **VCC**: Connected to the 3.3V power out on the Arduino
- **GND**: Connected to the ground on the Arduino
- **TX**: Transmit pin, connected to one of the digital pins on the Arduino
- **RX**: Receive pin, connected to one of the digital pins on the Arduino

Now let's look at all of the components that we will need for the projects that we will be doing in this chapter.

Components needed

For these, projects you will need the following items:

- One Arduino Uno or compatible board
- One HM-10 Bluetooth 4.0 module
- One DHT-11 temperature sensor
- One LED
- One 4.7K resistor
- One 3.3K resistor
- One 1.1K resistor
- One 330k resistor
- Jumper wires
- Breadboard

You will need a Bluetooth LE app for your phone/tablet or computer. I use the *BTCommander – Serial port HM10* (`https://itunes.apple.com/us/app/btcommander-serial-port-hm10/id1312640906?mt=8`) app on my phone. There are plenty of other apps, such as the *nRF connect* app for Android (`https://play.google.com/store/apps/details?id=no.nordicsemi.android.mcphl=en_US`) and iOS (`https://itunes.apple.com/us/app/nrf-connect/id1054362403?mt=8`).

Circuit diagrams

In this chapter, we will be doing three projects. The first project will be a simple serial communication project that will send a text to and from the Arduino through the Bluetooth radio. We will also show how to configure the Bluetooth radio in the first project. For the second project, we will show how to toggle a LED on and off remotely. For the final project, we will build a mini weather station, which will enable us to read the temperature remotely through the Bluetooth radio. Each project will have its own wiring diagram included with it; however, if you wish to connect all of the hardware at once, the following diagram shows how everything is connected:

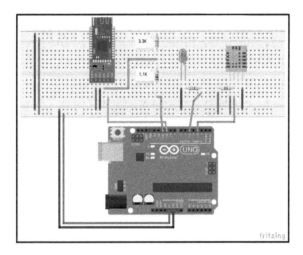

This diagram may initially look complex compared to earlier diagrams; however, if we break it down into three parts, it really is not that complex. The first part is the DHT-11 temperature sensor, which is located on the right-hand side of the breadboard. The second part is the LED, which is in the center of the breadboard. The third and final part is the HM-10 Bluetooth module, which is located on the left-hand side of the breadboard.

We have already covered wiring the DHT-11 temperature sensor in Chapter 9, *Environment Sensors*, and the LED in Chapter 4, *Basic Prototyping*. Therefore, we will repeat the explanation here.

To connect the HM-10 Bluetooth module to the Arduino, the **VCC** pin is connected to the power rail on the breadboard, which is connected to the 5V power out on the Arduino. The **GND** pin on the Bluetooth module is connected to the ground rail on the breadboard, which is connected to the ground pin on the Arduino. The **RX** pin on the Bluetooth module is connected directly to the digital **pin 10** on the Arduino.

Connecting the **TX** pin on the Bluetooth module to the Arduino is a little different. For this, we want to ensure that the voltage does not exceed 3.3V. Therefore, we use a simple voltage divider. A voltage divider is a simple circuit that will turn a larger voltage into a smaller one. For this, we use two resistors, a 1.1K and a 3.3K. These two resistors are connected in series, where one end of the 3.3K resistor is connected to ground, and one end of the 1.1K resistor is connected to digital **pin 11** on the Arduino. The **TX** pin is connected between the two resistors.

Project 1 – serial communication

For this first project, we are only going to use the HM-10 Bluetooth module and the Arduino. You will need to connect the Bluetooth module to the Arduino as shown in the previous circuit diagram. The following diagram shows this:

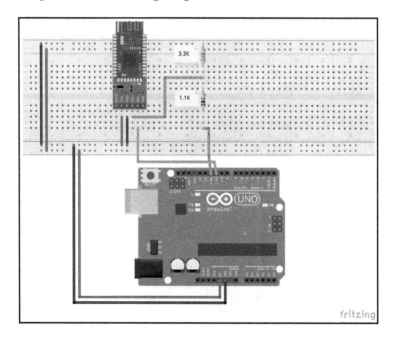

Now we need to write the code to access the Bluetooth module. We will be using the SoftwareSerial library to interface with the HM-10 Bluetooth LE module. This library was developed to allow serial communication on digital pins other than pins 0 and 1. There may be limitations to this library if you are using a board other than the Uno. You can reference the documentation (https://www.arduino.cc/en/Reference/softwareSerial) to see if your board has any limitations.

The code will need to start off by including the `SoftwareSerial` header file and then initiate an instance of the `SoftwareSerial` type. We also want to add a new line whenever a new command is issued from the serial monitor. Therefore, we will also define a Boolean variable that will be set to true whenever a new command comes in (this will make it easier to read the responses within the serial monitor). The following code will do this:

```
#include <SoftwareSerial.h>
SoftwareSerial HM10(10, 11); // RX | TX
bool addNewLine = false;
```

When creating the instance of the `SoftwareSerial` type, you need to define what pins to use for receiving (**RX**) and transmitting (**TX**) data. The first value is the `RX` pin and the second value is the `TX` pin.

Next, we need to initialize both the serial monitor and the `SoftwareSerial` instance. We will do that within the `setup()` function. We also want to let the user know when the application is ready to accept commands or connections. The following code shows the code for the `setup()` function:

```
void setup()
{
  Serial.begin(9600);
  HM10.begin(9600);
  Serial.println("Connected to HM-10.  Try connecting from any device or
  issue AT commands");
}
```

When we initiate the serial monitor and the `SoftwareSerial` interface, we need to define what the baud rate will be. Both the HM-10 Bluetooth module and the serial monitor communicate at a baud rate of 9600. Once everything is initiated, a message is displayed to the serial monitor letting the user know that everything is good to go.

In the `loop()` function, we will need to write anything that the user types into the serial monitor to the Bluetooth module and write anything that comes in from the Bluetooth module to the serial monitor. The following code shows the `loop()` function:

```
void loop()
{
  if (Serial.available()) {
    HM10.write(Serial.read());
    addNewLine = true;
  }

  if (HM10.available()) {
    if (addNewLine) {
```

```
        Serial.write("\r\n");
        addNewLine = false;
    }
    Serial.write(HM10.read());
  }
}
```

In this function, we use the `available()` function on both the serial monitor and the instance of the `SoftwareSerial` type to check whether either device has data to read. If so, we read the data and write it to the other device. In the section that reads the serial monitor and writes to the `SoftwareSerial` instance, we set the `addNewLine` Boolean variable to true so the next time we write to the serial monitor, we will write a carriage return and new line. In the section that reads from the Bluetooth module and writes to the serial monitor, we check to see whether the `addNewLine` Boolean variable is `true`, and if so, we write a carriage return and new line to the serial monitor before setting the `addNewLine` variable to `false`.

There are two ways that we can use this application. The first is to enter **AT (ATtention)** commands into the serial monitor, which enables you to get/set configuration settings on the Bluetooth module and also control the module. The second is to use the Bluetooth LE app on your phone to read and write values to the Bluetooth modules. Let's look at the AT commands first.

To send an AT command to the Bluetooth LE module, run the preceding code blocks and then open the serial monitor, which is part of the Arduino IDE. Once everything is initiated, you will see the `Connected to HM-10. Try connecting from any device or issue AT commands` message displayed in the monitor. This indicates that the module is ready, and everything is initiated. Once you see the message, type `at` in the input box and either click the **Send** button or hit *Enter*. You should see an `OK` response from the Bluetooth module. The output should look like this:

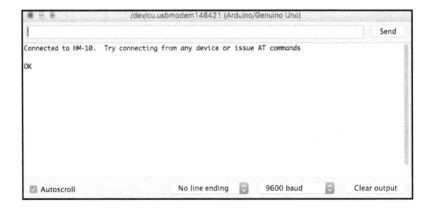

To send an AT command, you would use the following format:

```
Set item: AT+{command}{new setting}
Query item: AT+{command}?
```

To set an item, you type in the letters AT followed by the plus sign (+), the command and the new setting without any spaces. For example, to set the name that the Bluetooth module will advertise to "Buddy," we would issue the following command:

```
at+nameBuddy
```

Note: AT commands are case insensitive.

To query the item, we would type in the letters AT followed by the plus sign (+), the command and then a question mark (?). For example, to query the name that the Bluetooth module is advertising, we would use the following command:

```
at+name?
```

We can use the application that we just wrote to set the configuration manually from the serial monitor or we can set the configurations from within the application by using the print() function from the SoftwareSerial library like this:

```
HM10.print("AT+Name?\r\n");
```

Let's look at some of the commonly used commands. Any of these can be used from the serial monitor or within the code as we just showed.

Test command

Command	Response	Parameters	Description
AT	OK	None	This is a test command that can be used to test the connection to the Bluetooth module.

Query software version

Command	Response	Parameters	Description
AT+VERR	Version number	None	This command will return the version number of the firmware for the module.

Restore factory default

Command	Response	Parameters	Description
AT+RENEW	OK+RENEW	None	Restore the factory defaults.

Restart module

Command	Response	Parameters	Description
AT+RESET	OK+RESET	None	Restarts Bluetooth module.

Query MAC (Media Access Control) address

Command	Response	Parameters	Description
AT+ADDR?	OK+ADDR:{MAC Address}	None	This command can be used to query the MAC address of the Bluetooth radio.

Set name

Command	Response	Parameters	Description
AT+NAME{parameter}	OK+set{parameter}	None	This command will set the name for the module.

Query name

Command	Response	Parameters	Description
AT+NAME?	OK+NAME{parameter}	None	This command will return the name of the module.

Set the advertising interval

Command	Response	Parameters	Description
AT+ADVI{parameter}	OK+Set:{parameter}	0: 100ms 1: 152.5 ms 2: 211.25 ms 3: 318.75 ms 4: 417.5 ms 5: 546.25 ms 6: 760 ms 7: 852.5 ms 8: 1022.5 ms 9: 1285 ms A: 2000 ms B: 3000 ms C: 4000 ms D: 5000 ms E: 6000 ms F: 7000 ms	This command will set the advertising interval for the Bluetooth LE module. The parameter should be 0-F.

Query the advertising interval

Command	Response	Parameters	Description
AT+ADVI?	OK+get:{parameter}	None	This command will retrieve the current advertising interval and will return a parameter of 0-f.

Set advertising type

Command	Response	Parameters	Description
`AT+ADTY{parameter}`	`OK+set:{parameter}`	0: Advertising Scan Response, Connectable 1: Only allow the last device connect in 1.28 seconds 2: Only allow Advertising and Scan Response 3: Only allow Advertising	This command will set the advertising type.

Query advertising type

Command	Response	Parameters	Description
`AT+ADTY?`	`OK+get:{parameter}`	None	This command will retrieve the current advertising type and will return a parameter of 0-3.

Set baud rate

Command	Response	Parameters	Description
`AT+BAUD{parameter}`	`OK+set:{parameter}`	0: 9600 1: 19200 2: 38400 3: 57600 4: 115200 5: 4800 6: 2400 7: 1200 8: 230400	This command will set the baud rate for the serial interface of the Bluetooth module.

Query baud rate

Command	Response	Parameters	Description
AT+BAUD?	OK+get:{parameter}	None	This command will retrieve the current baud rate and will return a parameter of 0-8.

Set characteristic id

Command	Response	Parameters	Description
AT+CHAR{parameter}	OK+set:{parameter}	0x0001 -> 0xFFFe	This command will set the ID for the characteristic.

Set service id

Command	Response	Parameters	Description
AT+UUID{parameter}	OK+set:{parameter}	0x0001 -> 0xFFFe	This command will set the ID for the service.

Query service id

Command	Response	Parameters	Description
AT+UUID?	OK+get:{parameter}	None	This command will retrieve the current service ID.

Set role

Command	Response	Parameters	Description
AT+ROLE{parameter}	OK+set:{parameter}	0: Peripheral 1: Central	This command will set the role of the Bluetooth module.

Query role

Command	Response	Parameters	Description
AT+ROLE?	OK+get:{parameter}	None	This command will return the role of the Bluetooth module.

Clear last connected device

Command	Response	Parameters	Description
AT+CLEAR	OK+CLEAR	None	Clears the address of the last connected device.

NOTE: The at+clear command is only used when the device is in central mode.

Try to connect to last connected device

Command	Response	Parameters	Description
AT+CONNL	OK+CONN{parameter}	L: Connecting E: Connect Error F: Connect Fail N: No Address	This command will attempt to connect to the device that last successfully connected to it.

NOTE: The at+connl command is only used when the device is in central mode.

Try to connect to an address

Command	Response	Parameters	Description
AT+CON{parameter}	OK+CONN{parameter}	A: Connecting E: Connect Error F: Connect Fail	This command will attempt to connect to a device with the specified address.

 NOTE: The at+con command is only used when the device is in central mode.

Set pin code

Command	Response	Parameters	Description
AT+PASS{parameter}	OK+set:{parameter}	000000 -> 999999	Sets the pin code for connection.

Query pin code

Command	Response	Parameters	Description
AT+PASS?	OK+get:{parameter}	None	This command will return the current pin code.

Set module power

Command	Response	Parameters	Description
AT+POWE{parameter}	OK+set:{parameter}	0: -23db 1: -6db 2: 0db 3: 6db	Sets the power for the module.

Query module power

Command	Response	Parameters	Description
`AT+POWE?`	`OK+get:{parameter}`	None	This command will return the current module power.

Set bond mode

Command	Response	Parameters	Description
`AT+TYPE{parameter}`	`OK+set:{parameter}`	0: PIN code not needed 1: Auth without PIN code 2: Auth and PIN 3: Auth and bond	This command sets the authentication needed when connecting to this device.

Query bond mode

Command	Response	Parameters	Description
`AT+TYPE?`	`OK+get:{parameter}`	None	This command will return the current authentication needed to connect to this device.

Set notify information

Command	Response	Parameters	Description
`AT+NOTI{parameter}`	`OK+set:{parameter}`	0: Don't Notify 1: Notify	This command enables or disables the notification when a device connects are disconnects.

Query notify information

Command	Response	Parameters	Description
`AT+NOTI?`	`OK+get:{parameter}`	None	This command will return if the device will send a notification when a device connects or disconnects.

We can only issue AT commands to the Bluetooth module when another device is not connected to it. Once a device is connected to the application code that we wrote takes over, and the data that is typed into the serial console is sent to the connected device. Let's see what happens when we connect to the Bluetooth module from another device. I will be using the *BTCommander – Serial Port HM10* app to show how this works.

With the application running on the Arduino, start up the Bluetooth application on your phone/tablet or computer. The *BTCommander* app will look like this:

To connect to a device, press the blue connection button, which looks like an outlet plug, located at the upper right side of the application. Once you press the button, you should see a list of devices that the application can connect to. This screen looks like this:

This screen shows all devices that are advertising and are close enough to connect. Earlier in this chapter, when we ran the AT+nameBuddy command, we renamed our device to Buddy. Therefore, we know that is the device that we want to connect to. If we tap that device and then tap on the **Connect** button at the upper right side of the application, the application will attempt to connect. If the connection attempt is successful and the AT+NOTI setting on the Bluetooth module has the notifications enabled, we should see OK+CONN on the serial console as shown in the following screenshot:

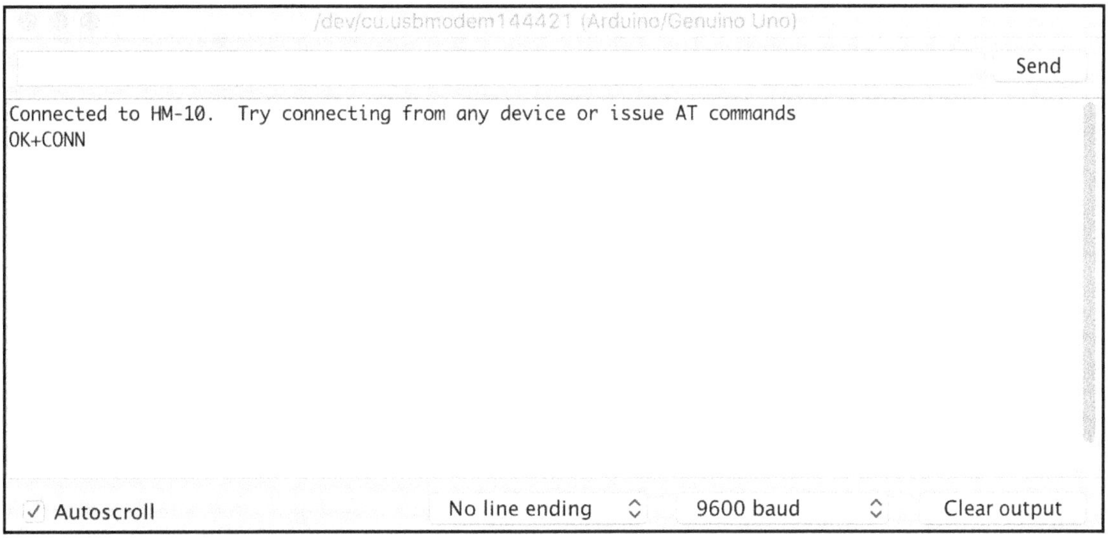

```
/dev/cu.usbmodem144421 (Arduino/Genuino Uno)

                                                                    Send

Connected to HM-10.   Try connecting from any device or issue AT commands
OK+CONN




✓ Autoscroll              No line ending   ↕    9600 baud    ↕    Clear output
```

When the connection is successful, the application will go back to the main screen. Now let's type a message in the input box at the bottom of the screen. For example, here we will type a simple `hello` message as shown in the following screenshot:

Once the message is entered, press the button next to the input box that looks like a paper airplane to send the message. If the message was successfully sent, we will see it in the serial console as shown in the following screenshot:

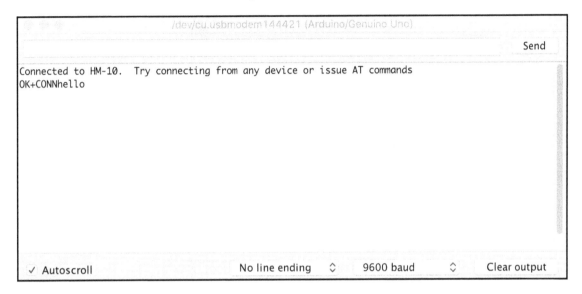

What is happening here is the message that is entered in the application is being passed from the phone application to the chrematistic on the HM-10 Bluetooth module, so our application can read it. The message is sent one character at a time.

To send a message back, type the message in the input box of the serial console and press the send button. If the message was sent successfully, we should see it in the application as shown in the following screenshot:

In this screenshot, we can see that the hello message was sent from the application and the Hello from Arduino was received from the connected device. When a message is sent from the HM-10 Bluetooth module back to the phone application, the application writes the message to the characteristic (one character at a time) and the Bluetooth module uses a notification to notify the client (the phone application) that there is new data.

If we press the connection button again in the *BTCommander* application to disconnect, and the AT+NOTI configuration is set to notify, we will see an OK+LOST message in the serial console as shown in the following screenshot:

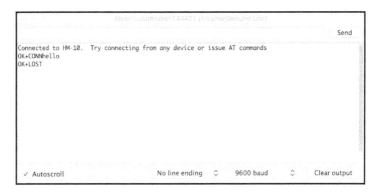

Now let's see how we can use the Bluetooth module to control an LED from our phone.

Project 2 – controlling LED

In this project, we will turn an LED that is connected to the Arduino on or off depending on the input from the phone. The first thing we will need to do is to add the LED to our circuit. The following diagram shows the new circuit:

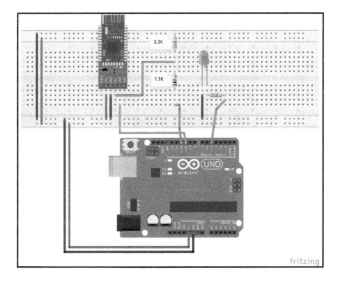

The LED is connected to the digital 5 pin on the Arduino through a 330-ohm resistor. Now we need to write the code to control the LED. We will start by setting up the `SoftwareSerial` library for the Bluetooth module and defining the pin that the LED is connected to. The following code will do this:

```
#include <SoftwareSerial.h>
#define LED_PIN 5
SoftwareSerial HM10(10, 11);
```

We can see that the Bluetooth module is connected to the same pins as the previous example, and the LED is connected to digital pin 5 on the Arduino. In the `setup()` function, we will need to configure the `SoftwareSerial` instance and the mode of the pin that the LED is connected to. The following code shows the `setup()` function for this example:

```
void setup()
{
  pinMode(LED_PIN, OUTPUT);
  digitalWrite(LED_PIN, LOW);
  Serial.begin(9600);
  HM10.begin(9600);
  Serial.println("Connected to HM-10");
}
```

This code starts off by defining the mode of the pin that the LED is connected to. It then configures the serial port for the serial monitor and the `SoftweareSerial` instance. We finally print a message to the serial console letting the user know that everything is configured and ready to go.

In our `loop()` function, we will need to check the `SoftwareSerial` instance, and if a 1 is received from the connected device, it will turn the LED on, and if a 0 is received, it will turn the LED off. If neither a 1 or a 0 is received, then it will ignore the input. Here is the code for the `loop()` function:

```
void loop()
{
  if (HM10.available()) {
    char val = HM10.read();
    if(val == '1') {
      digitalWrite(LED_PIN, HIGH);
    } else if(val == '0') {
      digitalWrite(LED_PIN, LOW);
    }
  }
}
```

In this code, we check to see whether a value is available from the Bluetooth module, and if so, we read the device to get the character that was received. If the character is equal to 1 (the character 1 and not the number 1), we pull the pin that the LED is connected to HIGH to turn the LED on. If the character is equal to 0 (the character 0 and not the number 0), we pull the pin that the LED is connected to LOW to turn the LED off.

Now let's run this application and use the *BTCommander* application to connect to it. From the *BTCommander* application, if we send a 1, the LED will light up, or if we send a 0, the LED will go off. This type of example can be used when we wish to have a phone application to control something that is connected to the Arduino such as an LED, DC Motor or some sensor.

Now let's see how we can retrieve temperature and humidity data from the DHT-11 sensor via Bluetooth LE.

Project 3 – environmental sensor

In this project, we will request, from the phone, that the Arduino send temperature or humidity information depending on the character sent. We will need to add the DHT-11 sensor to our circuit. The following diagram shows how to do this:

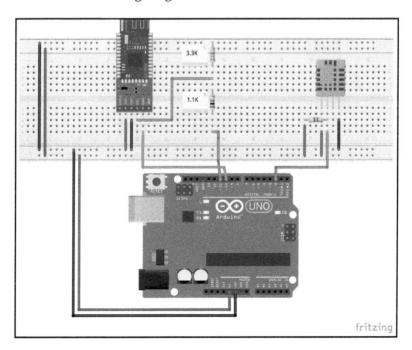

The DHT-11 temperature sensor is connected to the Arduino exactly as we did in Chapter 9, *Environment Sensors*. If you are unsure how to connect this sensor to the Arduino, please refer back to that chapter. Now we will need to write the code, so we can access the data from the sensor with Bluetooth LE service. We will start by setting up the SoftwareSerial library for the Bluetooth module and the DHT-11 temperature sensor. The following code will do this:

```
#include <DHT.h>
#include <SoftwareSerial.h>

#define DHT_PIN 3
#define DHT_TYPE DHT11
DHT dht(DHT_PIN, DHT_TYPE);

SoftwareSerial HM10(10, 11); // RX | TX
```

This code includes the libraries for the DHT temperature sensor and also the SoftwareSerial device. It then defines the pin that the temperature sensor is connected to and the type of sensor. Finally, it creates instances of the DHT and the SoftwareSerial types.

In the setup() function, we will need to configure the SoftwareSerial instance and the mode of the pin that the LED is connected to. The following code shows the setup() function for our example:

```
void setup()
{
  Serial.begin(9600);
  HM10.begin(9600);
  Serial.println("Connected to HM-10");
}
```

This function configures the SoftwareSerial instance and prints a message to the serial console when everything is initiated and ready to go. In the loop() function, we will want to read the input from the device that is connected to the service and then respond back with the appropriate information.

The following chart shows the input and what should be returned:

Input	Property Returned
f	Temperature in Fahrenheit
c	Temperature in Celsius
h	Humidity
F	Heat Index Fahrenheit
C	Heat Index in Celsius

From the chart, we can see that we will have five inputs and each one will return different information back to the remote device. Let's look at the code that will read the input and return the information requested:

```
void loop()
{
  if (HM10.available()) {
    char val = HM10.read();
    if(val == 'f') {
      float fahreheit = dht.readTemperature(true);
      HM10.println(fahreheit);
    } else if(val == 'c') {
      float celsius = dht.readTemperature();
      HM10.println(celsius);
    } else if(val == 'h') {
      float humidity = dht.readHumidity();
      HM10.println(humidity);
    } else if(val == 'F') {
      float fahreheit = dht.readTemperature(true);
      float humidity = dht.readHumidity();
      float hif = dht.computeHeatIndex(fahreheit, humidity);
      HM10.println(hif);
    } else if(val == 'C') {
      float celsius = dht.readTemperature();
      float humidity = dht.readHumidity();
      float hic = dht.computeHeatIndex(celsius, humidity, false);
      HM10.println(hic);
    }
  }
}
```

This code starts by checking the Bluetooth adapter to see whether there is any input available, and if so, it reads the character. If the input character is one of the characters listed in the previous chart, the code retrieves the appropriate value from the DHT-11 sensor and returns the value back to the connected device.

The output from the code in the *BTCommander* iOS app would look similar to this:

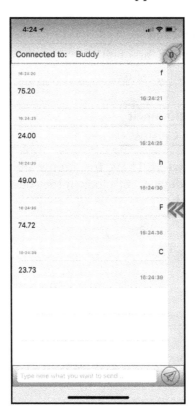

Everything we have shown here is compatible with Bluetooth LE 4.0 and above. As of the time of writing this book, there really are not that many low-cost Bluetooth LE modules for the Arduino that are compatible with the new Bluetooth LE 4.2 and 5.0 standards, which is why we stuck with 4.0 here. The good news is all of the newer standards are backward compatible with the 4.0 standard, so everything we talked about in this chapter will work as newer Bluetooth modules are released that are compatible with the newer standards. Let's look at what features are available with the newer Bluetooth standards.

What is new with Bluetooth 4.1, 4.2 and 5.0?

In this section, we will look at what is new with Bluetooth 4.1, 4.2, and 5.0. While these features are not compatible with the Bluetooth LE 4.0 module that we used in this chapter, eventually Bluetooth modules for the Arduino that are compatible with these standards will be released; therefore, it is good to know what features they offer.

Bluetooth 4.1

Bluetooth 4.1 mainly offers usability updates. One of the most important updates is to allow Bluetooth LE and LTE radios to coexist better. This update allows the radios to coordinate transmissions to decrease the chance of interference. It also makes the data transfer more efficient and allows for better reconnections after connection loss.

The big non-usability change with Bluetooth 4.1 allowed a device to be both a peripheral and a central at the same time.

Bluetooth 4.2

Bluetooth 4.2 offered numerous new features for IoT, security, faster speed and more capacity.

For IoT, Bluetooth 4.2 added **Bluetooth Smart Internet gateways**, which enables Bluetooth 4.2 devices a bridge to the internet. With the internet gateways, Bluetooth 4.2 also added IPv6/6LoWPAN, which enables IPv6 support over a Bluetooth connection.

Bluetooth 4.2 also added extra security with LE Privacy 1.2. The encryption standards with Bluetooth 4.2 comply with the **Federal Information Processing Standards** (**FIPS**), which is a US Government computer security standard.

The transmission packet size was increased by ten times as well. This allows for faster and more reliable data transmissions.

Bluetooth 5.0

Bluetooth offers a number of enhancements,quadrupling the range and doubling the speed. The catch with this is that if a device manufacturer increases the range of their device, the speed will go down; and likewise, if the speed increases, the range will go down.

Bluetooth mesh

One of the latest, and in my opinion, the most exciting, Bluetooth technologies is Bluetooth mesh. All previous Bluetooth technologies relied on a one-to-one or a one-to-many connection where there was always one master/central device. Mesh technology allows Bluetooth devices to establish many-to-many connections, which enables large-scale device networks that do not rely on a central controller. The Bluetooth mesh technology is still in its infancy at the time we are writing this book. However, I believe it is the future of Bluetooth and is a technology worth keeping an eye on.

One thing to note with Bluetooth standards higher than 4.0 is most of the new features are optional and not required to be fully implemented. For example, a manufacturer may say that their device meets the Bluetooth 4.2 standard. However, IPv6/6LoWPAN may not be implemented in the device. A good example of this is the iPhone. My iPhone X is Bluetooth 5.0 compatible; however, it is not capable of running Bluetooth mesh or IPv6/6LoWPAN.

Challenge

For the challenge, take the Nokia 5110 LCD display that we used in `Chapter 13`, *Using LCD Displays*, and the serial communication code that we used in the first project of this chapter and print any message sent from the phone app to the LCD display. This will require some modification to the code in this chapter to use the LCD screen rather than the serial console.

Summary

In this chapter, we learned a lot about Bluetooth LE, starting with a brief introduction on how the radio works and the network topology for Bluetooth LE connections. We learned how the GAP is used by Bluetooth LE devices to discover and connect to other devices. We also saw how the GATT uses attributes (services, characteristics and descriptors) to enable two Bluetooth LE devices to communicate with each other. We finally demonstrated how Bluetooth LE works with three projects at the end of this chapter.

Bluetooth LE is the technology best suited when we wish to use an external device, such as a phone, to control the device that we are building, because almost all smartphones have Bluetooth LE built in and the technology is easy to use. It is also a good technology to use when we wish to send short bursts of data from one device to another. If you wish to build a separate device, such as a remote control, to control your main device or stream a lot of data, then I would recommend a different Bluetooth technology that is known as Bluetooth Classic or Legacy, which we will see in the next chapter.

21
Bluetooth Classic

Bluetooth LE, which we saw in `Chapter 20`, *Bluetooth LE*, is an excellent choice when we need two devices to communicate wirelessly in short data bursts and where power consumption is a concern. There have been changes with Bluetooth LE with versions 4.2 and 5.0. That make it more appealing for devices that need to transfer large amounts of data or even stream data. However, there is another Bluetooth technology that has been doing this for very successfully for many years, this technology is known as Bluetooth Classic. While the name may imply that this technology is out of date, don't let the name fool you as Bluetooth Classic is used in many Bluetooth devices, and until there are more Bluetooth 5.0 modules available for the Arduino that also support some of the newer features, Bluetooth Classic will remain an excellent choice when we need to transfer large amounts of data between two devices.

In this chapter, you will learn:

- What the version numbers of Bluetooth Classic mean
- How the Bluetooth radio works
- The network topology of a Bluetooth network
- How to use the HC-05 Bluetooth module

Introduction

Bluetooth is a wireless technology standard that is used by two devices to transmit or receive data over short distances using a 2.4GHz wireless connection. While the design goal of Bluetooth LE was to create a low power wireless protocol, Bluetooth Classic had different design goals. Bluetooth Classic was created by engineers that work at Ericsson Mobile in Lund, Sweden, as a wireless alternative to serial (RS232) cables. This meant that this new protocol would be required to transmit large amounts of data, or even stream data, over short distances.

The Bluetooth Classic specifications are managed by the **Bluetooth Special Interest Group** (**Bluetooth SIG**) as part of the Bluetooth core specifications. As we mentioned in `Chapter 20`, *Bluetooth LE*, you can find information about both Bluetooth LE and Bluetooth Classic by downloading the specifications form from the Bluetooth SIG site at `https://www.bluetooth.com`.

At first, it may seem strange to cover the newer technology (Bluetooth LE 4.0) prior to covering the older technology (Bluetooth Classic). The reason Bluetooth LE was covered first is that you will find that it is appropriate to use it in the more significant majority of projects that you will be creating with the Arduino, as most projects will want to send short bursts of data, which is what Bluetooth LE is designed for. Bluetooth LE is also easier to integrate with smartphones using Bluetooth LE because every smartphone OS has an easy to use and well documented Bluetooth LE API, which is not the case for Bluetooth Classic. For the cases where you will want to stream data or share large amounts of data between two custom devices, Bluetooth Classic may be more appropriate.

When purchasing a Bluetooth Classic module for your project, you will have a choice of three different Bluetooth versions. These versions are:

- **Bluetooth 2.0 + EDR**: The core specifications for this version were released in 2004. This update to the Bluetooth core specifications contained a number of minor improvements to the Bluetooth standard. The only significant improvement was **EDR (Enhanced Data Rate)**, which increased the data transfer rate to 3Mbits/sec from 1Mbits/sec. The name of the standard reads Bluetooth 2.0 + EDR, which means that the EDR feature is optional. The HC-05 Bluetooth module that we will be using for this chapter is Bluetooth 2.0, compatible which means it does not include the EDR feature. For the vast majority of projects that you will build with the Arduino, Bluetooth 2.0-compatible modules will be fine and are actually preferable since we are able to avoid the secure pairing feature that was introduced with Bluetooth 2.1. While the new pairing feature may be called Simple Secure Pairing, it usually requires human interaction for the pairing process, which we may want to avoid since a lot of Arduino projects do not have the input capabilities to do this.
- **Bluetooth 2.1 + EDR**: The core specifications for this version was released in 2007. This version of the Bluetooth core specifications also offered a number of improvements on the previous version, with the featured improvement being the introduction of **SSP (Simple Secure Pairing)**. SSP overhauled the pairing process, making it both simple and more secure.

- **Bluetooth 3.0 + HS**: The core specifications for this version were released in 2009. The HS in the specification name stands for High Speed. Bluetooth 3.0 + HS can have a theoretical data transfer speed of 24 Mbits/sec, however the data is not transmitted over a Bluetooth connection. When in high-speed mode the data is actually transmitted over an 801.11 (Wi-Fi) connection. The Bluetooth link is only used to negotiate and establish the Wi-Fi connection. As with the Bluetooth 2.X + EDR specification, the HS feature is optional, and you will see devices that only meet the Bluetooth 3.0 standard.

As with Bluetooth LE, to really understand when to use Bluetooth Classic we need to understand the technology itself, so let's dive into in a bit more.

Bluetooth radio

The range of a Bluetooth radio is dependent on the class. The following chart shows the range of a Bluetooth radio by the class:

Class	Power (mW)	Power (dBm)	Range in meters
1	100	20	~100
2	2.5	4	~10
3	1	0	~1

As with any radio technology the area surrounding the radio has a substantial effect on the range of the radio. The range listed in the previous chart is the theoretical maximum range with ideal conditions. The typical range is usually less than this theoretical maximum range.

Where the Bluetooth LE radio operates from 2,402 MHz to 2,480 MHz with each channel being 2 MHz apart, the Bluetooth Classic radio uses 79 channels from 2,402 MHz to 2,480 MHz with each channel being 1 MHz apart. As with Bluetooth LE, the Bluetooth Classic radio uses frequency hopping, where the radio changes channels 1,600 times a second, to reduce interference.

With Bluetooth LE, the radio continuously turns itself off to reduce power, Bluetooth Classic does not do this. This makes the Bluetooth LE radio technology better at short bursts of data with low power while the Bluetooth Classic radio is better at transmitting large amounts of data or data streaming because the radio is continuously on.

All Bluetooth devices have a unique 48-bit address that is assigned to the Bluetooth radio by the manufacturer. The upper half of the address (the most significant 24 bits) is known as the **Organizationally Unique Identifier** and consists of two parts. These parts are the **Non-Significant Address** (**NAP**) and the **Upper Address Part** (**UAP**).

The NAP is the first 16 bits of the address and is used in frequency hopping synchronization. The UAP is the next 8 bits and is assigned to the radio manufacturer by the IEEE organization.

The last 24-bits of the address is known as the **Lower Address Part** (**LAP**). The LAP is assigned by the manufacturer to identify the radio uniquely. The following diagram shows how the Bluetooth address is made up:

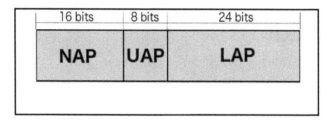

Now let's look that the network topology for Bluetooth Classic.

Network topology

The topology of a Bluetooth Classic piconet is very similar to the topology of a Bluetooth LE network where one device acts as a master and the other devices act as slaves to the master. In a Bluetooth Classic piconet, one master can have up to seven slaves for a total of eight devices in the piconet. The following diagram shows a Bluetooth classic piconet:

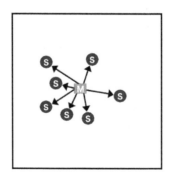

Piconets can interact with other piconets to form what is known as scatternets. A scatternet is one where the master of one piconet acts as a slave in another piconet. This does allow devices in one piconet to share data with devices in other piconets; however, this does require complex synchronization and bandwidth sharing, making these networks more complex and less efficient. It is good to know that we can create scatternets, but it is something that, in my experience, is rarely used.

There is a lot more to Bluetooth than what is described here; however, for the vast majority of use cases you will want to use Bluetooth LE as described in `Chapter 20`, *Bluetooth LE*. With the Arduino, we would use Bluetooth Classic when we want to connect two devices and stream data between them. Let's look at how we would do this with three projects. For the first project we will configure the Bluetooth modules, the second project we will learn how to send and receive data from the Bluetooth module, and in the third project, we will see how we can stream data from one radio to another. We will start off by looking at the components that we will need for these projects.

Components needed

For these projects you will need the following items:

- Two Arduino Uno or compatible boards
- Two HC-05 Bluetooth modules
- One Joystick breakout module for the Arduino
- Jumper wires
- Breadboard

Now let's look at the circuit diagram for our project.

Circuit diagrams

In this chapter, we will be writing code for three projects. In the first project we will be configuring the Bluetooth modules, in the second project we will create an application that will send data, in byte format, from one Bluetooth radio to another and in the last project we will attach a joystick to one of the Arduinos and stream the joystick position to the other Arduino through the Bluetooth connection. The following shows the circuit diagram for our projects:

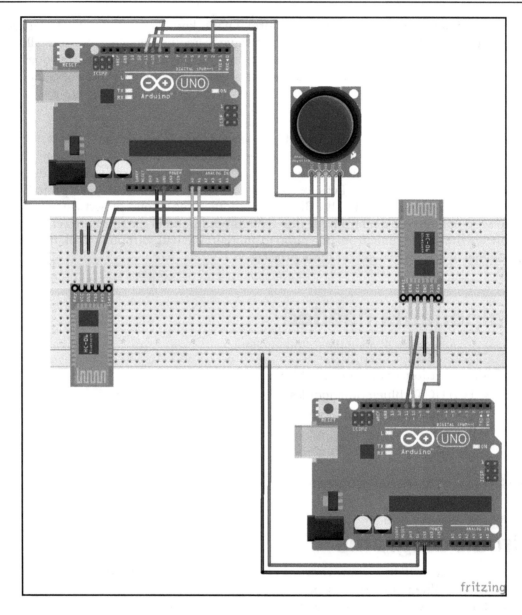

The two Arduino circuits are completely isolated from each other, therefore they do not need a common ground. Both HC-06 Bluetooth modules are connected to the Arduino in the same way where the VCC pin on the HC-06 Bluetooth module is connected to 5V out, and the GND pin is connected to the ground out on the Arduino. The key pin on the Bluetooth module is connected to the digital 9 pin on the Arduino, the RX pin is connected to the digital 10 pin, and the TX pin is connected to the digital 11 pin.

We will want to connect a joystick breakout module to one of the Arduinos. To do this, we will want to connect the VCC pin on the breakout board to the 5V out on the Arduino and the GND pin to the ground out on the Arduino. We will connect the SEK or SW pin, depending on your joystick module, to the digital 2 pin on the Arduino. Finally, we will connect the HOR or *x* axis pin on the breakout board to the Analog 0 pin on the Arduino and the VER or *y* axis pin to the Analog 1 pin.

Now let's look start with our projects.

Project 1 – configuring the Bluetooth modules

To communicate with the HC-05 Bluetooth module, we will use the same SoftwareSerial library that we used in Chapter 20, *Bluetooth LE*. The code that is used to communicate is very similar between the HM-10 (Bluetooth LE) and the HC-05 (Bluetooth Classic). How the two radios transmit and receive the data is a lot different, therefore understanding how the radios work and what they should be used for will define when to use the different technologies.

For this first project, we will be writing an application that will allow us to configure the Bluetooth modules. This code will start off exactly as we did with the Bluetooth LE code by including the SoftwareSerial library and creating an instance of the SoftwareSerial type. The following code shows how to do this:

```
#include <SoftwareSerial.h>
SoftwareSerial HC05(10, 11);
bool addNewLine = false;
```

The first line includes the SoftwareSerial library and the second line creates an instance of the type. The Boolean variable in the last line will be used to tell the application when to add a new line in the serial console.

Now we need to add code to the setup() function that will configure the serial console and the SoftwareSerial instance. The following code shows the setup() function for this first project:

```
void setup()
{
  Serial.begin(9600);
  pinMode(9,OUTPUT);
  digitalWrite(9,HIGH);
  HC05.begin(38400);
```

```
    Serial.println("Connected to HC-05.   Try connecting from any device or
  issue AT commands");
  }
```

This code starts off by setting up the serial console with a baud rate of 9600 and then define that the digital 9 pin will be an output pin and set it to high. The digital 9 pin is connected to the key pin on the HC-05. We pull this pin high to enable the Bluetooth module. We then configure the HC05 instance of the SoftwareSerial type with a baud rate of 38400 and print a message to the serial console letting the user know that everything is configured and ready to go.

You will note, in this first project we set the baud rate of the SoftwareSerial instance to 38400 because we are configuring the Bluetooth module. In the next two projects, we set the baud rate to 9600 because we will be sending and receiving data to/from the Bluetooth module.

In the loop() function, just like in the Bluetooth LE code, we will take any input from the Bluetooth module and print it to the serial console and any input from the serial console we will send out through the Bluetooth module. The following code will do this:

```
void loop()
{
  if (HC05.available())
  {
    if (addNewLine) {
      Serial.write("\r\n");
      addNewLine = false;
    }
    Serial.write(HC05.read());
  }

  if (Serial.available())
  {
    HC05.write(Serial.read());
    addNewLine = true;
  }
}
```

In this function, the first thing we do is to see if there is any data available from the HC05 SoftwareSerial instance (the Bluetooth module) by using the available() function. If there is data available we check to see if we need to add a new line to the serial console by checking the addNewLine Boolean variable. If we need to add a new line, we write a carriage return and line feed to the serial console and then set the addNewLine Boolean variable to false. We then write the data that was received from the Bluetooth module to the serial console.

Next, we check to see if there is any data available from the serial console, also using the `available()` function and if so we write that data to the Bluetooth module which is then transmitted to the connected device. We also set the `addNewLine` Boolean variable to true, so that the next time data is received from the connected device, we will add a carriage return and line feed to the serial console.

Before we plug the Arduino and run this code, we will need to set the HC-05 Bluetooth module into configuration mode. To do this, we will need to press and hold down the button on the Bluetooth module and then plug the Arduino into the computer giving power to the Bluetooth module. In just a couple of seconds, the light on the Bluetooth module will start to blink very slowly; the light will be on for two seconds and then turn off for two seconds. Once the light starts to blink, we can release the button, and the Bluetooth module is ready to be configured.

To configure the Bluetooth module, we issue AT commands similar to how we did it with the Bluetooth LE module. To send an AT command, you would use the following format:

```
Set item: AT+{command}{new setting}
Query item: AT+{command}?
```

To set an item, you type in the letters AT followed by the plus sign, the command and the new setting without any spaces. For example, to set the role of the Bluetooth module to a salve role we would issue the following command:

```
at+role0
```

Note: AT commands are case insensitive.

To query the item, we would type in the letters `at` followed by the plus sign, the command and then a question mark. For example, to query the role of the Bluetooth module, we would use the following command:

```
at+role?
```

To issue the command, we type the command into the input box on the serial console and press *Enter*. We will need to set the serial console to add both an **NL** (new line) and a **CR** (carriage return). The following screenshot shows how to issue an AT command:

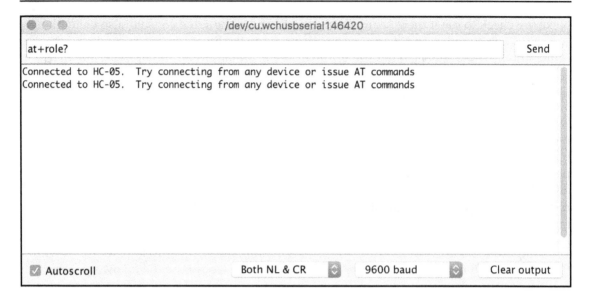

After we type in the `at+role?` command, we press the *Enter* key or the **Send** button to send the command to the Bluetooth module. The Bluetooth module will respond with the results of the query, as shown in the following screenshot:

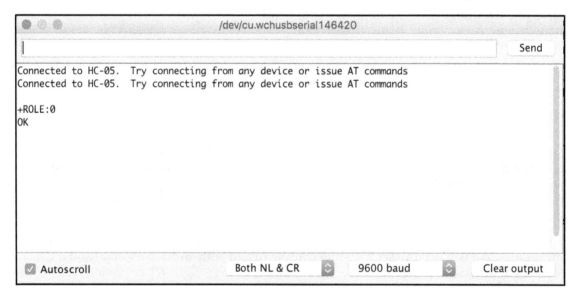

Before we configure the modules, let's look at some of the commands that we can issue to the HC-05 Bluetooth module.

Test command

Command	Response	Parameters	Description
AT	OK	None	This is a test command that can be used to test the connection to the Bluetooth module.

Reset command

Command	Response	Parameters	Description
AT+RESET	OK	None	This command will reset the Bluetooth module.

Query firmware

Command	Response	Parameters	Description
AT+VERSION?	+VERSION:<Param>	None	Returns the version of the firmware on the HC-05 Bluetooth module.

Restore defaults

Command	Response	Parameters	Description
AT+ORGL	OK	None	Restores the HC-05 Bluetooth module to the default settings.

Query module address

Command	Response	Parameters	Description
AT+ADDR?	+ADDR:<Param>	None	Returns the address of the HC-05 Bluetooth module.

Set/Query module mode

Command	Response	Parameters	Description
AT+ROLE?	+ROLE:<Param>	0 Slave 1 Master	Queries the role of the HC-05 Bluetooth module.

Command	Response	Parameters	Description
`AT+ROLE=<Param>`	OK	0 Slave 1 Master	Sets the role of the HC-05 Bluetooth module.

Set/Query UART parameters

Command	Response	Parameters	Description
`AT+UART?`	`+UART:<Param1>, <Param2>,` `<Param3>`	Param1 = Baud Rate Param2 = Stop Bit Param3 = Parity	Queries the UART parameters.

Command	Response	Parameters	Description
`AT+UART=<Param1>, <Param2>,` `<Param3>`	OK	Param1 = Baud Rate Param2 = Stop Bit Param3 = Parity	Sets the UART parameters.

Set/Query connection mode

Command	Response	Parameters	Description
`AT+CMODE?`	`+UART:<Param>`	0 Connect to Fixed Address 1 Connect to any address 2 Slave-loop	Queries the connection mode of the HC-05 Bluetooth module.

Command	Response	Parameters	Description
`AT+CMODE=<Param>`	OK	0 Connect to Fixed Address 1 Connect to any address 2 Slave-loop	Sets the connection mode for the HC-05 Bluetooth module.

Set/Query bind address

Command	Response	Parameters	Description
`AT+BIND?`	`+BIND:<Param>`	None	Queries the address that the module is configured to bind to.

Command	Response	Parameters	Description
`AT+BIND=<Param>`	OK	Fixed address	Sets the address to bind to.

Now that we have seen most of the AT commands let's configure the two Bluetooth modules. We are going to need to configure one of the Bluetooth modules as the master and the other one as a slave. For the purposes of the next two projects, I configured the Bluetooth module that is connected to the same Arduino as the joystick as the slave. This, however, is not necessary and either module can be the master or slave.

Let's start off by configuring the slave device. To do this connect one of the Arduinos to the computer, run the application that we wrote at the beginning of this section and then run through the command that we will outline in the next few paragraphs.

The first thing we will want to do is to issue the test AT command to the Bluetooth module. The module should respond back with an OK message. If you do not get a response back, check to make sure that the serial console is configured to send both the NL and CR. If you receive an error response, try issuing the AT command again.

Now that we are sure that the serial monitor and the Bluetooth module are talking, we will want to see what the UART settings are currently set to for this module. To do this send the AT+UART? command. For the examples in this chapter, we are going to assume that the UART settings are 9600 Baud, 0 stop bits, and 0 parity. If this is not how your module is configured then issue the following command:

AT+UART=9600,0,0

The next thing we want to do is to set the role of the device to a slave role. To do this, we issue the following command:

AT+ROLE=0

Finally, we will want to retrieve the address of this Bluetooth module. The following command will retrieve the address:

AT+ADDR?

Make sure the address is written down because we will be using it when we configure the master device.

The commands that we ran to configure the slave module are:

Command	Response
AT	OK
AT+UART?	+UART:9600,0,0 (if not, set it to this)
AT+ROLE=0	OK
AT+ADDR?	+ADDR:{address}

Now let's configure the master. To do this, connect the other Arduino to the computer (remember to press and hold the button as you power up the module), run the code we wrote at the beginning of this section and issue the commands that we will go through in the next few paragraphs.

As with the slave device, the first thing we will want to do is to issue the AT command to the Bluetooth module. The module should respond back with an OK message. If you do not get a response back, check to make sure that the serial console is configured to send both the NL and CR. If you receive an error response, try issuing the AT command again.

Now we will want to see what the UART settings are for the module. To do this send the AT+UART? command. For the examples in this chapter, we are going to assume that the UART settings are 9600 Baud, 0 stop bits, and 0 parity. If this is not how your module is configured then issue the following command:

```
AT+UART=9600,0,0
```

The next thing we want to do is to set the role of the device to a master role. To do this, we issue the following command:

```
AT+ROLE=1
```

Now we will want to set the connection mode to connect to a fixed address (mode 0). To do this issue the following command:

```
AT+CMODE=0
```

Since we are telling the Bluetooth module to connect to a fixed address, we need to give it the address of the slave device we need it to connect to.

To do this, issue the following command:

```
AT+BIND=????,??,??????
```

The question marks are the address of the slave device. When we queried the address of the slave device the address was returned separated with colons like this, 98d3:31:300e42. When entering the address in the BIND command, the address needs to be separated by commas like this 98d3,31,300e42.

The commands that we used to configure the master device are:

Command	Response
AT	OK

AT+UART?	+UART:9600,0,0 (if not, set it to this)
AT+ROLE=1	OK
AT+CMODE=0	OK
AT+BIND=????,??,?????? (question marks are the address of the slave device)	OK

Now if we reset both devices by recycling the power, the two Bluetooth modules should connect. Start off by recycling the power on the slave device, and you will see the LED blinking rapidly. Then recycle the power on the master and once the two devices connect the LED on both devices will blink rapidly twice, then turn off for two seconds and then repeat. This light sequence indicates that the two devices are connected.

If the devices do not connect, the most common mistake that is made is to type in the wrong address in the AT+BIND command. I would start off by checking that by running the AT+BIND? command and verifying the address is correct. If that is correct, then verify the AT+CMODE, and AT+ROLE commands ran properly by running the AT+CMODE? and AT+ROLE? commands. Now that we have the two Bluetooth modules connected let's go on to project two.

Project 2 – serial connection, sending data

For this project, in order to see the data going from one device to the other, you will need two computers. One connected to the master device and one connected to the slave device. If you do not have two computers, it is still worth reading through this section to understand the protocol that we are creating because we will be using the same protocol for the third project as well.

When we are streaming data or sending large amounts of variable length data, we need some way to tell the receiving device where a new message starts and where it ends. Luckily for us, there are built-in ASCII codes that allow for this. The 0x01 **SOH (Start Of Heading)** and the 0x04 **EOT (End Of Transmission)** codes can be used to tell the receiving device when a message starts and when it ends.

In this project and the next one, the protocol that we will define is when the receiving device receives a 0x01 ASCII character, it will know that a new message has started. When it receives a 0x04 ASCII character, it will know that the message has ended and everything between the 0x01 and the 0x04 characters are the message itself.

If you are not familiar with ASCII codes, the following chart shows the ASCII chart:

Dec	Hex		Dec	Hex		Dec	Hex		Dec	Hex		Dec	Hex		Dec	Hex		Dec	Hex		Dec	Hex	
0	00	NUL	16	10	DLE	32	20		48	30	0	64	40	@	80	50	P	96	60	`	112	70	p
1	01	SOH	17	11	DC1	33	21	!	49	31	1	65	41	A	81	51	Q	97	61	a	113	71	q
2	02	STX	18	12	DC2	34	22	"	50	32	2	66	42	B	82	52	R	98	62	b	114	72	r
3	03	ETX	19	13	DC3	35	23	#	51	33	3	67	43	C	83	53	S	99	63	c	115	73	s
4	04	EOT	20	14	DC4	36	24	$	52	34	4	68	44	D	84	54	T	100	64	d	116	74	t
5	05	ENQ	21	15	NAK	37	25	%	53	35	5	69	45	E	85	55	U	101	65	e	117	75	u
6	06	ACK	22	16	SYN	38	26	&	54	36	6	70	46	F	86	56	V	102	66	f	118	76	v
7	07	BEL	23	17	ETB	39	27	'	55	37	7	71	47	G	87	57	W	103	67	g	119	77	w
8	08	BS	24	18	CAN	40	28	(	56	38	8	72	48	H	88	58	X	104	68	h	120	78	x
9	09	HT	25	19	EM	41	29	)	57	39	9	73	49	I	89	59	Y	105	69	i	121	79	y
10	0A	LF	26	1A	SUB	42	2A	*	58	3A	:	74	4A	J	90	5A	Z	106	6A	j	122	7A	z
11	0B	VT	27	1B	ESC	43	2B	+	59	3B	;	75	4B	K	91	5B	[	107	6B	k	123	7B	{
12	0C	FF	28	1C	FS	44	2C	,	60	3C	<	76	4C	L	92	5C	\	108	6C	l	124	7C	|
13	0D	CR	29	1D	GS	45	2D	-	61	3D	=	77	4D	M	93	5D	]	109	6D	m	125	7D	}
14	0E	SO	30	1E	RS	46	2E	.	62	3E	>	78	4E	N	94	5E	^	110	6E	n	126	7E	~
15	0F	SI	31	1F	US	47	2F	/	63	3F	?	79	4F	O	95	5F	_	111	6F	o	127	7F	DEL

Basically, when we transmit character data between two Bluetooth Classic devices, we are actually sending the ASCII codes. For example, if we send the word "Dog," we are actually sending three bytes of data, which are 0x44 (D), 0x111 (o), and 0x67 (g). With the protocol that we are defining, if we send the word Dog, we would send five bytes of data because we need to start with the 0x01 character and end with the 0x04 character. The five bytes that we would send would be 0x01, 0x44, 0x111, 0x67 and 0x04.

Now let's look at the code to send and receive the messages between the two Bluetooth modules. This code will run on both the master and the slave devices. We will start off by including the SoftwareSerial library in the project and creating an instance of the SoftwareSerial type. The following code does this:

```
#include <SoftwareSerial.h>
SoftwareSerial HC05(10, 11);// RX | TX
bool newMessage = true;
```

The first line includes the SoftwareSerial library in the project, and then the next line creates an instance of the SoftwareSerial type. The third line creates a global variable that will define when a new message is started.

Now we will need to configure the serial console and the HC05 SoftwareSerial instance in the setup() method. The following code will do this:

```
void setup()
{
```

```
      Serial.begin(9600);
      pinMode(9,OUTPUT);
      digitalWrite(9,HIGH);
      HC05.begin(9600);
      Serial.println("Connected to HC-05. ");
}
```

In this code, we start off by configuring the serial console with a baud rate of 9600. We then define that the digital 9 pin will be an output pin and set it to high. The digital 9 pin is connected to the key pin on the HC-05 Bluetooth module. We pull this pin high to enable it. We configure the `HC05` instance of the `SoftwareSerial` type with a baud rate of 9600 and then print a message to the serial console letting the user know that everything is configured and ready to go.

The `loop()` function will need to monitor both the serial console and the `HC05` `SoftwareSerial` instance for new data coming in. If it receives new data from the serial console, it will need to transmit it out through the Bluetooth module, and if it receives new data from the Bluetooth module, it will need to display the data in the serial console. The following code does this:

```
void loop()
{
  if (HC05.available())
  {
    byte val = HC05.read();
    Serial.write(val);
    if (val == 0x04)
    {
      Serial.write("\r\n");
    }
  }
  if (Serial.available())
  {
    if (newMessage)
    {
      HC05.write(0x01);
      newMessage = false;
    }
    char val = Serial.read();
    if (val == '~')
    {
      HC05.write(0x04);
      newMessage = true;
    }
    else
    {
      HC05.write(val);
```

```
        }
      }
    }
```

In this function, we check to see if there is any data available from the HC05 SoftwareSerial instance and if so, it is read into the val variable. The val variable is then written to the serial console. We then see if the val variable is equal to 0x04 and if so we write a carriage return and line feed to the serial console because that particular message has ended.

Now we check to see if there is any data available from the serial console and if so, we check to see if we are starting a new message by checking if the newMessage variable is equal to true. If the newMessage variable is equal to true, we write a 0x01 character to the HC05 SoftwareSerial instance and then set the newMessage variable to false. We then read the character from the serial console and see if it is equal to the tilde (~) character. We are going to use the tilde character to specify that the message has ended therefore when the user types in a tilde we will write the 0x04 character to the HC05 SoftwareSerial instance and set the newMessage variable to true because this particular message has ended. If the character does not equal a tilde, we write the character to the SoftwareSerial instance.

Now if we run this code on both the master and slave device, whatever we type into the serial console on one device will be transmitted to the other device through the Bluetooth modules. The message will continue to be printed on one line of the serial console until the user types in a tilde signifying the end of the message.

Transmitting text back and forth is good but we can do that with Bluetooth LE as we saw in Chapter 20, *Bluetooth LE*. Let's do something that is a bit more useful by looking at how this can be used as a remote control by connecting an Arduino joystick module to one of the devices and streaming the joystick position to the other device.

Project 3 – joystick remote control

If you have not connected the joystick breakout module to one of the Arduino's you will need to do it before you start this project. Once the joystick breakout module is connected to the Arduino, we will write the code that will read the position of the joystick and transmit it to the other Arduino via the HC-05 Bluetooth modules; however, before we do this we need to figure out the protocol that we are going to use.

For this example, we will use the same protocol that we used in the previous project, where the message will start off with a `0x01` byte and end with a `0x04` byte and everything in between is the message itself. The message itself will contain two bytes, one that indicates the *x* position of the joystick and one that indicates the *y* position. Therefore, a complete transmission will contain a total of four bytes likes this:

```
0x01 - Start of header
0xDD - X position (221 decimal)
0xDD - Y position (221 decimal)
0x04 - End of transmission
```

Now that we have the protocol that will be used to transmit the joystick position from one Arduino to the other let's begin by writing the code that will run on the Arduino that the joystick breakout module is connected to. The position of the joystick is read through the two analog pins that are connected to it. We also need to bring the SEL pin, which is connected to the digital 2 pin, high.

The first thing we will need to do in the code is to include the `SoftwareSerial` library for the Bluetooth module, create an instance of the `SoftwareSerial` type and define the pins that the joystick module is connected to. The following code will do this:

```
#include <SoftwareSerial.h>
#define SW_PIN 2 // digital pin Joystick
#define BT_PIN 9 // digital pin Bluetooth
#define X_PIN 0  // analog pin
#define Y_PIN 1  // analog pin

SoftwareSerial HC05(10, 11);
```

In this code, we define the SEL pin for the joystick to be the digital 2 pin, the key pin on the Bluetooth module to be the digital 9 pin and the *x*/*y* axes to be the analog 0 and 1 pins.

In the `setup()` function we will need bring both the `SW_PIN` and the `BT_PIN` high and initialize both the serial console and the instance of the `SoftwareSerial` instance. Here is the code for the `setup()` function:

```
void setup()
{
  pinMode(BT_PIN,OUTPUT);
  digitalWrite(BT_PIN,HIGH);
  pinMode(SW_PIN,OUTPUT);
  digitalWrite(SW_PIN,HIGH);
  HC05.begin(9600);
  Serial.begin(9600);
  Serial.println("Connected to HC05.");
}
```

This code should look very familiar by now. The first four lines initialize the digital pins and pull them high. The next two lines initialize the `SoftwareSerial` instance and the serial console with baud rates of 9600. Finally, a message is printed to the serial console letting the user know that everything is ready to go.

In our `loop()` function, we will need to read the position of the joystick and then write the message to the Bluetooth module. The following code will do this:

```
void loop()
{
   int xpos = analogRead(X_PIN) / 4;
   int ypos = analogRead(Y_PIN) / 4;
   HC05.write(0x01);
   HC05.write(xpos);
   HC05.write(ypos);
   HC05.write(0x04);
   delay(500);
}
```

The first two lines read the *x* and *y* axes of the joystick module. When reading an analog pin the values that are returned range from 0 to 1024; however, we only want to send a single byte to represent the position of the joystick. A single byte can have a range from 0 to 255, therefore we divide the value from the analog read by `4`.

After we retrieve the values for the *x* and *y* axes of the joystick, we need to send the message through the Bluetooth module with these values. The next four lines of code writes a `0x01` (SOH), the value of the *x* axis, the value of the *y* axis and finally a `0x04` (EOT). After the message is sent, we pause for 500 milliseconds and then loops back.

Now that we have the code that will run on the Arduino that the joystick is connected to, we need to write the code that will run on the Arduino that will receive the data. This code will need to start off by including the `SoftwareSerial` library for the Bluetooth module and create an instance of the `SoftwareSerial` type. We will also need to define a buffer that will be used to store the data as it comes in through the Bluetooth module. The following code will do this:

```
#include <SoftwareSerial.h>
#define MAXBUF 255
#define BT_PIN 9 // digital pin Bluetooth
SoftwareSerial HC05(10, 11);
byte buf[MAXBUF];
```

This code starts off by including the `SoftwareSerial` library and then defines the max size for the input buffer, which is `255`. While we could limit the size of the buffer to four because we know that each message will be four bytes in size, we always want to have extra space in the buffer, especially with wireless communication, in case the message gets messed up in transmission. If this was a production system, I would probably limit the size of the buffer to 12 or 16 bytes.

We define that the key pin on the Bluetooth module is connected to the digital 9 pin on the Arduino. We then create an instance of the `SoftwareSerial` type and a `byte` array for the input buffer.

In the `setup()` function we will initialize the serial console and the `SoftwareSerial` instance. We will also need to pull the key pin for that Bluetooth module high. The following code does this:

```
void setup()
{
   Serial.begin(9600);
   pinMode(BT_PIN,OUTPUT);
   digitalWrite(BT_PIN,HIGH);
   HC05.begin(9600);
   Serial.println("Connected to HC05");
}
```

Now in the `loop()` function we will want to continuously read the input from the Bluetooth module until we receive and EOT (`0x04`) byte. As we read the data in, it will be stored in the byte array and once the `0x04` byte is read in we will print out the message and then loop back. Here is the code for the `loop()` function:

```
void loop()
{
   memset(buf, 0, MAXBUF);
   int counter = 0;
   while (counter < MAXBUF)
   {
     if (HC05.available())
     {
       byte val = HC05.read();
       buf[counter] = val;
       counter++;
       if (val == 0x04)
       {
         break;
       }
     }
   }
}
```

```
for(int i=0; i<counter; i++)
{
   Serial.print(buf[i]);
   Serial.print(" ");
}
Serial.println(" ");
}
```

This function starts off by using the `memset()` function to initialize the buffer with all zeros. We then create an integer variable that will count how many bytes are read in.

A `while` loop is used to continuously loop until the maximum number of bytes have been read. Within the `while` loop, we use the `available()` function from the `HC05` `SoftwareSerial` instance to see if there are any values to read from the Bluetooth module. If there is a value to read, we use the `read()` function to read the value in, store it in the `buf` byte array and increments the counter. We then check to see if the value that was read in is equal to `0x04` and if so we use the `break` statement to break out of the `while` loop.

Finally, we create a `for` loop that will loop through the values in the buffer and print them to the serial console. If we execute the code on both Arduinos and move the joystick around, we will see output similar to the following screenshot:

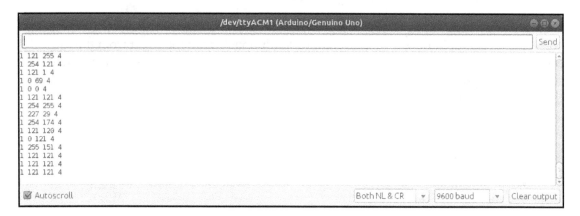

As we can see from the output, each message starts with the `0x01` byte and ends with the `0x04` byte. In between these two bytes are the joystick position on the *x* axis and the *y* axis.

We know that the packets are supposed to be four bytes in length. In a production environment we would want to toss out any messages that were not four bytes in length because we know that if the message is not four bytes in length, then the message got messed up in transmission.

We could also use a checksum to ensure that the message was received correctly. A checksum is some value that is calculated using the data that is sent. One of the easiest ways to generate a checksum is to add up all of the data bytes, storing the value in a byte that will cause the value to wrap around when it is greater than 255. Here is an example of a function that would generate a checksum:

```
byte checksum(byte *bytes, int buf_size)
{
  byte checksum = 0;
  for (int i=0; i< buf_size; i++)
  {
    checksum += bytes[i];
  }
  return checksum;
}
```

This function takes a pointer to a `byte` array and the size of the array as parameters. It then loops through the array and adds each byte to the checksum and then returns the value. A byte can have a maximum value of 255, therefore once the value gets above 255 the value will loop around. For example, if the checksum byte had a value of 252 and a value of 10 was added to it, the checksum value would then be 7. We could then send the checksum before the `0x04` value, and the device that receives the message could verify the message integrity by calculating the checksum on the receiving end and verifying that the two values match.

Summary

In this chapter, we learned a lot about Bluetooth Classic, starting with a brief introduction on how the radio works and the network topology for Bluetooth Classic connections. We demonstrated how we could configure the Bluetooth HC-05 Bluetooth module as both a slave and master. We also saw how we could configure the Bluetooth modules to connect to each other on startup automatically. Finally, we saw how we could stream data from one device to another using Bluetooth classic.

In `Chapter 20`, *Bluetooth LE*, and this chapter we looked at two different Bluetooth technologies, but the question may still be when to use which one. When we have a use case that defines that we want one device to ask another device for information periodically, like a weather station, we generally want to use Bluetooth LE. When we want to stream data from one device to another without waiting for the receiving device to ask for it, we generally want to use Bluetooth Classic.

Over the course of this book, we have looked at many different items from a microcontroller to sensors and from motors to wireless communication modules. The idea was to expose you to a number of different items to hopefully give you ideas for your own projects. The best thing about the Arduino, is the projects that you do are only limited by your imagination, so start imagining what super awesome projects you can do and then create them.

Another Book You May Enjoy

If you enjoyed this book, you may be interested in these other books by Packt:

Building Smart Drones with ESP8266 and Arduino
Syed Omar Faruk Towaha

ISBN: 978-1-78847-751-2

- Includes a number of projects that utilize different ESP8266 and Arduino capabilities, while interfacing with external hardware
- Covers electrical engineering and programming concepts, interfacing with the World through analog and digital sensors, communicating with a computer and other devices, and internet connectivity
- Control and fly your quadcopter, taking into account weather conditions
- Build a drone that can follow the user wherever he/she goes
- Build a mission-control drone and learn how to use it effectively
- Maintain your vehicle as much as possible and repair it whenever required

Leave a review - let other readers know what you think

Please share your thoughts on this book with others by leaving a review on the site that you bought it from. If you purchased the book from Amazon, please leave us an honest review on this book's Amazon page. This is vital so that other potential readers can see and use your unbiased opinion to make purchasing decisions, we can understand what our customers think about our products, and our authors can see your feedback on the title that they have worked with Packt to create. It will only take a few minutes of your time, but is valuable to other potential customers, our authors, and Packt. Thank you!

Index